HALO

Lighting up Heaven on Earth

Compiled by: Brian Calhoun

LWL PUBLISHING HOUSE
Brampton, Canada

H A L O – Lighting up Heaven on Earth
Copyright © 2017 by LWL PUBLISHING HOUSE
A division of Anita Sechesky – Living Without Limitations Inc.

All rights reserved. No part of this publication may be reproduced, distributed or transmitted in any form or by any means, including photocopying, recording, or other electronic or mechanical methods, without prior written permission of the publisher, except in the case of brief quotations embodied in critical reviews and certain other noncommercial uses permitted by copyright law. For permission requests, write to the publisher, addressed "Attention: Permissions Coordinator," at the address below.

Anita Sechesky – Living Without Limitations Inc.
lwlclienthelp@gmail.com
www.lwlpublishinghouse.com

Publisher's Note: This book is a collection of personal experiences written at the discretion of each co-author. LWL PUBLISHING HOUSE uses American English spelling as its standard. Each co-author's word usage and sentence structure have remained unaltered as much as possible to retain the authenticity of each chapter.

Book Layout © 2017 LWL PUBLISHING HOUSE

H A L O – Lighting up Heaven on Earth
Anita Sechesky – Living Without Limitations Inc.
ISBN 978-0-9939648-9-3
ASIN 0993964893

Book Cover: LWL PUBLISHING HOUSE
Inside Layout: LWL PUBLISHING HOUSE

CONTENTS

LEGAL DISCLAIMER 1

FOREWORD 3

GRATITUDE & ACKNOWLEDGMENTS 7

DEDICATION 9

INTRODUCTION 13

ONE 19
Tuning In – Fiona Louise

TWO 25
My Journey to Wellness – Julie L. Dudley

THREE 29
Food is Medicine – Jennifer Dahl-Kowalski

FOUR 35
Rediscovering Old Patterns
and Finding Ways to Heal Them – Nicole Black

FIVE 39
Mary Me – Georgie Deyn

SIX 45
The Healing Power of Song Writing – Robyn Dewar

SEVEN 49
A Journey through Time – Vonne Solis

EIGHT 55
Gratitude of a Stranger – Robert Hickinbotham

NINE 57
Magic in Trauma: Writing to Heal – Manpreet Komal

TEN 63
Magic in Trauma: A Prayer Story – Manpreet Komal

ELEVEN 67
The Ascension of Lost Souls – Louise Lajeunesse

TWELVE 73
The Flower of Thankfulness – Jamieson Wolf

THIRTEEN 77
Souly Reconnected – Kimberly Hutt

FOURTEEN 83
Miracles Happen Every Day
(All You Have to Do Is Appreciate Them) – Mary Willemsen

FIFTEEN 89
The Grand Illusion: Part One – Brian D Calhoun

SIXTEEN 93
The Grand Illusion: Part Two – Brian D Calhoun

SEVENTEEN 97
The Energy of Money – Michelle Scarborough

EIGHTEEN 101
You Can Rewrite Your Story – Maggie Power

NINETEEN 107
Out of Despair Came Prosperity – Marie-Hélène Fortin

TWENTY 113
Abundance is Destiny – Michelle Mayer

TWENTY-ONE 119
Have Faith, Dear One – Bonnie Scarborough

TWENTY-TWO 121
The Adventures of Discovering My Passion - Ivana Risianova

TWENTY-THREE 127
Creating a Life with Passion and Purpose – Cheryl Sinfield

TWENTY-FOUR 133
Creating Abundance – Michelle Scarborough

TWENTY-FIVE 137
Angels of Abundance – Georgie Deyn

TWENTY-SIX 143
Mahsi Choo: A Northern Thank You! – Regina Wright

TWENTY-SEVEN 151
The Healing Power of Love – Angie Carter

TWENTY-EIGHT 157
The Love Tree – Jamieson Wolf

TWENTY-NINE 161
Love – Sharon Hickinbotham

THIRTY 167
Creating Your Love Masterpiece – Julie L. Dudley

THIRTY-ONE 171
The Transforming Power of Love – Quin Van Hagan

THIRTY-TWO 177
The Day I Learned to Love Myself – Nicole Black

THIRTY-THREE 181
Awakening to Authenticity – Tracey Nguyen

THIRTY-FOUR 187
Speaking from the Heart – Jennifer Dahl-Kowalski

THIRTY-FIVE 191
Animal Speak – Valerie Cameron

THIRTY-SIX 195
My Soul Journey:
De-Rooting My Authentic Seeds Authentically - Natalie Bélair

THIRTY-SEVEN 201
Love Continues On – Fiona Louise

THIRTY-EIGHT 205
Everything Happens for a Reason – Sharon Hickinbotham

THIRTY-NINE 213
When Spirit Has a Plan – Michelle Evans

FORTY 219
Imagine, Listen and Let It Be So – Menna Glyn Andrews

FORTY-ONE 223
Saved! – Melisa Archer

FORTY-TWO 229
My Journey Within – Valerie Cameron

FORTY-THREE 233
On a Spiritual Journey - Louise Lajeunesse

FORTY-FOUR 239
The Silent Journey to the Soul - Ivana Risianova

FORTY-FIVE 245
Experiencing the Soul – Jennifer Dahl-Kowalski

FORTY-SIX 249
Awakening Forgiveness – Melisa Archer

FORTY-SEVEN 253
Angels' Rule of Empowerment:
Stand in Your Own Power – Brenda Rachel

FORTY-EIGHT 259
Bobby's Heart – Kelly Gregory

FORTY-NINE 263
One Dimension Away – Robyn Dewar

FIFTY 267
Rainbow Blessings – Angie Carter

FIFTY-ONE 273
We Are All ONE – Fiona Louise

CONCLUSION 277
Brian Calhoun

Compiled by Brian Calhoun

LEGAL DISCLAIMER

The information and content contained within this book *H A L O - Lighting up Heaven on Earth* does not substitute any form of professional counsel such as a Psychologist, Physician, Life Coach, or Counselor. The contents and information provided does not constitute professional or legal advice in any way, shape or form.

All chapters are written at the *discret*ion of and with the full accountability of each writer. Anita Sechesky – Living Without Limitations Inc. or LWL PUBLISHING HOUSE is not liable or responsible for any of the specific details, descriptions of people, places or things, personal interpretations, stories and experiences contained within. The Publisher is not liable for any misrepresentations, false or unknown statements, actions, or judgments made by any of the contributors or their chapter contents in this book. Each contributor is responsible for their own submissions and have shared their stories in good faith to encourage others.

Any decisions you make and the outcomes thereof are entirely your own doing. Under no circumstances can you hold the Compiler, LWL PUBLISHING HOUSE, or "Anita Sechesky – Living Without Limitations Inc." liable for any actions that you take.

You agree not to hold the Compiler, LWL PUBLISHING HOUSE, or "Anita Sechesky – Living Without Limitations Inc." liable for any loss or expense incurred by you, as a result of materials, advice, coaching or mentoring offered within.

The information offered in this book is intended to be general information with respect to general life issues. Information is offered in good faith; however, you are under no obligation to use this information.

Nothing contained in this book shall be considered legal, financial, or actuarial advice.

The author or Publisher assume no liability or responsibility to actual events or stories being portrayed.

It may introduce what a Life Coach, Counselor or Therapist may discuss with you at any given time during scheduled sessions. The advice contained herein is not meant to replace the Professional roles of a physician or any of these professions.

Compiled by Brian Calhoun

FOREWORD

What kind of thoughts come to you when you think about the title of this book, specifically the word *"H A L O?"* For me, I imagine Angelic beings and the serenity that comes from being in their presence. The energy changes in the way I am currently looking at things and turns into the bliss of that evoked perception of Angels, Source, or something bigger, like God, who is ever-loving. Then the subtitle *"Lighting up Heaven on Earth"* brings me into another realm of majestic possibilities where all things truly are possible. The rush of joy, love, and total emotional and spiritual awareness allows me to escape from the present moment and accept the world that is waiting to unfold around and within me.

When you open up this beautiful book, you will be translated into a world of so many realities which are possible for you, despite your present circumstances. The thirty-three international co-authors in this book have presented so many perspectives that you will be delighted in the energy that oozes from the pages before you.

As the Publisher of this book, I would love to share a little story with you. I first met Brian Calhoun when he co-authored another beautiful book, published by LWL PUBLISHING HOUSE, entitled *"Guided By the Light – Following Your Angelic Guides"* which was compiled by Jewels Rafter. Brian knew quite early on that he was ready to step into the courageous role of being a Compiler of his own anthology, and taking on the leadership responsibilities required, because he had a very clear vision of what his book was going to bring into the world. When you have a vision, it becomes even more beautiful as it unfolds and develops into the finished product. This why having a supportive and professional team to collaborate with your vision is the most productive way to go. Often times, our vision must evolve to reflect the people who are also helping to bring it to life. This does not mean the original intention is of less value, it actually means it has been through a refining process to perfect it into becoming something that suits a larger audience, if that was the intention to begin with. The vision never really changes but the presentation may. Therefore, the goal is still accomplished. It has then become a multifaceted vision enveloping all the loving energy contributed by each beautiful soul helping to fashion it, much like a diamond gemstone that reflects all of it's glistening qualities, as each aspect of its valued contribution is perfected into bringing the whole vision to life from conception to birth.

"H A L O, Lighting up Heaven on Earth" will encourage you to not give up so easily, but to look for that silver lining when all hope seems lost. You may find it in the most unlikely of places and when you least expect it to show up. You may choose to read this book section by section, or one chapter at a time, determining which story speaks to your life at that very moment. Sometimes, the unpleasant people we are connected with and cannot really see their perspectives may result in our greatest life lessons. Sometimes the experiences of others are where we find our greatest treasures for a life better lived. Your journey is always fascinating, but it's up to you to decide how you will grow and evolve into your most beautiful self. By staying in constant gratitude, you can train our emotions to attract so much more abundance, joy, love, and bliss. Healing is a natural flow of these conscience behaviors when you choose to live without expectations but in appreciation of all, for all.

I must say that this book is one of our biggest anthology projects to date, with over 300 pages, and I am pleased that it has accomplished its purpose. I do believe that all of our self-healing books at LWL PUBLISHING HOUSE, like #*Love – A New Generation of Hope Continues...*, and others bring inspiration, insight, and well-needed information to our readers to enable them to determine the destiny for their own lives. Our books do not replace any professional guidance and are merely for the pleasure of our readers. Should you find any of the chapters speaking to your soul, please feel free to connect with the individual co-authors.

It has been a delight to work with Brian and his co-authors in bringing his collaborative book to light. A special note of appreciation to each contributor for coming along side Brian and partnering with LWL PUBLISHING HOUSE in sharing their stories that are being published on an International platform. Many blessings to you our dear readers for allowing your hearts and spirits to be open to learning and understanding the significance and possibilities that await you, if you believe.

If you would also like to have the vision of your own anthology sponsored by LWL PUBLISHING HOUSE, (Valued at $650 CAD + HST) with you being the Compiler/Visionary, please contact:

Anita Sechesky, CEO, Founder & Publisher @ LWL PUBLISHING HOUSE or visit our website: www.lwlpublishinghouse.com

Anita Sechesky, RN, CPC, Publisher

Anita Sechesky is the Founder and CEO of Anita Sechesky - Living Without Limitations Inc. She is an RN, CPC, Best-Seller Publisher, Book Writing

Compiled by Brian Calhoun

Mentor, Multiple International Best-Selling Author, Conference Host, Keynote Speaker, as well as a Law of Attraction and NLPP.

Anita is also the CEO, Founder, Owner, and Publisher of her company LWL PUBLISHING HOUSE.

Currently, her company has successfully branded approximately 300 International Best-Selling authors in the last four years. LWL PUBLISHING HOUSE is a division of her company, in which she offers coaching, mentoring, motivation, marketing, and of course publishing services for her clients. 2016 marked the addition of LWL KIDz and the introduction of non-fictional single author books.

Working with Anita at one of her "LWL INSPIRED TO WRITE" workshops, MasterClass, Webinars, or one-to-one support, will equip you to step out of your comfort zone fearlessly! Anita's solo book entitled "Absolutely YOU! - Overcome False Limitations & Reach Your Full Potential" was written in less than four weeks and she can teach you how to do the same! Join Anita's "Absolutely YOU!" MasterClass at: www. http://lwlpublishinghouse.com/masterclass/

Join my Private Facebook group: LIVING WITHOUT LIMITATIONS LIFESTYLE. With over 950 members, we offer exclusive prizes, co-authoring opportunities, Random Contests with FREE Publishing possibilities, "Inspired To Write" Webinar classes, and more - http://bit.ly/1TlsTSm

Please visit our Facebook page: LWL PUBLISHING HOUSE

Website: www.lwlpublishinghouse.com

1(647) 822-2897

Email: lwlclienthelp@gmail.com.

Join my Private Facebook group:

LIVING WITHOUT LIMITATIONS LIFESTYLE: Exclusive prizes, co-authoring opportunities and Random Contests with FREE Publishing opportunities: http://bit.ly/1TlsTSm

YouTube Channel: http://bit.ly/1VEGHew

Website: www.anitasechesky.com

LinkedIn: https://ca.linkedin.com/in/asechesky

Twitter: https://twitter.com/nursie4u

Compiled by Brian Calhoun

GRATITUDE & ACKNOWLEDGMENTS

I would like to take a few moments to thank those that I have encountered along the path that encouraged me to write and share my wisdom, tips, and stories with the world. Thank you for believing in what I have to offer.

Thank you to all my clients, students, and everyone that I have ever been or will be in service for. Thank you for trusting and having faith in my gifts, abilities, and all that the Divine guides through me. Thank you for listening and answering the call of your heart to connect.

Thank you to my family for being in my life growing up. For you all helped to shape me to be the person that I am. You helped me to have stories to share with the world, which can inspire, uplift, empower, and enlighten others along their journey. Many of you have moved from the physical level back home to Spirit, however I am very grateful that you are still with me, loving, supporting, and guiding my journey from your new perspectives.

Thank you to those that I went to school with and were a part of the earlier years of my life. Without the connections and experiences that we all shared in, life as I know it may be extremely different. Some of you were villains, some played supportive roles, and many were inspirations or heroes in my story but each of you had a very important role to play, so thank you!

I would like to thank my parents, teachers, and elders for the wisdom and love that you each offered me in life, for the lessons that you helped me to learn, and for being supportive even when I may have been a stubborn student or rebel at times. Without your persistence to see the best in me, and help me to truly find myself, I may not have made it this far in life. Thank you very much for sticking with me and never giving up. You showed me a strength in myself I didn't know was there many times while guiding me along the path of loving light.

Thank you to my #TeamHALO Co-authors and publishing team. Without each of you believing in the vision for this book, and following your heart, this book would still be in concept only. Thank you for stepping up to help bring this vision from within me to the world. Thank you for your stories, supportive love, and for aspiring to help Light up Heaven on Earth. Together, I know that every word in this book will touch the hearts of all to bless all in their lives to look at circumstances differently and see the light within that much brighter. Thank you for taking a leap of faith and for spreading your wings to soar. Your stories are a gift to the world. Thank you for all the time, energy, and resources that you gave to this project. It is much appreciated by myself and the entire world.

Thank you to my Angels, Guides, and my Divine Spiritual Support Crew. I am so blessed to be an instrument for the divine energy and to be able to help others along the pathways. Thank you for being a part of my service work. Thank you for guiding, protecting, and blessing my life in the infinite number of ways that you do. Thank you for answering my soul call to be of service in this lifetime, along with the numerous other lifetimes that we experienced together. Thank you for the many signs, synchronicities, and everything encompassing my life that you have had a hand in.

Thank you to Mother & Father Creator, the Divine that goes by many names and who is nameless, omnipresent, omnipotent, and omniscient. Thank you for the divine inspiration, guidance, and all that you have blessed me with in this lifetime. Thank you for the wisdom, healing, and enlightenment along my own personal journey and in all ways in life. Thank you for the time, energy, and resources that you grant me each day to accomplish all that is mine to do. Thank you for all the clients, students, and people that have blessed my life in amazing ways. Thank you for all the blessings, treasures, gifts, and miracles. Thank you for Lighting up Heaven on Earth through this book and for guiding us together to share our messages of love and light with the world in an inspiring, uplifting, empowering, healing, and enlightening way. Thank you for the Health, Abundance, Love, and the Oneness with everything through the divine connection that is you within us all.

Lastly, I would like to thank you the reader for opening your hearts and allowing us into your sacred space. Thank you for all the time, energy, and support you have given #TeamHALO and myself in every way. It is such an honor to be welcomed into your homes, your hearts, and your lives in some small way through this book.

I truly hope and pray that as you read these stories, you will begin to live a life of Heaven on Earth in all areas of life and that you receive healing, inspiration, empowerment, and enlightenment for your own personal journey, and integrate the energy contained within these pages. You are very worthy and deserving of such divine blessings. Thank you for everything from our hearts and souls to yours.

Brian D. Calhoun

Compiled by Brian Calhoun

DEDICATION

This book is dedicated to those that have come before us, those that have been a part of our stories, and those who come after us. Together with you, the reader, we shall Light up Heaven on Earth.

Compiled by Brian Calhoun

Compiled by Brian Calhoun

INTRODUCTION

Welcome to H A L O: Lighting up Heaven on Earth

This book began its journey to creation in the spring of 2015, when Spirit gave me vision to bring together a group of people to share their stories on topics of Health, Abundance, Love and the Spirit Connection to all that is. The pages that you now hold in your hands is the product of that vision.

Each of the authors will bring to you some of their most touching and personal stories. I would encourage that you keep an open mind and heart as you read through them. By doing so, you are allowing yourself to receive the gift that is held within their words for you from Spirit.

You will often find that as you read their stories, there may be a connection to your own personal journey in some way. Sometimes it is obvious right from the get go, other times it is mid-way through when you will make the connection, and often it will be when you step back to ponder what the story and author was sharing on a deeper level.

Every time, Spirit will bring to the surface what one is meant to be aware of in the perfect way and time, especially when we take a step back and get out of our own way; remembering that words often will have multiple layers and meanings to them that only time and space will to show us.

This book has four main themes. Each one focuses on a certain area of the vision that Spirit guided to me.

Within the first theme, you will find stories on Health and Wellness. This section will hold personal stories of the co-authors' journeys to heal and embrace the natural state of well-being that lies within the divine soul.

As you read the chapters contained within this section, you may find yourself sharing some similar feelings and experiences with the author. You will find that the writers open up their hearts to connect with yours as they share their health and wellness experiences. You are sure to find some inspiration, feel uplifted, empowered, or even being blessed with healing and enlightenment as the words hold many blessings for you and your journey.

The next theme is on Abundance and Prosperity. When one is truly living an abundant life, they will hold thoughts of abundance and prosperity at all times. They will connect and feel that there is more than enough of everything for everyone. They will be living a rich and prosperous life in health, love, wealth, and so much more. Abundance will just naturally flow for these people as they will be connected to the source of it all within, Spirit.

In this section, you will find that the authors share about how they found their life purpose, opened up to abundance and what it means to them, and so much more to help everyone to receive and feel heaven's abundant riches on earth. This section is sure to raise you up and help you improve the quality of your life in divinely perfect ways.

Love and Romance is our third section. Love is our natural state of being: it is who and what all is made of, what heals, connects, and blesses the world in amazing ways. Love is compassionate, understanding, and always expanding. Think about it, without love we wouldn't be on the earth here and now. We are conceived with love, born into love, experience love, and will leave the earth embraced by love.

There are many facets of love and in this section, you will find the authors sharing their own journeys to finding, expressing, and experiencing love in life. From self-love to romantic love and more amazing love possibilities, this section is sure to touch your heart.

Our final section is on Oneness and the Spirit.

At the Heart and Soul of everything is the energy of Spirit; aka God; aka Love; aka Universe; aka Source; and so many other names one may call the grand energy of the I AM. Through this omnipresent, omnipotent, and omniscient source, everything is ONE. This includes all the health, abundance, love, relationships, animals, food, and so much more than we could ever imagine on this earth and in heaven. This all-providing source is where our entire good comes from and is all that is, isn't, and in between.

So, within this section you will find chapters on a variety of subjects from Oneness, Messages from Heaven, Angels, Faith, Miracles, and more.

I encourage you as you read through all the chapters within this book and find yourself comparing your journey to take a moment after each chapter to think about your own story.

- What are the similarities between your story and the authors?
- What is Spirit showing you about yourself through this account?
- What did the author learn through their experience?

- What is it that Spirit is helping you to learn?
- What gift are you being granted or find yourself receiving?
- What is the message that the author is sharing with you the reader?
- What is it that you perhaps need to shift in order to light up your heaven on earth life?
- What is your next step to get from where you are to where you want to be?

These are just a few questions to help get you started integrating the blessings of each chapter that you are reading through. These chapters are like seeds you plant. It isn't enough just to read through the words, but it is in the nurturing of the seeds that you grow and experience more of the blessings of Heaven on Earth.

You will also find that sometimes it is beneficial to read a story multiple times as you meditate upon the words and ask yourself the questions. Think about it like an onion; we need to peel away at the layers to get to core and truly be able to understand, shift something, or break free and move forward.

I would like to encourage you to take the time to love yourself in order to free yourself through this journey. Remember, this isn't a race. It is a journey and you are truly worth it.

Now let's get you going on your venture of Lighting up Heaven on Earth.

Brian.

Compiled by Brian Calhoun

HALO
HEALTH - HEALING

Fiona Louise

Tuning In

As part of my own healing process from grief, depression, and several auto-immune conditions, I studied and became a Nutritionist and Natural Therapist, specializing in stress management and relaxation therapy. Using myself, as my main case study, means I can truly say that the strategies I've used do work!

I've also changed the way I think about myself, which provided the opportunity to shed negative people and experiences from my life, open up to new possibilities, change professions, and discover a life path which fulfils me. I'm sharing my personal story with you, so that if any of it sounds familiar, you may find the courage to begin your own healing journey, regain vibrant health and wellness, discover your life purpose, and begin to live once again, with love and peace in your heart and soul. That is my wish for you.

I now know through first-hand experience that what we focus on, and what we believe about ourselves, has direct consequences and manifests physically. This concept is supported by quantum physics. Many years ago, I was a typical A-type personality: life revolved around career and charitable work. I was also stuck in the grieving process and not moving forward. I didn't give myself time to rest and recuperate as I was working fulltime, which included travel, and volunteering with charities. Yet, I was deeply dissatisfied, limited by conditioning and beliefs that shaped my identity throughout my life. I longed for something worthwhile and to feel joy again, but I didn't know how. I thought that owning my own house, achieving a high status at work, and being independent would do that, but I was wrong. So, I sold the house, quit the job, and moved overseas intending to travel and have fun, without taking on any responsibilities. But as I took all my baggage with me, I was just as unhappy and unsatisfied there and within five months, slipped into another staff-management position! I still hadn't dealt with my grief, and I ignored my body's warning signs.

As my energy dwindled my caffeine intake increased – I was chain-drinking coffee just to stay awake. Starting as stiffness and aching, pain became my constant companion. Impatient, frustrated, and very depressed, I was unable to shift the dark feelings, and slowly lost joy and hope. Everyday activities became a huge deal. Often at weekends I lay in bed exhausted, unable to move. Trying to work through this haze became extremely arduous and flat-lined my immune system, seriously compromising my health. I was physically, emotionally, and spiritually depleted. I well-and-truly burned out. I could no longer work and became bedridden for six months because I had nothing left to give.

However, being empty meant something new could fill me. Thus, I began my spiritual journey and return to health. Once I realized I did want to live, just without suffering, my healing could begin. I was open to anything and everything to make this happen!

I studied Eastern and Western philosophies and medical practices. I went to counselors to make sense of the really hard stuff, and I began to feel again. For years, I pushed emotions down but they continually bubbled under the surface. It was high-time I acknowledged, processed, and released them. It was actually a huge relief to let go of the heaviness that weighed me down and burdened my shoulders. I felt lighter and clearer as a result. Being empty meant there was now room for new experiences; enabling me to start from scratch, relearn what is truly important, and listen to my inner guidance and my body. I learned to change my thoughts and beliefs, which brought me back to the right path and life purpose.

Deep down, we all know how to heal. Once we've cleared out all the limiting beliefs and old conditioning, and let go of other people's opinions, we begin to hear our inner guidance. When we let go of all that is holding us back, we can take control of our lives, redefine our priorities, and live the life we once dreamed about but believed impossible. This is what I am doing and I wish this for you also.

My body was so depleted that I started my healing journey with something very simple, yet very effective, which we often take for granted: breathing. First I noticed how I was breathing, some days fast and shallow, other days slow and laboured. I didn't try to change it, just paid attention for a few minutes. Whilst lying down I drew in a deep breath filling my lungs, expanding my belly outwards towards the ceiling, held, and then exhaled all the air out, drawing my belly towards my spine. Deep breathing like this, for a few minutes per day, increases oxygen flow, which helps us think more clearly, and feel lighter. Often when stressed we breathe shallowly from our chests, which can cause hyperventilation, and anxiety attacks. When agitated, we can simply return to this deep breathing process, calming our minds and bodies. And because it is so simple, we can practice it standing in line at the grocery store, during rush hour traffic, at work, or cooking dinner – anywhere!

One of my favorite places to practice breathing is whilst sitting in the garden. I always feel at peace surrounded by nature, my soul yearns for those precious moments sitting perfectly still, with the sun on my face, listening to the birds sing, and the wind whistling through the trees. This is also where I learned to meditate. Starting with the breath, I introduce a simple mantra "Om": the sound of the universe. In chorus with our breathing, we can mentally or out loud, say or sing "Om" lengthening the "m." Doing this for a few minutes focuses our minds so that the chatter falls away. In time, we can introduce other mantras to train and calm the mind, simple words like "love", "peace", "joy." With practice, we can lengthen our meditations from a few minutes to 20 – 30 minutes, once or twice per day.

Following on from meditation, I introduced gentle body movements and stretches. Imagining a twenty-centimeter ball cupped between my hands, with my left on top and my right under the imaginary ball, I gently rotate moving my hands in a fluid motion to switch positions. I would also stretch my arms above my head as if trying to catch hold of something just beyond my reach, and then gently bend to touch the ground. Strengthening my body through these simple manoeuvres several times per day meant I could introduce yoga and exercises.

For my body to find its own rhythm again, I cut out the artificial energy. Caffeine and sugar provide constant waves of highs and lows which are detrimental to our body's natural rhythms, and they dehydrate. Filtered water keeps our body hydrated and energized, and helps with mental clarity. I began my detox by substituting the 8 – 10 daily coffees with black tea. Then I replaced one tea with herbal tea, and so on until all teas during the day became herbal. This enabled me to slowly withdraw from caffeine and sugar, and increase my water intake. I started with a small glass of water gradually increasing, and now I drink a litre or two per day and only two hot drinks. I still treat myself to a decaf coffee or hot chocolate occasionally, but I find the more water I drink, the less I crave caffeinated or sugary beverages.

Next I introduced more nutrients into my diet through berry and green smoothies. My chocolate craving reduced significantly, with my increase in green vegetables, until I no longer "needed" any chocolate. It's only when I slip back into bad habits of convenience food that my chocolate craving returns. When I'm eating healthily and nutritionally: fresh vegetables, legumes, berries, nuts and seeds, and fish, I feel at my very best, with energy and a lightness of body and soul! Each person has individual nutritional needs, and I recommend working with a qualified nutritionist or dietician to find what works best for our metabolism, and to ensure an adequate daily supply of vitamins and minerals. I choose to be vegetarian, obtaining protein from beans and lentils instead of meat. Eliminating processed foods, and consuming only real foods makes me feel so much better!

As my body strengthened, I began the mind-work: processing limiting beliefs, prioritizing goals, and finding meaning in small gestures, whilst being gracious for all the lessons and experiences I've had so far, which make me, me. I've learned that what we project into the world, returns to us tenfold. If we don't feel worthy, and don't value our own opinions, we meet people who validate our unworthiness, never listen to our point-of-view, or criticize it when we do voice it, bully, and push us around. I worked with, lived with, and befriended bullies and narcissists, and they reflected how I felt about myself.

When I made the conscious effort to heal, retrain my mind, and affirm my worth and loveableness, I began treating myself with love, kindness, and respect, and valuing my place and space in the world. As we love, respect, and honor ourselves, so will the people we meet. As we start to believe in ourselves, and infuse all our thoughts with love, our friendships change: the drama-filled, manipulative people realize they can no longer control us and leave. New people matching our latest way of thinking, enter.

So where to start? We can write a list of things we currently think about ourselves, aspects of our body/personality we don't like, and then, on the other side of the paper, change the sentence to a positive. For example: I am unlovable to I am loveable. I hate my nose/legs, to I accept myself just the way I am.

When we create I AM statements with conscious awareness, we project that belief out into the world. It takes twenty-one days to form a habit, so repeating our affirmative I AM statements daily, creates a natural routine.

Writing is very cathartic for experiencing raw emotions fully and completely, acknowledging them, and releasing them. Composing enables me to express myself. I write something down that is bothering me, and then rip up the piece of paper, burn it, or if I've typed it on the computer, close it without saving. The act of disposing is as important as the writing, because we are physically releasing the emotions and thoughts that have held us back when we delete or rip it up. The simple act of giving them space to come forth enables us to let go. I write about all aspects of my life that I feel grateful for, even the hardships and losses, as they are opportunities to learn.

I focus on things I desire: good health, happiness, love, abundance, supportive friends, and experiences which bring me joy, make me laugh, or fill me with warmth and love. Things I desire include going for a walk in nature, looking up into a starry night, listening to uplifting music, being embraced in a loving hug, cuddling the cat, sitting by the fire, and watching a sunset. Writing gives me focus to acknowledge where I am now, where I want to be, and the action steps in between.

I've learned that I am worthy and deserve to occupy space in this world.

Compiled by Brian Calhoun

We all have a reason to be here, we all have opportunities to learn, and experience, and when we do all of this from a place of love, we not only heal ourselves, but we gift that healing to others through our kindness, gratitude, words, and actions. Self-care (tuning in to the needs of our bodies, minds, and souls) provides us with the first step in the healing process. In time, although it may sometimes feel like a struggle, we blossom and grow, healing all aspects of our lives, learning, letting go, and moving on to new and wonderful experiences.

Fiona Louise is a writer, student, natural therapist and blogger of both fiction and non-fiction. She has co-authored three International Best-Selling books. With a background in marketing and management in the science and property industries, Fiona left the corporate world to heal from auto-immune disorders, learn natural therapies, and write. Re-evaluating her life in order to heal put Fiona back on the spiritual path which she now shares with others. She facilitates creative workshops locally as she sees a need for people to unwind from hectic lifestyles, de-stress, and have fun! Fiona is currently studying Educational Psychology.

http://www.fiona-louise.com

Julie L. Dudley

2

My Journey to Wellness

Just a couple years ago, I was in so much pain I couldn't function properly. I was dizzy, had slurred speech, and experienced numbness in my fingers, face, and legs. It started with dizziness, chronic fatigue, and progressively got worse each year. I finally met a doctor who was determined to get to the bottom of things and he requested an MRI. That year, I was also drawn to deepen my connection to my Guardian Angels, and was asking the Archangels for their assistance in feeling better. I called on Archangel Michael to stay with me during the MRI because I was so anxious.

A week after having the MRI, I received a call to see a neurologist the following day. When I got to the office, the neurologist told me to sit down. He explained that the innumerable lesions in my brain and spine alongside the white matter issues were consistent with Multiple Sclerosis. He told me about further testing and asked if I was open to having a spinal tap, to which I agreed. On my way out he told me, "Don't lose your smile."

I started intensely researching anything and everything to do with healing. I already had an extensive collection of Health and Wellness books. During my research, I came across inspiring stories of people who recovered from autoimmune diseases. One of the first things I did was adjust my diet. I also realized I needed to switch my perspective from feeling helpless to feeling empowered. I started working with Archangel Raphael and his emerald green healing light daily. I realized it was time to make big changes in my life. I had to slow down, manage my anxiety, and show my body love. Self-love didn't come easily for me.

One day, I did a card reading exchange with a friend whom I'm so thankful to have met. She's been tremendously supportive. The healer card came up for me. I told her that I used healing light and crystals on others but that I was now afraid of transferring my illness. We talked about Reiki, which is a healing technique that activates the natural healing processes in your body. She told me that there was no risk of transferring anything onto others with Reiki. When I got home, I began my quest to find a teacher that would teach me about Reiki in depth. My intuition guided me to the right one who helped me on so many levels. My symptoms gradually faded as I did several Reiki treatments and self-treatments.

Finally, I had the spinal tap, alongside with a series of other tests including another MRI. When I went to my appointment for the results, I found out the lesions had shrunk and the results were no longer showing Multiple Sclerosis. I decided that day to devote my life to healing.

I'd like to share seven things that helped me on my path to wellness:

1 - Start the day off with 1 – 2 positive affirmations.

> It's okay if you don't completely believe the words right away, but try to find something somewhat believable for yourself. You can experiment with it to find what works best for you.

2 - Gradually adjust your diet.

> Do some research on any conditions you have and how diet factors in. Some of the basics that helped me reduce chronic pain:
>
> - Eat lots of fresh organic fruits and vegetables.
> - Reduce or eliminate caffeine, alcohol, and soda intake.
> - Reduce the salt in your diet. I prefer to use Himalayan salt.
> - Reduce or eliminate refined sugars, bleached or dyed breads, and snacks.
> - Eliminate pork, as it can add to inflammation problems.
> - Avoid highly processed foods.

3 - Treat your body lovingly and be kind to yourself, especially when you feel unwell.

This may mean searching for a less stressful job, or taking a walk in nature more often. Always listen to what your body is trying to tell you. It truly has the capacity to heal itself, if you believe and follow the guidance.

4 - Welcome the Divine into your life.

> - Prayer is a great way to get stuff moving.
> - Ask your guardian angels for assistance.
> - You can call on Archangel Raphael to help you. Ask him to surround

you in emerald green healing light, once or twice a day.

5 – Keep your Energy Fields Clear

- Release the toxic and unhealthy relationships. Surround yourself with healthy balanced relationships that are supportive;
- Cut negative cords regularly by calling upon Archangel Michael to cut and clear all cords at their root and to strengthen love cords. He can also clear all psychic debris with his energy vacuum.
- Try to avoid keeping clutter around your house, especially your bedroom.
- Salt baths are beneficial in maintaining a clear aura.
- Burning Sage, Cedar, or Palo Santo regularly will help keep your environment clear.

6 - Reduce the Chemicals in your Environment.

Read the ingredients in your cleaning products, makeup, shampoo, laundry detergent, etc. I like to look for paraben-free and sulfate-free products, equally avoiding polyethylene and potassium sorbate.

7 - Find something you like doing that relaxes yourself. It could be meditating, tai chi, yoga, or painting.

The decision to take responsibility for one's own health can feel overwhelming, but it's a choice to be free. Each of us has an inner guidance system – all you need to do is tap into it. You're guided to certain things for a reason, whether it's a lesson that may help others or aid you on your own healing process. Never give up – the universe is full of miracles and magic and there's hope for everyone. It's a matter of discovering what works and sparks joy for you. Healing can be gradual and requires continuous effort, but is well worth it.

When we share what sparks joy inside of us and helps us in our healing process, that love spreads and expands, which the world needs more of.

May all be blessed with Health and Healing.

Julie L. Dudley is a Reiki Master-Teacher and IET Practitioner who offer sessions and classes in the Gatineau/Ottawa area. She is a Certified Fairylogist and Realm Reader. Julie offers Angel Card Readings and is a clairvoyant with over twenty years' experience working with Tarot Cards, Rune stones, and Crystals.

www.Mystiquedreams.com

Jennifer Dahl-Kowalski

3

Food is Medicine

The predictable world I grew up in, a place of guaranteed safety and security, instantly shattered into tiny, rough-edged glass pieces when I became ill. The life I knew vanished from my existence and I was left feeling confused, scared, and alone. My illness made no sense to me. Why was I ill? How did I get here? What do I have to do to overcome it? These questions felt empty when I asked them. There was no path to follow and no certainty of an answer. I had no previous experiences to draw from, no friend with similar symptoms that I could seek advice, nor any given diagnosis to research. I was falling fast down the rabbit hole with no Alice skirt to keep me afloat.

After spending three unsuccessful months taking an onslaught of medical tests and answering doctors' questions, I willingly turned to alternative healing methods for answers. I found a naturopathic doctor who worked close to where I resided and booked an appointment. After hearing my complicated story, she proposed that I consider changing my diet. She had worked with other patients with similar symptoms, which included tiredness, low energy, feeling bloated, and no appetite, and witnessed large improvements to their health when they switched to a gluten-free and dairy-free diet. If I chose to take her advice, she also recommended that I monitor my intake of fiber and that I start taking a B vitamin supplement. And lastly, she handed me an information sheet on the eight most common allergens: eggs, milk, soy, wheat, tree nuts, fish, shellfish, and peanuts, and suggested that I refrain from eating these foods for one month to see if I notice a difference in how I felt.

I left the naturopath's clinic completely stunned by her recommendation. I never considered my diet as a possible suspect to what ailed me. Instantly, I felt overwhelmed as a growing number of questions rose inside of me in an attempt to digest what I just heard.

Was it possible that food could have this much of an impact on my health? Could I heal simply by making a change to my diet? Did the food industry go too far in interfering with the food cycle?

Could certain categories of food pose a health concern for the population? Furthermore, in the future, would it be the consumer's responsibility to educate themselves on how their food was grown and processed in order to make healthy choices that are right for their bodies?

Regardless of how confused I was about her recommendation, there were no other options that presented themselves to me and so I chose to follow it. Within one week of changing my diet, I noticed significant improvements on how I felt and how I related to the world. A lightness grew inside of me replacing a heavier feeling that I had previously believed to be the norm. Conversations with others flowed effortlessly and for longer periods of time without any distracting thoughts intercepting my concentration. I could absorb and recall more information at one time. I felt this renewed sense of purpose and clarity about life. It was easier to assert what I wanted and how I desired to live. And for the first time since I fell ill, I had energy.

This swift change of events left me in disbelief. I not only felt better from being ill, I felt better than I had ever experience…in my entire life! How could a simple change to my diet lead to such a dramatic shift to my well-being in such a short period of time? How was this possible?

I vowed to learn everything I could about food. I read books on how to create a balanced meal, watched movies on how food is grown and produced, attended seminars about allergies, and took online courses on nutrition. As well, shortly after my appointment with my naturopath, I met with a dietician who thought I displayed symptoms consistent with leaky gut syndrome. She explained that food sensitivities, including gluten, can cause inflammation in the mucosal lining of the small intestine and result in intestinal villi damage, which interferes with the absorption of nutrients. In these cases, the intestinal villi will absorb all digested as well as partially digested food particles into the bloodstream causing havoc to our immune system. Our body's response to this invasion is to create antibodies that eliminate these foreign substances, resulting in additional food allergies. This vicious cycle will continue until we eliminate the foods we have become allergic to and allow the small intestines time to heal.

Moreover, she continued to explain that it is not only our food sensitivities that can cause intestinal permeability imbalances but our emotions, thoughts, and hormones can play a role as well. She suggested that I start taking notice of my thoughts and my feelings before and after a meal. Am I feeling stressed and anxious about my day? Am I distracted by watching television, texting on my cell, or working while I am eating? Also, am I taking the time to savor the smells, taste, and texture of the food, or am I rushing through the meal? Am I putting my fork or spoon down after every mouthful to ensure that I am taking the time to chew and swallow before the next bite? At the end of our session, she asked me to consider the following questions:

Compiled by Brian Calhoun

What am I having troubles digesting in my life? What areas of my life am I resisting? What areas am I having difficulty absorbing?

Again, I left another appointment feeling flabbergasted, lost, and confused. My medical history did not correlate with the advice I was being given. I never had any issues eating food growing up. I had never been allergic to any foods before. And I rarely got sick. Why was all of this showing up now? Also, I rarely felt negative or upset. Which part of life was I not accepting? Overall, I was happy with the way my life was going. None of this made sense. What was I missing?

Since I could not see how my emotions played a role in my illness, I chose to divert my attention to improving my eating habits. I recognized that I tended to eat quickly, usually distracted by the Internet, and I often felt tense due to stress at work. I also realized that I rarely wanted to spend time eating. Eating felt like an unnecessary chore and I would much rather get back to work. Therefore, I committed to making a concerted effort to eating slower during each meal, to taking time to breathe between each bite, and to being present with the food while I ate. I also began repeating an affirmation before each meal. I would say with conviction, "I willingly and joyfully digest and absorb all aspects of life with ease." After stating my affirmation, I also gave thanks for all the nutrients I would receive from the meal.

Despite my best efforts, I had difficulty in integrating these new rituals in my daily routine. There were days when I felt unmotivated, days when I felt like I did not have enough time, or days when the distractions seemed more appealing than the rituals. Occasionally, my saboteur would find ways to sneak into my thought patterns. I would feel anxious before my meals and because I could sense my anxiety, I would start to worry that this nervousness would cause further food allergies. And this vicious cycle would lead back to having more anxiety. Thus, I would feel sick after eating and I would dread my next meal. And when I did finally eat again, I would overeat.

I wanted to eat my stress away so that I could no longer feel frustrated. I wanted to feel the high I got from eating sugar or fat because it offered me small doses of feeling hopeful and good again. And in truth, I just wanted to run away from my situation. I did not want to have to deal with the illness that I created through my own neglect and ignorance. I missed feeling well and would give anything to feel that way again.

Over time, food became the only thing on my mind. I would spend my days thinking about what I was going to eat and contemplate the likelihood of it making me feel sick. And while I was eating, I would feel anxious, overeat, and then regret my choice. And it did not stop there. I would then feel guilty about overeating and would continue eating to suppress the guilt.

This vicious cycle lasted longer than I would like to admit. And the more that I would try and resist the food, the more I craved it. I had created a mess and I had no idea how to fix it.

After months of emotional eating, I surrendered to the idea that I could tackle this problem directly. Instead, I chose to focus my attention on other aspects of my life. And I made a personal promise that if I did overeat, I would no longer judge myself for it. I would let it be as it is and move forward. At first, this was not an easy task and I continued to overeat everyday but I stuck to my commitment. I began to open my mind and explore new topics on spirituality, mindset, intuition, etc. I took a 30-day yoga challenge and I continued to practice yoga on a daily basis after the challenge was over. I practiced daily gratitude and recorded five reasons why I was grateful in my journal every day. I also began meditating and would set aside time to focus my mind on staring at one object while emptying my thoughts. These new activities led to a reduction in stress and a happier peace of mind.

As months passed, I began to feel filled up, renewed, and happy. Through incorporating challenging rituals into my life, I witnessed my own strengths and felt the power within me. Life began to make sense again. And when I felt strong enough, I took the time to start tackling my inner conflicts that I had never chosen to admit to before - my inner child issues, my unresolved emotions, and my pains. I stood up to each of them and I confronted my fears. I was no longer willing to run away from them. Instead, I was willing to make new choices, regardless of how difficult it would be.

And as I began to honor my soul and stop ignoring what it had to say, my anxiety and stress levels began to diminish. With each major shift that I made, my food allergies began to disappear. I no longer felt sick when I ate. I no longer overate. My diet became my choice again. I ate based on what I intuitively felt was right for me. I no longer had to think about it. I continued to refrain from eating all processed foods, grains, caffeine, sugar and alcohol because it no longer interested me. Everything else, I left on the table.

Upon reflection, I realized that my illness had nothing to do with my relationship with food. My food sensitivities, my emotional eating habits, and my self-indulged food anxieties were merely a byproduct of what was actually going on underneath the surface. The truth was that I was unconscious to how little attention I was offering my soul. I rarely felt the need to tune into how I was feeling after I started my career years back. I thought that my life would naturally figure itself out and I could finally relax. However, as I discovered from my illness, this was not the case. And even though it was a scary thought, I knew what I needed to do next. I would recreate my entire life, starting fresh, and I vowed to begin today.

Jennifer Dahl-Kowalski became conscious of her gifts following an unexplainable illness in 2013. With no clear diagnosis, she ventured into unchartered territories and searched within to uncover her own innate healing abilities. Through utilizing the power of thought, tuning into her intuition, and mastering her sensitivities to energy, she was liberated from her sickness. Dedicated to sharing her wisdom, she helps others release anxiety, stress, and childhood traumas by breaking through old patterns and offering powerful practices that lead to a life with meaning. Jennifer currently resides in Canada as an intuitive coach, certified energy therapist, public speaker, and author.

www.ignite0your0light0.com

www.facebook.com/ignite0your0light0

Nicole Black

Rediscovering Old Patterns and Finding Ways to Heal Them

I think one of the biggest keys to fixing a pattern you are tired of repeating is to recognize it. Once you see the pattern, you can then look a little deeper and see where it's really coming from. It's uncanny to me that most of the time our physical ailments aren't coming from the place where it hurts. Once we start chasing symptoms however, the pain seems to run in circles and it becomes almost like a merry-go-round, never knowing when it will end.

I felt my body slightly shifting to the left as I was walking down the street. I really slowed down because I wanted to feel into my own body and find where the angst was really lying low, dormant, and ready to pounce at any moment. The words came back to me and it was as if someone was whispering them into my ear. "You're a pain in the neck."

"No! I am not!" I shouted indignantly. But it didn't matter, the damage had been done and until recently, I would walk around with my neck pain and had no idea where it was coming from. When I felt like I was a pain in the neck for asking for something from another person, I noticed my neck would always clench up.

No matter what, the neck pain would consistently come back. I never knew if I was going to wake up in the morning and feel like a million dollars, or if I would feel like my head weighed one hundred pounds and that I couldn't lift it off the pillow. It seemed nothing would take the pain away until I discovered a system of soft tissue therapy. I had to wait patiently until the seventh session to have the entire lesson devoted to my neck, but for the first time in years I felt a relief that can only be described as heaven sent. I was able to turn my head and look over my shoulder. I didn't think it would be possible but my neck was finally starting to feel better. And it felt better for years. Until it didn't.

I noticed that I had gained a few pounds and I was really getting upset with myself for this. The fact that ten pounds isn't a huge difference was followed by the realization that I wasn't following what I wanted to do for my life. I was once again letting other people tell me how I should live my life and guess what else showed up at the same time? Yes, the neck pain came back and it was stronger, harder, and more intense than the previous time. I needed to make a change quickly because I had worked too hard to rid myself of that pain.

It was only ten pounds but to me it felt like one hundred again. And I couldn't let myself slip back into those old, dark, familiar patterns. It started with the late night snacking and that was just the physical way it manifested. That was how I would stuff down all the old feelings of insecurity that had reared their ugly head. The insecurity was like a ball and chain around my neck; I didn't want to be seen but I did want to have my voice heard. I was constantly waiting for it to be my turn, but it didn't materialize the way I was attempting to manifest it. I needed to know the "why" behind why I gained so much weight in the past, which was after another major life shift, similar to the one I've just gone through.

In order to break the cycle, I took my body, mind, and spirit back to the place where I was at my thinnest. I was one hundred and twenty-two pounds, and I willed myself to remember what was happening. I know I was incredibly happy and then it hit me like a freight train. I was busy living my life the way I wanted to live it. I was seeing the man I wanted to see long distance and working the amount of hours that I wanted to work. I was so busy honoring myself that I forgot that I sometimes slip into old patterns.

The old patterns were rhetorical questions, things like, "Does this person or that person like me? Am I good enough? Why is this happening to me?" And the answers were all so simple and right in front of me that I felt like kicking myself. When you live in your true sense of self and highest vibration, you want to show the world that your body, mind, and spirit are at peace. So, I decided to go back to peace and remember to live in this moment right now because in the immortal words of Eleanor Roosevelt, "Today is the oldest you've ever been, and the youngest you'll ever be again." Make that time count.

I had to develop a set of "rules," so to speak, to follow because I was tired of the neck pain but even more tired of the insecurity that was the source of the pain.

In closing, I would like to gift you with the guidelines that I set up for myself. Consider it a cheat sheet of sorts, an easy thing to be able to refer back to if you find yourself not taking care of you first.

1. Know yourself and honor yourself first. This includes living your powerful truth.

2. Only you can decide how much you want to weigh.

3. Remember back to your thinnest weight (realistically) and imagine all the things that were happening in your life at that time.

4. Now move heaven and earth to get back to where you were so that you can feel that sense of happiness, or calm, or stillness, or whatever word you want to attach to it.

To love yourself is to put yourself first in order to inspire others to begin to break free to live their happiness today.

Nicole Black is a certified Rolfer™ Massage Therapist, and writer. She lives in southern California with her daughter and when Nicole isn't writing, she enjoys traveling to distant lands, Pilates, and chasing butterflies.

www.NicoleBlack.com

Georgie Deyn

Mary Me

I've always believed in Angels. I would invite them into my life to help me with my healing work and to guide me along my spiritual pathway. But never could I have imagined that Mary, the Queen of the Angels, would have such a special place in my heart as she does now.

For back in 2006, I was given a gift from the angels, delivered to me by a dear friend. It was to be a turning point in my life that sparked a series of events. Life has never been the same since. A flame was ignited in my heart, changing my life from the mundane to the sacred. I remember the moment like it was yesterday.

"Georgie, I have been given a great idea for a song title for you, during my meditation," my friend excitedly told me.

"Really, what is it?" I asked curiously.

"Mary Me. It will be a healing song and you will channel Mother Mary's words and love, as you sing it to your clients."

"Oh ok, thanks." I thought to myself, "I don't have a connection to Mother Mary! My only recollection of Mary was from the nativity plays at school." I didn't really take much notice of the wacky idea.

However, a few days later I found myself effortlessly channeling beautiful words. I knew it wasn't me. I wasn't a writer, I was a singer, but a writer – no way! The song, my first ever, was written in a matter of minutes, the tune was simple and the chorus catchy.

Within days I found myself singing the song during healing sessions. I would spontaneously begin to sing the song and it would take my client into a time in their childhood that needed healing in some way. During these sessions, I was guided by Mary to help the clients reclaim a part of their child within that had felt abandoned or hurt. We often found the wounded child hiding somewhere, stuck in a past moment. I could feel Mary's presence during the song and many clients reported being rocked in the arms of an angel.

I was soon guided to sing "Mary Me" during my group healing meditations. If Mary wanted me to sing the song, I would find myself in an altered state and hear myself from a distance. Many clients and students asked me if I had recorded the song, as they wished to listen to it again at home. But something stopped me having the courage to record the enchanting song. I just never thought the healing magic could be captured and given justice. So I continued to sing my song when Mary made her presence felt and I was guided to do so.

My connection with Mary was soon to become stronger, for in the summer of 2008, I was guided to read a book about a well-known medium and his healing center. I remember how strong the pull was to go and visit. I felt the guides of the healing center in my bedroom at night, as I eagerly read through the pages. Within a week my flights were booked and so was my accommodation. I flew out to Brasilia airport in August and had a magical spiritual healing experience.

The angels and Divine Mother had orchestrated a little surprise for me upon my arrival. The room that I had been given happened to be next to the Mother Mary shrine, in the garden of the guesthouse, where I was staying. It was a beautiful grotto, which had been built on the land where people had seen visitations of Mother Mary.

A few nights into my stay I had the most beautiful dream. Mother Mary came to me in my sleep. She told me to spread love and healing with our song guiding me to share the song at the center. On the Sunday afternoon at the meditation and service I was encouraged to sing. I could feel my throat becoming dry and tight. I prayed for support, took a deep breath, and started the first verse. I do not remember the whole experience as I drifted into an altered state. I was informed later that it touched many hearts. Even those who did not understand the English words began to cry, as the unconditional love stroked their souls.

During my stay at the healing center, I had asked for a deeper understanding of my spiritual path and journey; praying to be healed of everything that was holding me back from being the purest channel I could be. This understanding and healing came, but more dramatically than I could have predicted. At first, I felt my life crumbling around me, a bit like "The Tower" in the Tarot and then I was like a butterfly coming out of a chrysalis.

In February 2010, I found a spiritual group in London that I joined. It was the highlight of my week, for it was in this circle that I connected with my new guide "Love." Her message to me was as follows:

"Sing, sing, and sing! For when you do it heals you and those who listen."

I began to channel tones and sounds. Everyone in the group felt the presence of Mary. My angel, Love's job was to help me raise my vibration to be able to channel the Divine essence once more. I felt incredibly overwhelmed with love and a sense of unconditional compassion like never before. I knew Mary wanted me to believe in myself and help me heal my inner child too. So I started singing for myself as a form of meditation and a way to go into an altered state to channel the messages from Love, Mary, my other guides, and the Archangels.

I was still reluctant to record the special song and finding a musician to do it justice was proving difficult too. So, I plodded on being a channel and kept things fairly low key. At times my path felt lonely, but my connection with Mary was becoming stronger and deeper.

A few psychics told me that they saw a nun around me and that her name was Mary. I, however, knew deep in my heart it was Our Lady. I never quite had the courage or self-belief and confidence to tell them. After all, who was I to be channeling the Queen of the Angels? Why would Mary give me the song, when she could have given it to someone famous, who could share it to their followers? Surely she would have gone to someone world-famous, not little insignificant me! My inner child was still not feeling worthy or good enough; I can see that now.

I needed more confirmation and proof. Another piece of the puzzle came to me through a dear friend. I was invited to take part in a healing day with her on the magical Island of Ibiza. Here is where I was to connect with more people who needed Mary's magical touch; the wounded inner children who desperately needed the loving tender care of Mary found their way to myself and the song.

It was whilst in Ibiza I felt free to talk about the fact that I was channeling the Divine Feminine, through my singing and messages. At home, in the UK, I was concerned that people would think that either I had an over inflated ego or that I was crazy and delusional. Yes, I had the support from my group, however, there were not many people I could openly discuss my spiritual connection with. So, in the UK, I sang the song under the disguise of my Angel Love, as that seemed less egotistical. But, In Ibiza, I could openly say, "I channel Mother Mary through my singing and speaking and together we can help love, heal and nurture your inner child."

Whilst in Ibiza I had a clear message from Mary that I was to write about my story and channel her words in written form – a book to heal and love the child within, including examples of my clients' sessions and channeled messages about self-worth, love and healing. Although, I wanted to write, I just never knew how to start, so I procrastinated.

Back in the UK, I was still very much low key with my "Mary work." I was asked to sing and run a meditation "Healing the Inner Child" at a charity

MBS night. To be honest I felt a little bit despondent as most people were not interested in my healing meditation. Instead they went to listen to a medium give messages from loved ones and only a few people attended the session I was to run. However, at the end of the session another earth angel approached me and asked about my song.

"Have you recorded it? Well you must and I know the perfect musician. I'll give you his number now. Give him a call." So I did. We connected musically and he came up with a beautiful piano piece that enhanced the melody and words perfectly. Not only did we record Mary Me together, but another three albums, all of which have healing qualities.

However, it was not until I visited Fatima in May 2016 that I was given the final push to put Mary Me on the map. My first day there was spent in the village where the three children of Fatima had lived. It was an enchanting place and the area that marked the angelic sighting gave me an overwhelming sense of peace and security. As an empath amidst the vast number of pilgrims, it was difficult for me to be amongst big crowds who were visiting the shrine. But somehow I felt protected, held and safe.

Excitedly on my second day, I visited the sanctuary and here is where I shed tears of joy. I had never had such a profound sense of urgency from Mary. She was insistent that I share our song with the world and talk about its healing quality. I felt her presence so close, as if the veil between our worlds was finer. It surely was one of the most precious and sacred moments in my life.

So that is the story behind the song and this is the start of the new chapter of my life and my book *"Mary Me."* I decided to ask Mary for help in sharing her love. I asked her from my heart, "Mother, where do I start? How shall I begin to channel and write for you? Show me the way please."

"Where do you start dear one? Now is the time. Now is the time to truly, truly shine your light. This message is for many. These words are infused with love, hope, peace, and eternal light. I wish to make the words and the expression accessible. I will create a portal of light for those who read the words of love. When you hold the book in your hands, you shall feel the love emanating from the pages within. This is my sacred wish. Have faith child I am with you."

The story continues, as does my connection with the Queen of the Angels.

I have also been guided to co-create a celestial sound healing modality named "Angelic Harmony Therapy" which is spreading around the world and other practitioners are learning this beautiful therapy.

The blessings continue to shower an abundance of spiritual riches upon me in the form of friends and opportunities.

My message to you now is never give up on your dreams; follow them and nurture them. For I believe in you and so does Mary!

Georgie G. Deyn is a Singer, Healer, Teacher, and Channel of Love in its purest forms. She works with the Light and Sound of the Highest Realms, including the Archangels, Seraphim, and that of the Divine. She has been inspired to channel Angelic Harmony Therapy, a celestial sound healing, into fruition by the light. Since 1999, Georgie has worked with groups and individuals of all ages to help them connect to their most Divine selves. She brings healing and inspiration through the messages, meditation, music, and movement from her angels, guides, and Divine Feminine collective consciousness to all.

www.angelicharmonytherapy.com

https://www.youtube.com/user/AngelicHarmonyHeals

Robyn Dewar

6

The Healing Power of Song Writing

Song writing has been a gift in and of itself on my journey of self-love. I never feel alone during the creation process. The vibrational lift I receive from strumming chords on my guitar nurtures every cell in my body. Music has supported me through the darkest moments of my life and has comforted me in times of tremendous grief or sadness. Writing music connects me with my highest self, offering me a way to communicate through the frequency of love.

I began my song writing journey at the age of seventeen. I was elated when I discovered a constructive and healthy way to release bottled up emotions. Up until this age, words did not come easy for me. My preferred method of communication was by thought and feel. As an empath, I naturally took on the pain and suffering of others, which distanced me socially. It wasn't until my early forty's (over twenty years later) that I learned how to participate freely in social settings without weighing myself down with heavy energy. I am grateful to my teachers and guides for their lessons about energetic shielding.

In 2007, I noticed myself transitioning to a new way of thinking. I slowly felt an openness to the shift of a new thought pattern, which professed that "life is happening for me." It was during this time that the lyrics to my song titled *U R Free* poured out me.

The words to *U R Free* became my anthem for the next four years. I found myself singing these words when shadowy moments crept in. I began to trust the thought of no longer being a victim of my life, but rather embrace the moment with gratitude and celebrate the ride. For the first time in my life, I was able to look into a mirror and tell the little girl reflected there that she is safe and loved. I was able to look into her eyes and say, "I love you." This was an incredibly empowering and healing time in my life.

U R Free

Are we free to believe in anything?
Can we trust what we know to survive?
When the world's closing in,
It feels like a sin to want to change this life of mine.

Wishing on a shooting star,
I see in the distance it's not far.
A hope, a gleam of happiness for me.
All of my faith in this great world,
Tells me a scared little girl,
Be brave, be strong, you are free.

Chorus

Free to change the world,
Free to make a difference one day.
Free to raise your voice,
Free to make a choice someday.
All the powers that be will help you to see that you are free.

When the world's closing in,
Then it's time to begin,
To change your view.
What you've got to do,
Is sit in the dark for a while.

Then you will see the light,
It will be shinning so bright.
Open your eyes for you will see,
Who you are truly meant to be.
And you'll know this in your heart
That dreams are meant to be FREE.

Chorus

******

It was just two short years after I wrote *U R Free*, my Mom left this earthy realm. She is with me often in spirit. One early spring morning, she was with me. It was then that the words and music flowed to create the song *Words Not Said*. I am deeply grateful for the gifts that she continues to give me as she is just one dimension away.

Words Not Said

The rain is falling down, tears are all I taste.
I know that in my heart, I've come to the right place.
With every piece of me, you sparkle in my soul,
For what you've given me, is not for me to hold.

Chorus

Let me wrap you up in the sunshine,
Let me wipe away your tears,
Let me fill your soul with gladness,
And comfort your buried fears.

It's the fear of never knowing, just who we truly are.
But a crystal clear reminder that's gifted by a shooting star.
This mystery that we've been solving, since words are never said.
It's the quilt that we've been weaving, connected by tiny threads.

Bridge

Oh I don't know, where to go from here.
If I raise my hands up high, will the world disappear?

The rain is pouring down, tears are still all I can taste.
And the salt that's on my lips, takes me to another place,
Where the waves come rolling in, the sand is always white.
It's where I think of you the most, your wings took flight.

CHORUS x2

Life truly is a journey where music fills my soul. Song writing helps me express my truth and singing helps me share it. ♥ I wake up in the morning, grateful for each day. I am so in love with today and celebrate healing through self-love. I invite you to listen to the songs that allow you to connect with your heart, and invite the healing power of music to flow into your life.

Robyn Dewar easily shares her passion for a fulfilled life as an International Singer / Songwriter and Entrepreneur. She is an educator of integrative wellness and savvy network marketing professional. Robyn happily resides in Haileybury, Ontario with her husband Shawn and their two daughters.

http://www.robyndewar.com

Vonne Solis

7
A Journey through Time

My story today is considerably different from my story eleven years ago. While many of the elements remain the same (the characters, setting, plot, and conflict), the resolution to this mostly drama and sometimes comedy has yet to be written.

The topic of my story, *Overcoming Loss & Grief* was a theme I chose with some reticence, given the degree to which our society, in general, reacts to loss and grief. It doesn't, at least not to any measurable extent. For those that do consider the impact of loss and its untold complications of lingering grief, the mere idea that its associated pain can be overcome is unthinkable to most.

My daughter died by suicide on July 26, 2005. That was the death of me too. She was beautiful, talented, creative, gentle of spirit, and only twenty-two years old. I missed all the signs of trouble brewing; as did the doctors, extended family, and friends. While this isn't a story about blame, regret, anger, hopelessness, despair, confusion, frustration, bewilderment, defeat, and all the other untold destruction that suffering brings to those left behind, any story of loss would not be worth telling if these elements were not mentioned. They are the ugly part of grief. The darkest parts of the soul that nobody wants to talk about or even acknowledge to themselves. It takes courage to face one's demons in grief head-on and even more to openly talk about our vulnerabilities in our deepest sorrow.

Often, in the early days after loss, grievers turn to loved ones they believe are their strongest supporters. It is not uncommon to find through time that they are not. They are usually just as damaged as those closest to the loss. In my story, as the bereaved mom who is spiritual by nature, I am both the author and protagonist. I carry a lot of weight as to how the plot unfolds; the characters develop within the setting (home, heart, family, healing, and environment); how all conflict gets resolved; and critically, how the outline will take shape to bring a positive resolution for my happy ending. Often, I feel like a lone lighthouse that without a bright and flashing inner light could not possibly guide those nearest me to the safety of the shore.

There is a huge responsibility that comes with accepting loss, and becoming a bright and shining light by choosing to heal from as much pain as possible, in order to guide others to do the same. I used to think it was possible to heal from all pain. Today, eleven years into my grief, I still believe that to be true. However, I also believe that the degree to which we choose to and can heal from pain is relative to the impact of our loss. And this impact rests entirely on the relationship we had to the person who died through the enormous love we had for them and/or the unresolved issues that emotionally bind us to them.

After my daughter's death, I lost my parents, other family members, and several people close to me. In fact, I've started to think there's a party to be enjoyed on the other side when I get there and my daughter is certainly not alone, which has brought me a whole new measure of comfort. By opening my mind to the probability of life beyond death (expanded consciousness) and accepting the instantaneous power of the Divine to teach and guide us, my grief took on new meaning. Understanding the gifts that are ours for the taking, from the humility we experience succumbing to our greatest vulnerability in the darkest of times, and knowing the freedom we can enjoy as we trust we can soar despite the constraints of our physicality, I learned to honor the sacredness of all suffering. I found that the challenges we endure are designed solely to entice and enhance our spiritual growth. Knowing all this and more, I now want to accept my daughter's death so that I can fully embrace living again with the joy, ease, and contentment that is how life is meant to be lived.

Acceptance of any loss means giving up the emotional ties to our dreams and the longing for what was. This is especially difficult after the death of a child, but I have known people to suffer severely after the loss of a spouse, parent, or sibling. In this way, pain is universal, as are the challenges to overcome the loss experience.

Without the *willingness* to want to heal from the pain of a loved one's death, it is almost impossible to enjoy a fulfilling and meaningful life. We can try and even find some aspects to living that feel rewarding and purposeful. However, without committing fully to healing the mind, body, and soul from any loss experience, we cannot authentically take part in the riches of what's been left behind to create something more, now and in the future.

I remember after my daughter's death, sitting on my verandah looking at the gardens I had planted and loved so much. I could not fully see the colors of the flowers nor enjoy their scents, or feel delight at the sight of birds feeding. I couldn't appreciate the warmth of the sun amidst the clear blue sky. There was a veil between me and the world that numbed me to all of my senses. I had no feeling towards my loved ones except my surviving son. And these were largely centered on the guilt I carried for no longer being able to provide for him the way I had. I felt and looked like a vacant being with nothing to offer anyone. All of my relationships had shattered. I no longer functioned in a way I recognized. Former friends dropped by the wayside as I could no longer anchor them to me. I instantly isolated myself from the world and those I loved because I felt so alone in my loss. I was weak, broken, confused, angry, and desperate to leave the planet to be with my girl again.

This was not a short-lived experience. It took years for me to unravel all of the complicated feelings and emotions related to my grief and find the strength I never knew I had to try to overcome the experience of what I was left with after my daughter died.

My own body of work is centered on empowering grievers to heal from their pain through a metaphysical and spiritual understanding of loss and grief. More recently, I have found that it is equally necessary to embrace the physicality of the experience to give full justice to our chosen existence in incarnate form. This is not easy. With head in the clouds, it is preferable to revel in the certainty of ongoing consciousness after death, commune with the angels, enjoy visits with spirit loved ones, feel heart-centered peace through the constant feelings of unconditional love and compassion for the self and others, where there is no pain.

After years of making solid strides in my healing through my spiritual practice, more recently I was forced to face my grief in the physical. I collapsed in the fall of 2015, no longer able to carry on the pace of my daily living. I decided to pull my head and heart out of the ethereal for a while and focus only on the physical aspects of my loss and grief. This decision felt daunting and terrified me, largely because I felt sure that once I let myself fall into that pit I'd lose all control. And control is very important to managing grief in the long term or ignoring it altogether.

With the help of medical professionals that understood me better than I thought, I let myself become vulnerable to my physical needs. I have long been critical of the lack of understanding in the medical community about grief, suicide, and it's after effects, and to a large degree I still stand by this opinion. Choosing to work with a doctor and therapist was not an easy decision for me. However, I have discovered that for authentic and integrated healing, this must include tending to the physical and mental components of pain alongside the spiritual and emotional. Professional help is available, but it is our job as grievers to find the doctors and therapists we can trust and actively guide them to help us tear down the walls of our suffering. In many cases, they learn about grief by the trust we show them to help us in this way. However, this may not be a journey many grievers can embark on for years to come in their bereavement, if ever. Along with control, establishing trust is an integral part of and critical to the healing process in grief.

I love a happy ending to any story. Who doesn't? The way my resolution outline is shaping up looks like it's going to bring just that – a happy ending. Recently, my strides are getting bigger, with my feet rooted solidly to a foundation that is starting to feel safe. That foundation, I've come to realize, is me. It's my faith, courage, confidence, vision, and readiness to be more. Not for others (though they benefit), but in respect of the incarnation and experiences I have chosen and now must courageously accept.

On my daughter's angel anniversary this year, I decided to honor me as well for the bravery I've shown this far in accepting an incarnation no one in their right mind would willingly choose in human form (and I know every other bereaved parent would concur). In spirit form, where our contracts are agreed before incarnating, it's a different story. It is not one of pain and suffering, but rather growth and enlightenment, wisdom and knowledge, not only for the self but countless others. We gladly and enthusiastically accept our chosen roles and responsibilities.

The burden of loss is a certainty that each one of us will carry at some point in our lives. Who we lose, when, and how is not. That we all will endure grief to some degree makes the need for our culture to start having a more open discourse on grief and loss palpable. Grievers need to feel free to be in pain (the same as with all physical ailments) and treated with respect in identifying and managing their changing needs throughout the healing process. If we were to start talking more about grief, it would make it a lot easier for grievers to seek the help they need, even if this start is in trusted and intimate surroundings (talking to friends and family members). Stepping out larger they may feel encouraged to find a support group that promotes enlightened healing, work with medical professionals that will listen to their needs and prescribe an appropriate course of treatment, help to create their own supportive work environment, or lend a hand to others.

My desire in sharing my story is that anyone suffering will choose to understand the hidden blessings in every loss experience. While pain has its place, its value eventually runs out. We were not meant to be a mere shell of existence on this planet. All of us have chosen specific lessons to learn and teach others in our various roles.

I learned long ago never to underestimate the relevance of all experiences we have chosen in our combined lifetimes as a means to connect to each other through heart and soul, joy and love, triumph and purpose. This obliges us to share our stories; find courage to lead as required and follow when inspired to live as enlightened and purposefully motivated as possible. We can create what we want, including living a blissful life after loss. I invite you to experience this magic unfold on a journey through time, step by step, as you become willing and ready for more.

Vonne Solis is an author and Angel Therapy Practitioner®. After losing her twenty-two-year-old daughter to suicide in 2005, Vonne dedicated herself to becoming a voice for the grieving to change our cultural view on loss and grief. Her work offers a thoughtful discourse and self-help practice for transformation based on the insights of Divine wisdom. Vonne's goal is to assist individuals in raising their consciousness to live as joyous a life as possible after loss. The foundation of her work is based on the principles of self-responsibility and the choice we have to heal and transform from all suffering.

http://www.vonnesolis.com

http://bit.ly/divinehealingbook

Robert Hickinbotham

8

Gratitude of a Stranger

Some people won't understand this simple thing called Love.

With the weight of the world on their shoulders, people are busy with life. But it is with every choice they make that could bring a change to someone's whole day.

I am the type of person that will say a joke about probably the worst racist, sexual, and inhumane thing possible. It is funny at the time, but that's not what I believe. Myself, I don't care about a person's race, belief, gender, orientation, or any other so-called personal status.

As I think about it, and I may be wrong, I believe there are two types of people – good or bad. I have seen both kinds: bad people present themselves when needed and good people hide when needed. Sometimes, I think I'm a bad person because of what goes through my thoughts, but I live in a major city where often times, nobody gives a crap about anyone else. Everyone is just going about their own lives.

I find a lot of laughs and a bit of happiness just by talking or even helping a random person I felt drawn to at the time. It's not hard to say, "How's it going?" or, "Lousy weather, hey?"

I was inspired to write about this today as I thought about an elderly man who walked up to a crowded bus stop and as soon as he looked confused, people either got their phones out or looked down. So, I looked at him and said, "Are you alright, buddy?" This turned into a quick chat and as it turned out, he needed the same bus as me and wouldn't get off until three stops before mine. He commented that he walked my way because, "I had a friendly face." **Wow**, I didn't expect that.

Anyways, we all got on the bus, and I sat three seats behind him. As he stood up to get ready to depart the bus, he turned around, looked at me and said, "You are a good person," to which I replied the same back to him. After he slowly got off the bus, he leaned back in and tipped his hat forward towards me to say these words, "Takes one to know one."

I thought about this and his words for the rest of my trip, until I realized that it felt good to hear those simple five words to me.

This simple act of love and conversation from a complete stranger is what keeps me going in a big city, as it reminds me that there are still people out there in this world who make your day better. The best thing is that it costs you nothing but you gain a lot in return.

With each gift that you share, you might help to heal or repair someone's broken heart. Love, kindness, a gentle smile, or even a simple "Hello" to a stranger is all it may take to change someone's day or even their whole life.

Over the years, I have witnessed both decent and bad people and events through personal experiences that have shown me that goodness and wickedness are all around us.

People are drawn to me not because I am different from anyone else, but because they see my true inner spirit. They see someone who is a kind and honest person wearing his heart on the sleeve, and is willing to give a hand when needed.

I believe that when one goes through such things as I have over the years, it makes us better people. I know I have a soft spot for others because of some of these experiences. I just want to help even when it is a stranger like the man wearing the hat at the bus stop, or just by having a conversation with someone to make them smile or laugh. It's the simple things in life that can change someone's day or even their life.

Gratitude, to me, is giving a free act of kindness and being mindful that we all go through stuff in our lives. I encourage everyone to regularly take some time to share gratitude in your day-to-day tasks. It's simple and most of all, it's free.

It doesn't take much to be gentle or kind to another, to help others in need, and can even be as simple as giving up your seat on the bus for a stranger who needs it more. If other people continue to be drawn to me, that's okay. Who knows? They may even help or bless my life in some way.

Robert Hickinbotham is a loving, kind, and generous-natured soul who helps others along their life's journey, often without realizing he is doing so. Happiness and sadness shape us into the person we are, which inspires Robert to write stories from the heart to reach many souls around the world.

Hick186@gmail.com

Manpreet Komal

Magic in Trauma: Writing to Heal

Our deeper wounds don't just go away and sometimes we don't even know they exist.

During my meditations, in June 2014, twice in the same week, I had a clear vision of standing on top of a hill at an Inn in Big Sur. I had been there once three years before. I researched the Inn to understand more about it and after my second vision, I read up that it attracts a lot of writers. I knew I was meant to go there to write, so I ended up booking the first date they had available, which was two months out.

As the trip got closer, I started getting nervous, thinking, "What am I going to write about? Me? Writer? Maybe I will write a book for women."

Two weeks prior to my departure, I decided to start writing about my life from the time I was born. As I got to the age of twelve, when I moved to USA, I wrote about a trauma I had experienced. The more I wrote, my body resurfaced the trauma, screaming as if I just went through it in the present moment. I was in fight or flight mode; triggered, breathless, and scared.

I was alone at home. I tried to meditate and take deep breaths to calm myself down. Not knowing how to deal with the trauma resurfacing, I felt helpless, powerless, and in shock. Somehow I found myself strolling through a blog by a spiritual advisor I had worked with and I clicked on a song from her blog. That song brought me back into ease and grace. As I look back now, I can see that the Universe was working with me to support me in my helpless and courageous moment.

Four days before my trip, I started getting anxious, doubting my ability to write again. I then decided to call a local institute close to the Inn to see if they had any writing courses during that weekend. There were no such courses that weekend but there was one called "Way of Story" that had already started. As much as I wished I could take off and attend that course, I knew I couldn't as I had other work commitments.

I went on the author's website and discovered that she wrote for writers. I ended up watching her one hour interview twice the same night and time flew by. She specifically talked about how people in prison had picked up her book and healed their traumas. I was in awe, thinking this is meant for me. So, that night I ordered her books.

I was having difficulty sleeping. It was 3 a.m. in the morning and I was listening to spiritual radio. I had dozed off to sleep when in my half asleep/half-awake state I heard a woman saying 8.22, 8.22, and 8.22. Eight stands for Infinity, Twenty-Two is a master number and that it was Angel's day. It was a perfect day to start a book and make it a forty-four day project.

Later in the day, I was writing a date on a paper when it occurred to me the message I heard in my half asleep state. I looked at my arrival date at the inn. I connected the dots and was amazed once again. From the vision, Inn, trauma resurfacing, song, to the author's website, to 8.22 – something was clearly supporting me behind the scenes.

I felt the mysterious forces nudging me along. It was as if the Universe was saying, "Manpreet, this is for you and for us, don't take this trip lightly and make use of it – just trust."

I didn't have a topic or writing experience but I knew my meditations, the 8.22 message, and the book I had found days before were all leading me to something greater than me. Sometimes you just have to trust the messages, and follow your higher calling and signs of the Universe to something larger in play than your human body can comprehend.

I decided to call the inn and get there a day early on 8.21 and truly let the 8.22 day surprise me. After settling in my room, I went to the restaurant. The server generously poured me a nice glass of champagne as I admired the gothic art shining through a long white tapered candle flickering along. I found myself speaking with her about Angel's day and how the next day, 8.22, was the perfect day to start a book. She got excited and wanted to start her own music project that day.

I woke up the next morning warm in my comforters and didn't really want to get up. Suddenly, I heard something ringing in my head, "Who moved my cheese" – a reference to a short book I had just reread recently. Clearly whoever was sending me that message didn't want me lazing around in that room but getting to it. I got up, ate breakfast, and went to the top of the hill. It was very exciting to be led on this journey and to not know what was awaiting me there. I still remember going to that spot three years before and taking a picture of myself in a purple dress and two purple flowers on each of my ears.

After finding a nice rustic bench to sit on next to a tree overlooking the vastness of the magnetic ocean, I took out my journal and the book I had

Compiled by Brian Calhoun

ordered. Chapters 1 – 8 really flew by. These were exercises to make you look deep within your soul and your past uncovering the deepest moments of your life. This book helps you rewrite specific incidents from your life while connecting you to the other person involved. It is like writing a dialogue from both perspectives while reshaping how you see your life in the present moment.

I found incredible wisdom and inner peace in rewriting the chapters of my life with a different perspective. The meditations, exercises, and talking to my inner self from a higher perspective was powerful, healing, and transforming.

The next morning I woke up feeling much lighter and happier. I walked into the restaurant and looked at the beautiful flowers and greenery outside, and made a silent wish to come back here every 4 – 6 weeks to write.

I sat having an amazingly delicious breakfast at the corner table next to the piano where I met "G", whom I had been introduced to by a restaurant's employee whose birthday was on 8.22. "G's" stories were full of excitement, romance, and adventure. Like little girls, together we car pooled to her favorite spot of the day, her daily shower in a cold waterfall built by surfers overlooking a sexy and deep valley facing the deep ocean behind the trees.

The day had arrived. It was time to make my way back to San Francisco. I was sad to leave and happy what I uncovered during this trip. I went to the restaurant to eat breakfast. I felt called to sit at the same table as day before but noticed an older couple sitting there and having breakfast. I thought to myself that I should talk with them as it could turn out to be a fun conversation, but then I realized it might be interrupting their peace. I went back to the other room and waited for my warm oatmeal to arrive as I continued to read and write.

Minutes later, a short woman with the white hair from that same table walked up to me. She had a genuine smile and greeted me with her warm hands. I could feel her energy run through me as she held my hands. She said, with a very genuine smile and some honor in her voice, "I hear you are looking for a place." I was stunned, as I understood how difficult it was to find somewhere to stay in Big Sur. She told me she had no website as she did not market this place and it was by invitation only. She then handed me a vanilla-colored folded card with a beautiful hand sketched picture of a yurt. I immediately asked her about the month of September.

Later on, I found out that some very special people have stayed at the yurt. I was stunned, excited, and honored all at the same time. One could think that all these gifts along the way were rewards that Universe was giving me. The more courage I took to heal parts of me while rewriting my life and forgiving the old hurt, the more of such coincidences were occurring.

The Universe was saying "Yes" along with me, and encouraging, guiding, holding, and supporting me. I had to follow the signs, trust, and take action.

September 15th was the day I was scheduled to arrive on my first visit to the yurt. As I drove up hill, on the left side was a deep beautiful valley of green trees and behind it, the view of the ocean. The owner of the yurt walked me in and gave me a sacred tour reflecting on her memories of the yurt. I was in awe.

After a few hours and few chapters into healing through the writing my book, I was invited for tea by the yurt lady and her friend at a local bakery. She said, "Manpreet, very few people follow their dreams. The key is to not be attached to the outcome. When you follow your dreams, the Universe sends you help in unimaginable ways." She gave me an example of how she knew Big Sur was her lover long before she moved there. She bought a piece of land there and for thirty years, people came and helped her build her dream home. She never had to go look for help.

The last day of my stay was September 19th. I had already worked my way through Chapters 1-8 of the book exercises but was resisting the next chapter on "Trauma." Hours before I was supposed to take off, I opened chapter nine. I knew I had to do this chapter at the yurt, next to my crystals, while the sandalwood incense and candles were burning. It was as safe and as sacred as it could get.

At first, I found myself talking to my inner twelve-year-old self and then I spoke to someone very close to me. Tears flowed as I wrote from his perspective in seeing his innocence and his pain. After journaling, the exercise in Chapter Nine asked to send light to the people with the same experience I had. To pray for others with the same situation was something I had never imagined. I had been stuck in pain and fear in my subconscious, not even knowing it was affecting me.

As I meditated, my eyes still closed, I saw a yellow and blue circle rotating around me. It was yellow on one side and blue on the other, as if an oval shaped energy was revolving around the front of my body. Tears flowed and I let them. Messages came and I let them.

From being guided to the hill, writing the book to heal, to the yurt, I can see clearly now that all these steps were leading me to find the courage to heal myself. I was being prepared to trust the signs of the Universe, allow, and use my healing to spread messages of finding hope in what seemed to be a deep dark well of my life. I was taught in the process of healing that it in fact it was a teacher, for me, showing me my true courage and willingness to reveal the pain to myself that had been long hidden. No doctor, counselor, or healer could have given me what I gave myself with the support of God.

Compiled by Brian Calhoun

Manpreet Komal was born in Amritsar, a city in India, called land of the Golden Temple. One of her life purposes is to help people find light in the dark. She loves discovering everyday treasures in the little moments of bliss connecting with the Ocean and the mountains. Manpreet is a contributing author of two International Best-Selling books and is working on her first book. She is a Keynote Speaker, Dancer, Writer, Traveler, an Intuitive coach, and has over 100,000 people that share her journey on her sacred Facebook page called *Magic Is Everywhere*.

http://www.facebook.com/universesendshelp

http://www.manpreetkomal.org

Manpreet Komal

10

Magic in Trauma: The Prayer Story

The healing journey continued and I finished all the chapters of the book designed to help me heal through writing.

I had learned to do Reiki on myself and I started trusting the process of praying for others. I then started combining prayer for others with sending distance Reiki energy to the world. I especially enjoyed sending Reiki to those who had experienced trauma like me. As I started praying and sending light to all people suffering, I thought of the difficulties I had experienced, and how others could be going through the same. I prayed for God and the Angels to bless all with healing love and light and for a miracle cure.

It was now the month of December. The rains were pouring heavily, and my apartment had experienced several leaks making it unliveable for weeks. I was back and forth with my landlords and was forced to live in a hotel for days. It was frustrating.

I had a spa appointment booked around Christmas day and before driving to the spa, I went to my regular coffee shop for a walk and breakfast. I was enjoying my sip of coffee when suddenly my eyes glanced over at the newspaper underneath my coffee cup. It had half the word of the same trauma listed in the headlines. It drew my attention so I picked up the paper, and it spoke about a miracle cure recently discovered. I was in awe reading this. For the first time in my life, I had prayed for those affected like me, more or less, and here it was – a miracle cure right in front of me. I was happy, excited, humbled, and in grace of magic answers showing up right then – just in time for Christmas.

Later in the day, I was sitting on a couch after getting a massage at a local spa. I was doing Reiki on myself and then sent prayers and distance Reiki to endless people around the world. I called upon angels to assist me on my mission to help the world; to make it clear to me what that it was and how to go about it. After thirty minutes of deep connection with my body and deep healing, I was feeling a high vibration inside.

I then went to the main relaxation area. I had picked up my phone and connected it to Facebook. I was still in a very deeply intuitive state when the first Facebook post showed up was for a non-profit organization. They were asking for funds to help hit their million-dollar fundraising goal by the end of the year. I felt a strong urge to donate not $1, nor $100, or $500, but $1,000 – the maximum possible for myself. It hadn't been the best month for me financially. I couldn't help myself, but I felt strongly this was a message from the angels. I needed to donate that precise amount. It was as if the angels wanted me to show a sign that I was listening to them. I went and got my credit card and didn't overthink it. I told the angels intuitively that this was for them. I got home and told my husband about this donation, but he wasn't happy and reminded me of all the times I had stopped him from overspending.

A few weeks later, I was trying to resolve a dispute with our landlord over the work they needed to finish to our apartment caused by all the leaks in December. Every time I tried to open my email to write them an assertive letter, I couldn't get into my email. When I did log in, I saw an email from the leasing office. It said, "Manpreet, A Resident Inconvenience Reimbursement was issued for $1,900.00."

I was amazed! I couldn't believe their level of generosity. They had given already given me the option to leave my apartment over the holidays due to the level of discomfort. They had given me $900 to cover hotel expenses which I expected, but they also gave an additional $1,000 for the inconvenience. My husband was amazed just as much as me at this synchronistic coincidence. I knew the angels were watching and telling me I did the right thing by donating $1,000 for the cause.

When we follow our guidance to support others unconditionally without thinking of what's in it for oneself, we are rewarded with gifts from God that are beyond our imagination. There is power and beauty in prayer. Prayer connects us to our ultimate force – God, source, spirit. It takes us out of our heads and connects us to a higher power of faith. When we have faith, we can imagine the impossible. And often, we will find that the impossible is possible.

Compiled by Brian Calhoun

Manpreet Komal was born in Amritsar, a city in India, called land of the Golden Temple. One of her life purposes is to help people find light in the dark. She loves discovering everyday treasures in the little moments of bliss connecting with the Ocean and the mountains. Manpreet is a contributing author of two International Best-Selling books and is working on her first book. She is a Keynote Speaker, Dancer, Writer, Traveler, an Intuitive coach, and has over 100,000 people that share her journey on her sacred Facebook page called *Magic Is Everywhere*.

http://www.facebook.com/universesendshelp

http://www.manpreetkomal.org

Louise Lajeunesse

11

The Ascension of Lost Souls

When departing the earth plane, not all souls follow the path to "the Light." Some linger patiently in the lower dimensions trying to figure out what their unfinished business is. Others linger because they haven't found their way to the light, most often not certain if they are dead or not.

On some occasions, I found lingering souls still searching for departed loved ones, not knowing if they had moved on or not. Some may feel that their earth friends and family are still in need of them and not realize that their presence may be having a negative effect by staying attached to the earth and causing interference with the earth soul's healing and journey since their death. With the help of the source energy it is possible to assist them in their transition into the Divine Light.

I was privileged to witness this state of being and how the angels showed me that, us as mortals, can assist departed souls with the transmutation of attachments, fears, and other unknown reasons, to guide them to the Light, where they can be reunited with their loved ones.

One day I was assisting my dear friend with some healing energy when the angels showed me a powerful technique to help release souls to the light. She had suffered most of her life from powerful panic attacks and always felt an unpleasant energy presence dragging her down. During this healing session, I suddenly realized the main cause of her trauma originated from trapped souls surrounding her.

I began to focus on their energy and reasons for being, when a cry for help emerged. I discovered they weren't present to cause any mischief or to impact her negatively. They were simply attracted to her light as a beacon of hope to guide them to "the light."

With this realization, a question was raised. *How can I best offer assistance?* My guides showed me in response to my question a beautiful golden elevator slowly coming down from above, guided by Divine Light and two beautiful angels. An inner excitement filled me. It's then, with curiosity and disbelief, that the rest of the scene unfolded.

With the inner knowing this was the tool to help free them, I started to lovingly guide these souls towards the elevator. It was a man, a woman, and a child; the man had the strongest presence. A magnificent beam of white light was glowing above and within the elevator, as they hesitantly made their way into it with the assistance of the angels. They were transported to the end of the beam of light where their departed loved ones were awaiting their arrival. The energy we could feel of the reunion in Heaven, was truly overwhelming.

At that moment, a feeling of extreme peace and relief came over my friend. She finally felt free of the immense burden that had plagued her all her life. Although upon further checking in, we knew that additional work was required despite the newly found feelings.

Searching the cause, we were called to extend the cleansing to her surroundings. As I proceeded to lower the elevator to below the earth surface, a dark cave appeared. Sensing there was no fear to be had, we slowly saw the soul of a woman, who seemed to pull itself from the rock wall formation, to come forward. With love and excitement, we naturally guided her into the elevator, while the angels were welcoming her with loving energy.

An enthusiasm and belief in a higher purpose came over me. I started paying better attention to this large and dark underground area. Slowly, with a felt hesitation, an increasing file of lost souls with no end suddenly appeared. More seemed to be coming off cave walls! It was certainly a blessed opportunity to help these souls pass over.

Seeing this was now an important and urgent task to be accomplished, we joined our releasing intentions and increased the number of elevators to three. Clearing the area lasted a few days, as we set the intention for the elevators to continue their freeing effort until all souls in that area, ready to move up, had reached their destination. The more souls were freed, the better my friend felt. The energy was now lighter and more peaceful.

Following this experience, whenever symptoms of inner turmoil comes over my friend, combined with feeling drained, extremely tired, or a wave of heaviness around her solar plexus, she knows a lost soul is calling for help. She then calls upon the magnificent liberating energy of the elevator to come forth. As earth angels, our ability to sense energy surrounding us and others makes us a beacon for these lost souls searching for a transition mode to the Light.

Not long after this first experience, my friend asked for another intervention, feeling again the presence of that man around her. Tuning in, it felt as though the departed father was back, searching for something. We were then guided to the possibility of a missing part of the family who hadn't yet joined them. It's at that moment that we saw another young child surface.

Shivers run through my body as I write these words, and the remembrance of it brings back tears to my eyes! What a joy when we saw them both meet the mother who was finally reunited with her whole family, sending us love and gratitude. They had perished during the war from the collapse of the building they were in. The cycle was now complete.

When this amazing experience was shared with my other earth angel friends, they were each called to clear many surrounding areas and parts of the globe, where lots of tragedies occurred. This Divine elevator is a wonderful tool added to our healing tool box.

As we are amidst the ascension process, I received the confirmation that the release of these souls was divinely guided and necessary for Mother Earth, to free herself of the heavy and dense energy.

On February 7, 2017, as I was ready to make my way home from work, I felt a strong presence against my right arm and cheek. It was a small fairy, sitting on top of my purse, beside me. As I asked what the reason for his presence was, my mind's eye was directed to a mine, where many miners had been submerged. Automatically sensing the requirement for the elevator, I proceeded to bring one down. The poor miners seemed to rise one by one, blinded by the light. Once they realized the reason for this brightness, I could see them crawl over one another to reach it. In no time, the area was cleared, cleansed, and peace restored.

My fairy friend accompanied me home, all happy to be in my presence and the work that had been done. His feet were dangling and he was happily looking out to the way ahead. With his continued presence and the addition of a second fairy friend, I felt that another chapter of my life was about to open. It's with excitement that I prepare for it and the mischievous attitude of my new-found friends.

On February 10, 2017, a friend with whom I had just discussed the benefit of the elevator with, asked me to help someone she knew suffering from *Post-Traumatic Syndrome Disorder* (PTSD).

While focusing on this man's energy, I could see many black shadows suffocating him. Although some were released with the help of the elevator, others who remained still had lots of anger within them. Having a powerful energy, he attracted the souls of people killed in the areas where he was in service. I came to the realization that this exercise would be of great benefit to all soldiers and first responders, but would likely require more than one release attempt.

If you, as a reader, feel some of the symptoms described within this chapter, it might be in your calling to assist with the liberation of souls, or just to free yourself of dense energy. Knowledge and experience is not a necessity; holding the intention is all that is required.

When souls are attached to us, it can cause us to feel depressed, anxious, a sense of heaviness, and maybe plain right that something wrong is going on! This can also affect us in other areas of our lives, such as unpleasant repeating patterns, lack of flow, not understanding an inner state of confusion, weight issues, food disorders, feeling stuck, addictions (alcohol, drug, food, sex, gambling, etc.), feeling lower emotions of sadness, grief, and unhealthy relationships.

Doing this exercise could break the cycles of confusion and inner turmoil, by bringing a sense of relief and help you heal.

One never knows when they will be called to assist. Just be open, prepared, and ready. If curiosity gets the best of you, it might be the Divine Light finding a way to help open you to the possibilities of the Universe.

****

It's important to remember that not all souls are ready to move up and whether you see the release being done or not, have no fear! If the request was sent, the work will get done. Focus your energy on love and being of service. Although many ways can be used to perform this exercise, if unexperienced, you can follow these simple steps.

Sit quietly by taking a few relaxing breaths and visualize powerful white and golden roots shooting down from your feet to Mother earth and above your crown chakra, to ground you.

Begin by focusing on your heart chakra; ask Archangel Michael to assist and protect you during this exercise, from everything that is not in harmony with the Divine. Ask that everything in need of transmutation be done with love and forgiveness, in all dimension of time.

Once centered, call upon the Divine Light to lower the "Golden Elevator" to the desired area, whether your house, a person, your surroundings, or in a dark part of the world. Visualize it coming down from a ray of white light. As it flows down in all its glory, guided by two magnificent angels with the powerful white light rising above it, see it pause gently on the ground. As the golden doors slowly open, pay attention to the surrounding.

You may have to implore a sense of trust, infuse an increase amount of loving energy, and mentally communicate with these souls how their loved ones are patiently awaiting their arrival, as you lovingly guide them to the path leading to the elevator.

Watching them make their way to the Light, a sense of gratitude, love, and wellbeing will feel you, as you receive thanks from the awaiting family members or receiving party.

On occasion, while using this practice, you might be faced with what seems to be negative energy. These souls appear lost and uncooperative, often caused by frustration, fears of not being able to find someone to assist, or not understanding the state they are in. Sometimes, multiple release attempts may be required in order to fully clear the energies.

The Law of Free Will prevents us from forcing someone to reach the Light for their own good. By sending them light and offering the opportunity to ascend, if they are not ready, can create a sense of hope which will grow as required. Do not feel failure if this occurs, but feel blessed for all the ones you'll have the opportunity to assist. You can also call upon the Angels to guide them further to prepare to ascend to meet with their loved ones.

May love and light help you find success with this Divine tool and guide you on your spiritual path.

Louise Lajeunesse is a certified Angel Guide Practitioner, Reiki Master-Teacher, Spiritual Messenger, and Therapeutic Touch Practitioner who utilizes her vast wisdom and experience gained through her journey to those that she is in service for. People who have been fortunate to cross her path know that her wisdom, light touch, and gentle loving nature is a Divine Grace. Louise is multi-talented beyond the healing realm and it is her diversity that allows her to reach people on many levels. She is a true visionary, powerful Goddess Healer, and hidden gem on our planet with many gifts still being discovered.

www.louiselajeunesse.com

louiselajeunesse444@gmail.com

Jamieson Wolf

The Flower of Thankfulness

People are mystified when I tell them that I'm thankful I have Multiple Sclerosis.

It was a long road, though. When I was struck with MS on January 1st, 2013, I was bedridden for a month and a half. I could barely walk and found it difficult just going to the living room couch. I had no balance, vertigo, and nausea. My vision and hearing were affected as well; I went deaf in one ear and I was partially blind. I couldn't write, although I used to be able to type out 25,000 words in a weekend. Now I couldn't write anything. The stories still wanted to be told, but there was no way to do that. This was the most painful thing to me, beyond all else that I couldn't do. I am a writer and words are how I truly live.

After six weeks, when I started trying to get better, I had to force myself to get out of bed every morning. I walked with a cane and was still partially blind. I needed help with simple things like doing the dishes, taking out the garbage, and groceries. Even bathing was a chore as I kept falling when I would try to lower myself into the tub.

I did not recognize my life anymore. I had no idea who I was, who this monster was inside of me that had taken control of my life. I was finally diagnosed with Multiple Sclerosis in April, after months of not knowing what was wrong with me. May should have been a month of sunshine and brightness, but I call May 2013 my dark month. I almost took my life.

I thought that I would be okay with having Multiple Sclerosis, having been born with Cerebral Palsy. What was a disease on top of a disability, right? Turns out, it was more than I could deal with at the time. I had spiraled into a deep depression and all I could see were shadows and darkness. I had cut all of my friends out of my life. I thought that no one deserved to be around me, that I didn't deserve anyone.

They had prescribed pills to help with the spasms. I remember sitting on the bench outside of work on my break and the pill bottle was sitting there.

I did the only thing I could think of and called my mother.

When I told her that I wanted to end it, that I was so tired, she told me something that will forever stick with me: "I didn't raise a quitter. Don't you quit on me."

From that day forward, I fought. I clawed with tooth and nail. I would not succumb. I was stronger than this. So I set about learning to do what I used to be able to do, all over again. I remember the first time I took out the garbage all by myself. It took me thirty minutes to do it, but when I finally lifted up the trash can to the dumpster and back down again, without falling down, I experienced a moment of euphoria that is hard to describe.

I started to write again. I could only do a handful of words at a time and I was able to stitch those together to become poems. I started walking on my breaks at work. It was slow going at first, but every step helped. I began to change my diet, eating healthier foods and quit smoking. However, I was forgetting to heal my Spirit as well as my body.

So I began with Tarot classes, submerging myself in anything that called to my Spirit. I took manifestation workshops and followed that up with Reiki. Throughout all of the spiritual learning, I began to notice a change in myself.

It started off small at first, like a seed inside of me. That seed grew into a bud and then the bud began to flower. I started to love myself, all of myself, even the Multiple Sclerosis. This didn't happen overnight – there were still many dark days and self-doubt was in plenty. But I resolved to love everything about myself, even if I didn't like it very much.

When the flower inside of me was in full bloom, I started to look at the world in a different way. Every sunrise, every sunset was a gift, as was every good book, every story, every wonderful meal. I began to notice things I hadn't before or had just taken for granted: the stars at night, the sound of people talking, and birdsong. The world was the same, but I was seeing it through different eyes.

I tried to put a name to this feeling inside of me, tried to find a way to put into words what I was experiencing and kept falling short, a frustrating thing for a writer. Finally, it occurred to me what the flower was called: Thankfulness.

It was such a foreign concept to me. I realized over time that I had taken everything for granted, had just accepted everything as it was and didn't think any further than that. Sure, I was grateful for a lot of things in my life, but I had never been thankful. I just accepted everything as it was and thought it was due to me.

I am not the person I was before the Multiple Sclerosis hit. I look back at my past self and don't recognize him. Had I known then what I know now, I would have told him to cherish every moment, every day and not to take anything for granted.

When I had to fight, to really dig down inside of myself, just to do every simple task, I learned how strong I was. When I overcame obstacles that had stood in my way, I learned about courage. When I was finally able to look back at everything I had been through and everything still to come, I was thankful.

Jamieson Wolf is a Number One Best-Selling author of over forty books. He is also an accomplished artist and storyteller. When not telling tales or creating art, Jamieson is a Tarot consultant helping others find clarity in their own lives.

www.jamiesonwolf.com

Kimberly Hutt

13

Souly Reconnected

Sitting in quiet contemplation, reflecting on what contribution I would make to this anthology as I embarked on my journey to become a published author, my ego and subconscious mind had to ask the proverbial question "What could you possibly have to contribute that would be of enough importance to make a difference in the lives of these readers?"

As waves of self-doubt, fear, and questions of my value would have continued to surface and overwhelm me even a few short months ago, I actually found myself chuckling inside and heard a soft quiet voice soothingly speak, "Dear Child - Shhh! You have the tools and the support of so many. Quiet yourself, ask for assistance and guidance, and keep going."

I come to you from a space of love, light, and peace; divine guidance and assistance share this journey and healing of my heart as I reflect and share my story. Please bear with me as my humanness is exposed.

Many of you may be able to relate and connect to the words that will follow; I hope to inspire you by holding sacred space for you to recognize and move any stagnant or old energy patterns, beliefs, or conditioning that may still be holding you back, as it had me.

Let me explain. As I began to write and the internal dialogue began to bubble and froth forward, I reflected and remembered many occasions throughout my forty-eight years in this lifetime – where other people's beliefs, patterns, and social conditioning had formed and shaped my perception of self-worth and confidence. I had completely relinquished my power and expectations of who I was supposed to become and who I was to external circumstances; not trusting the essence of who the Creator knew me to be.

As a small child, I had a extremely vivid and creative imagination. I was very connected to spirit and source; spending much of my time engaged in story writing, painting, arts and crafts, or playing with my imaginary friends. I could see and sense many things that others could not – I often shared stories of my friend "Blah Blah" with my mom and sisters – until I attended school! My Mother often tells the story of asking me, after several days of attending school, where my friend was. I replied quite matter of factly that, "He ate a piece of rotten cheese and died." At six years of age, I believe my social conditioning had begun.

As I moved through public school, I loved learning and sharing; although socially I knew I held myself back in many ways with sitting as an observer rather than a participant. I felt different from others and didn't always fit in. I was a good student, tried hard, and remember playing sports. I loved floor hockey and may have been a bit aggressive at the age of tem, but I was competitive and wanted to win. I remember a teacher scolding me for not being a team player. This again contributed to fortifying my perception of who I was.

My family and I moved the year I was in 6th grade to a large city thousands of kilometers away – my perception of this was terrifying for a small town country girl. I was constantly in a state of fear and paranoia. The list was endless: What if I take the wrong bus? What if I get lost? As a young girl, I remember thankfully returning to our small town life fourteen months after moving.

This is where several of my health symptoms and conditions began to appear. I woke with terrible pains in my tummy, sharp intense pains in my sides, and headaches. Doctors believed it was kidney issues and prescribed a pharmaceutical "cure" for my issues. It did not help, and eventually appendicitis was diagnosed. I had surgery a few years later, while in grade ten, to remove an almost bursting organ. Yet again the abdominal pain and migraine headaches continued as I missed school.

I struggled with intense feminine issues and was terrified to grow up or to be a woman. My self-confidence and self-esteem contributed to the poor body image I carried – in today's world, I would have been diagnosed with borderline anorexia or body dysmorphia for sure. I was so shy and nervous at this time in my life that when our annual class Public Speaking assignments happened, the teachers would allow me to stand at the back of the classroom to deliver the 5 minute topic. Otherwise, I would be in the washroom sick to my stomach and ready to faint.

The loss of my grandmother that year, as well as what I now know was depression, triggered a series of dreams and visitations from the other side. My intuition had been shaken to the surface and awakened again. I would sit up and read all night so I didn't have to fall asleep. This began an arduous battle with insomnia and contributed to eating issues, which left me tired and missing classes.

Compiled by Brian Calhoun

Our family situation was experiencing many difficult issues and we attended family counseling sessions. I remember telling the counselor how I felt: everyone's life would be so much better if I were not here. The suicidal thoughts had begun. My perception of the situation was to blame, complain, justify, and judge myself so that I took all responsibility for the dynamics of the situation – believing fully that I was to blame for everyone's unhappiness. I complained about what I wasn't doing right so I could justify that I had not done my share, thereby judging and convicting myself. There were many circumstances contributing to the situation – the least of which was me!

I mysteriously came down with a medical condition that was unknown and left me in the hospital for five days in isolation. Any family or visitors had to wear masks and gowns, and could not make skin contact in case I was contagious. I was in a room by myself with a small rented TV – being spoiled by nurses and family. I was quite content and in my element there!

By my own accord, and certainly no one else's, I was positive there was something wrong with me and that I was unlovable. My self-esteem diminished. I had a close group of a few friends that had been very supportive and loved me unconditionally through my high school journey; I spent a lot of time bouncing from house to house each weekend.

I had little to no self-esteem or confidence, and money was not available to pay for college. I was the first in my family to graduate from high school, let alone college. I should be satisfied with that, or so I told myself.

I decided to wait another year and come back for a "Victory Lap." Grade 13 was an option for students who wanted a year of pre-college classes or to fill in until they knew what they wanted. I had no idea what I wanted, so more education couldn't hurt. That spring I began having issues with my teeth and had to have all four Wisdom teeth pulled. I was forced to sit and take care of me for several days.

My self-esteem and confidence were still extremely shaky but I could see parts of myself realigning and filling with love. Early in the year I met and fell in love with my "Knight in Shining Armour" – my now husband, who changed my life.

I was opening myself up to possibilities. My identity and self-esteem began to rise, and I started to see that I was a positive contributing factor in life. I had a placement in Fashion Design with great mentors and enjoyed it immensely. I applied to several colleges and got accepted to all, rebuilding parts of myself that had slowly shut down.

My fiancé and I traveled to tour the college. He would take Welding and I would take Design. We would get an apartment and life would be wonderful. We had become engaged at this point – unfortunately, our conditioning and belief systems both kicked in and we decided to stay close to home. I accepted a college program locally and he went back to work. I applied for student loans and when the funds did not arrive on time, my parents borrowed money to pay for the initial semester and books. I felt an overwhelming guilt, a lack of deservedness, and quickly dropped out after only weeks. I had no driver's licence and no desire to get one – my fear of this stemmed from a failed attempt when I was sixteen years old. I was quite content to have others chauffeur me around. I went back to my part-time job working in Fashion, my fiancé went back to school six weeks later, and we got married in December. My survival zone was safe, but my comfort zone was not ready to expand.

I was codependent. Looking back throughout my childhood, adolescence, and early married life, I can see the health patterns and symptoms for what they are now. I had completely closed off the possibilities of creation and creativity by accepting and believing that what I had to contribute was of little value to society. I closed off my connection to spirit and creator wisdom, and stopped trusting that I knew what I needed most in my life. I played into the expectations and codependent needs of myself and others around me, discounting my value and worth at the Creator's level.

Since then I have reawakened my value or worth and to my soul. This connection with energy and spirit has afforded me valuable insights and allowed for healing to take place on many levels. Through in depth self-awareness, journaling, Meditation, Yoga, and Qi Gong, I have learned to heal many parts of myself and realign with who I am.

When I began the journey of self-discovery, I repeatedly felt a need to validate and prove myself. Some thirty years later, with over thirty-five Certifications and trainings under my belt trying to overcompensate my right to be here, my awakening came while working with private clients, some facing terminal illness or palliative, as well as, everyday folks just like myself. I quickly realized that many people struggle with the same perceptions and belief patterns: fear of rejection, judgement, and self-worth issues are common denominators in each person's journey and I found that I was not alone in my travels.

I would sit with each person holding space for regrets, guilt, and deep dark secrets to surface and be expressed. I found that most people, no matter age, gender, or stage in life, were seeking very similar things: *to be heard, to be seen, to be understood, and to be loved*. As we co-created the sacred space, the layers of masks and cloaks of insecurity from sometimes decades of hiding would gently slip off and the raw pure essence of the authentic soul would come to light. Physical pain and suffering would ease from level ten to level two. Emotional baggage that was carried for generations began to release and unfold into tears. Mental clutter and chaos became connection and love.

Levels of spiritual oneness and inner acceptance allowed for healing to take place. Some people got well, others transitioned back to spirit world and creator, lighter and gentler, than they thought possible.

Through humble grace and gratitude, I have become the observer and spiritually connected person creator set out for me to be. I am very honored to say that I am continually working toward the divinely imperfectly perfect reflection of who I am. I am a work in progress. I am who I am.

Be who you are. In each moment: Live your truth, know your worth, shed the masks of fear, and be all you are as the Light!

Blessings,

Kim

Kimberly Hutt is a Relaxation Therapist, Natural Health Care Consultant, and Intuitive Counsellor of Energy Therapies. She helps co-create a sacred space where the essence of your soul and authentic voice of your spirit can be seen and heard. Kim travels across Canada as a Guest Speaker, Facilitator, and Instructor. Sharing many Ancient Healing modalities and old wisdom, as well as using modern Medical practices and technology, Kim creates customized individual and group programs and trainings for Corporate and Business clients, Medical Professionals and Patients, Educational Staff and students, as well as personal clients in her private home practice.

www.soulyreconnected.com

www.facebook.com/soulyreconnected

Mary Willemsen

14

Miracles Happen Every Day (All You Have to Do Is Appreciate Them)

I was having one of those mornings. Things were not going as planned. I tried a new recipe from a favorite website that I had been having good luck with lately. The recipes were gluten free, high fiber, great tasting, and chocolate. My four favorite food groups!

Yet, my mixture was not looking like the pictures on the website. The recipe for unbaked chocolate brownies started off with 2 ½ cups of dates, 1 ½ cups of walnuts, and cocoa. I prefer using cacao instead of cocoa. The real stuff tastes so much better, more chocolaty, and more nutritious with added fiber.

I am not a big fan of walnuts, although I realize they are nutritious and contain lots of vitamins and minerals. My daughter had recently asked me, "Mom, why don't you like walnuts?" I stopped and thought about that for a minute. Did I not like them because of their aftertaste? They seem to be rather bitter tasting to me. Or, did I not like them because when I was quite young and walking to the bus stop to go to school, I had to pass under the branches of a walnut tree. I remember its branches were heavy with an abundance of nuts. And as I walked under the tree, the walnuts would fall off and hit me on the head! Definitely not a fan of walnuts.

I measured out the dates and pecans into the food processor and pressed the "ON" button. It whirled for a bit and then made a strange screeching noise. The mixture was not moving, and the dates and pecans were still the same size as when I put them in the food processor. What happened? The machine would "whirr", but nothing moved. Did the motor burn out? No, I didn't think so or there would have been a burning smell. Did I fill the bowl of the food processor too full? No, there was still room for more ingredients. Was the mixture too compact? It was pretty solid. I not only had used copious quantities of dates and pecans, but real cacao too! What to do?

I work with my Angels every day. I am an Angel Messenger, so I asked my Angels, "How can I fix this problem?" As I was thinking of ways to salvage these brownies, my Mom's date bar recipe popped into my mind. In her recipe, she cooked the dates on the stove for about ten minutes to soften them. Perhaps that would work. I needed to soften the dates and chop the pecans, so I dug the sticky, ooey gooey mess out of the food processor and tossed it all in a large saucepan on the stove. I warmed it up for about ten minutes, stirring constantly and trying to break up the dates and pecans, all while thinking about my Mom and pretending I was making my mom's date bar recipe. Mom passed away a few years ago and it was nice to think of her and how much she enjoyed life. One of her famous recipes is her *Date Bars* recipe.

The mixture softened enough that I was able to pour the thickened mass into a pan generously greased with coconut oil. The brownies cooled on my kitchen counter while I prepared the chocolate frosting, which was easy to make and lovingly spread over the brownies.

Clean up time! What a sticky, gooey mess to clean up. Usually, I will just toss the food processor blades and bowl into the dishwasher if I am ready to turn it on. But, today I wanted to use the machine for another recipe. So, I decided to wash the dishes by hand instead.

As I started to fill the sink with hot water, a voice in my head said, "Put on your rubber gloves." Was that my guardian Angel talking to me? I thought, no I don't need rubber gloves today. I didn't listen to the voice in my head. I was concerned about the recipe, wondering if it would turn out okay. I listened to my ego instead – the voice that said, "You don't need gloves. You're fine."

As I washed the dishes, all of a sudden I felt a sharp pain in my finger. The blade of the food processor had sliced my finger! I pulled my ungloved hand out of the dishwater and yelled "HELP!" as I watched bright red blood gushing out of my finger. I grabbed paper towels to staunch the flow of blood, but the blood kept rushing out. I ran to the bathroom for a towel while my husband raced upstairs to discover the scene with blood all over the kitchen floor, all over me, and bloody paper towels littering the floor.

Compiled by Brian Calhoun

The blood, my life force, just kept flowing unstopped!

Remembering what I learned from taking a first aid course, I held my hand above my heart as I pressed towels into the wound to staunch the flow of blood. Yet, nothing seemed to be working for me, until I looked up and said, "Help, Archangel Michael, Archangel Raphael." I looked at my finger, the blood stopped flowing immediately! I looked again in amazement. The bleeding had stopped! I looked up with relief knowing I was truly blessed and said, "Thank you Angels." No need for stitches. My finger has healed without a scar. Thank you, Angels.

Next time, I will ask the Angels for help *before* I begin creating in the kitchen. I am sure the job will be much easier with their help.

Your Angels are with you always. They are ready to help you and be of service to you in any way you may need. All you have to do is ask them and remember to thank them.

Mary Willemsen is a Reiki Master, Angel Messenger, Intuitive Reader, and Fairyologist. She works from her Reiki studio in Ottawa, Ontario and offers Distance Healing to clients all over the world. Mary enjoys bringing the Angels' love and light to the world while helping her clients unleash their inner strength.

www.reikirelaxation.ca

Compiled by Brian Calhoun

HALO
ABUNDANCE

Brian D Calhoun

15

The Grand Illusion: Part One

Sometimes life will bring you down a path that isn't always so fun and light filled. In fact, you can find yourself in a truly dark and scary place where you may feel that you are lost in the dark alone, as though no one truly understands what you are going through. Your thoughts may be negative, fearful, and worrisome at times. You may be telling yourself and others the reality of the situation "like it is" even, or so you may think at the time.

Throughout life, I have gone through said times myself, like many of you surely in your own journey. This chapter is about one particular dark period of my life, where spirit led me down a path that was actually a blessing in disguise. This period of time was not unlike other periods of my life where I had encountered similar experiences, perhaps in different ways. The difference this time being that I was more spiritually aware of the laws of the universe and how we play a key role in the life that we are co-creating with the divine part of us.

Growing up, my family wasn't rich in any sense of the word, particularly during my teen years where we often struggled financially to make ends meet. My mom and step father had gone their own ways a couple of years earlier, for reasons that I won't go into at this time. The point being because of their forced separation a catalyst for one of my life lessons was revitalized. I say revitalized as I believe a part of me had dealt with a portion of it and put it on the backburner. Waiting for another event to bring it back up to be healed and cleared.

I think a part of me had always felt insecure on some level because of the fact that I had gone through various sorts of abuse starting in the foundational years of my life. So, when the experience of my parents parting ways came up, it triggered some of the old stuff from when my mom and biological father divorced, when I was a baby. One may not think that such an experience at such a young age would trigger life lessons, but that is exactly what unfolded.

I kept to myself for the most part of my childhood as I never felt secure, confident, good enough, or whatever the case may have been at the time. But, I never would have thought that it would have had an impact on my financial security as well, until I started to understand the bigger picture and see how all the puzzle pieces that is life fit together. However, when my sister and I ended up in foster care for a brief period of time, and the security of my family was removed from me, well that just added to the many layers of mental and emotional stuff. Talk about feeling rejected from your family who couldn't or wouldn't even take you in during a rough period in life. This just caused me to retreat further inward.

I had already started down a darker path at the time, much like many teenagers trying to find themselves and their life path. These recent events just added to me feeling alone, lost, and confused on top of puberty. My schools where changing from Senior Public School to High School at the same time as all this moving around from home to foster homes to home again. I just wanted something or somewhere I could feel stable once again. I had always been blessed with creativity and thus forth found myself using it in a variety of ways, during these times.

Once my sister and I were returned to Mom, things were still not the same. Mom was trying to support a family by herself while looking for love at the same time. There were many men that my mom dated for brief periods of time. She eventually found someone to settle down with, have another child, and create a life with. However, I feel she was never truly settled as she had lost the love of her life when she and my stepfather separated.

We definitely still didn't have security in our life. That is for sure. As if we didn't move around enough in foster homes, now we were being evicted from our home because the owner was selling. Mom couldn't afford to purchase it with barely being able to make ends meet. So here is a family of four, with a newborn due soon, and we are moving from a three bedroom house to a two bedroom apartment, temporarily, before moving into the city housing system. Here, we started to have a bit more stability once again.

By this time, I was moving into my early adult years and had also started to work when I was seventeen years old. This definitely helped me out financially to be able to afford some of the stuff that I had wanted such as my driver's licence, a computer, music, and eventually my own apartment. However, there was a part of me that still felt unsettled or unstable. Perhaps, a part of me felt that it was because I was bullied growing up, the lack of a stable home structure, or something else related to my life. But I now understand that it was because I was seeking what I once had, and that was the feeling of safety and security.

Sure, I was making money, but I was blowing it at the same time; not truly appreciating what I had right here and now. I was trying to fill my life with stuff and appreciating the fact that I was truly abundant in so many ways. I had an abundance of love in my life from my mom, family members, and friendships that truly did love, accept, and appreciate me as I was, faults and all.

I found myself repeating the same patterns over and over in life still, as I began my journey into the world of working for a living. I would save up, spend and try to fill the empty void. What the void was, I couldn't tell you at the time. Looking back, I would say that I was seeking my spiritual and life purpose, to know myself as perfect, whole and complete, as well as abundant, safe, secure and happy in every way.

Throughout my life, I was always in the kitchen providing food for the family and enjoying using my creative gifts in this way. As I got older, it just made sense that I would end up working in the restaurant industry. After all, it would feed my soul in two ways: It would give me a sense of purpose and I would be using my creative talents that came naturally to me. Or so one would think. I didn't feel fulfilled yet. I still felt myself feeling lost, confused, unaccepted, and out of place.

Sure, I was making money, but I still didn't feel safe and secure even in this industry. Perhaps it was the fact that I had a boss who was tough on her employees, bullied and belittled us at times. Or perhaps it was the fact that some of the staff treated me like a loser and called me names, talking behind my back, or something else. This all in turn played with my mind and emotional state. It caused me to feel unworthy and undeserving of my good. Which, in truth, I now understand was my choice. We have the power to allow others to make us feel a certain way or not. In my case, having low self-esteem certainly did not help at all.

I found myself sabotaging myself and my good in life, including my financial good. At the age of twenty-three, I found myself declaring bankruptcy because I let myself spend beyond my means with credit cards, loans, and such forth. I felt myself hiding this dirty little secret from some of my family and friends, and only a select few even knew how bad it got. I didn't feel comfortable talking about what was going on within me, or in my life with others. This came from the fact that every time I did feel safe in opening up or in expressing myself in some way, I was consistently shut down.

Even though I ended up rebuilding my financial life and eventually moved away from where I grew up, the past would continue to play out in my patterns and cycles. It wouldn't just be financially, or emotionally, it would also play out in my relationships, health, and in many other ways. Much like the onion, there are many levels and until we get to the core of them and gain the full understanding, we will repeat, repeat, and repeat.

This doesn't always need to be the case. We can take the wheel and step into our power as the creator of our own personal heaven on earth at any time. The universe will continue to help us to learn and grow as spiritual beings having the human experience. It does so by showing us parts of ourselves that are still active and alive within us in our relationships and experiences.

Let me say this to you: Pay attention to what is it that keeps showing up and repeating in your life. This is a part of what the universe is mirroring back to yourself that you may have been ignoring or unaware of on some level of your being. Once you understand the message being shared, take responsibility and start to shift within – you will break free.

It took me many trials and errors to learn this, but I think I am finally starting to get it. I state that because sometimes when you think you got it, another layer will come up to show and teach you more about what is active within.

Before continuing on to part two, take a few minutes to think about what has been some of your own personal catalysts for your life lessons? Have you figured out what your life lessons are? If not, think about what is it that keeps on repeating in your life and perhaps what some of the messages contained within them are trying to speak to you.

Reflect on your life both the positive and negative to discover more about why certain things had to play out in your life, from a new perspective; think bigger picture perspective. What is it you are learning? How are various aspects of your life interconnected to help you grow and expand as a soul having a human experience?

A writer's life lesson may be learning to communicate what it is they are holding within, whether thoughts or feelings, and putting a voice to it. Many people have communication lessons in play in their life in a variety of ways. A writer is no different, because they may just find it easier to put down on paper what they can't speak out loud. It gives a voice for their truth. I know that this has been also one of my lessons that has been in play.

Brian Calhoun is a Heart-Centred International Psychic-Medium who has dedicated his life to bringing high spiritual truths and messages of loving light for the purposes of healing & enlightenment to the world for over fifteen years. He is a Reiki Master, ANGEL THERAPY PRACTITIONER®, Certified Personal Trainer, Chef, Ordained Minister, Spiritual Teacher, Speaker, and International Best-Selling Author. He has released Guided Meditation CDs, published articles, contributed to books, and been a repeat guest on International Radio and Local Television. Raised in the City with the literal Heart of Good – Timmins Ontario, Brian now calls Ottawa, Ontario, Canada his home.

www.angelswithin.ca

www.facebook.com/angelswithin

Brian D Calhoun

16

The Grand Illusion: Part Two

When I was in my mid to late thirties, I was following my heart doing what I felt guided to be doing on my life path as a Psychic-Medium, Energy Worker, and Spiritual Teacher, when life began to repeat again. I started to struggle financially again, this time while on my spiritual path.

This is a pattern that I noticed many people on the spiritual pathways often have. We would focus on the higher spiritual chakras or journey, and will often neglect the lower chakras, physical and earthly stuff. This would lead us to encounter challenges of some sort; in part because we are not fully grounded and connected to the earth, as we were before we "awakened." Part of what is needed is to balance the two, as yes, we are spirit, but we are also on the earth still.

That is exactly what happened to me as I awakened, and thus I created a financial mess of things once again. I ended living beyond my means using credit cards and not having the ability to pay things on time or in full. I even manifested an eviction notice at the time. I had been consistently following the guidance of my angels and guides, or so I thought at the time. However, there was a part that I hadn't been listening to, that our thoughts, beliefs, emotions and words create, from both conscious and unconscious levels.

You see the law of attraction was beginning to make its notice in my life, and the universe was trying to teach me about it further. This would be a blessing and a curse. A blessing, as it would help me move forward and help others that I would be in service for, or sharing the story along the way. A curse, as it caused me to go into fear and darkness, not to mention financial instability and insecurity once again in life.

Like many of you, surely, I had been reading books on the subject, watched "the Secret," and would find other like-minded materials finding their way into my life. I would try to implement the information into my life, only to have it fail to create the promise of a better life in whatever area of focus.

Little did I know that the universe wasn't only listening to one part of the equation; it was listening to the sum of the wholeness of all my subconscious, superconscious, and conscious levels of my being. It would then take the sum of all parts, and whatever was strongest in energy at the time, and translate that into some life experience. Whether negative or positive, it is always in our highest and greatest good according to the divine plan we set forth spiritually.

For me, it allowed me to experience financial hardships and struggles to help me understand the law of attraction further, to help me help you, and to help me heal further the life events that were tied to safety, security, and stability. It also helped me to get to a better place financially as well as on all levels of my being. It helped me to truly understand that I am abundant and prosperous in so many ways in my life, and that financial abundance is just one small part of the equation of abundance or prosperity. It taught me that I hold the power to manifest and create anything I want by becoming aware of where I am giving my time, energy, and focus on all levels of my being. It helped me to shift my perspectives where needed, and so much more.

You see, I am perfect, whole, and complete, as are you in all ways. We sometimes may not always feel that way, but our true nature and divine self never waivers from this divine truth. We may be spirit having a human experience, perhaps sometimes losing ourselves along the journey feeling unsupported, unloved, or whatever else we may feel disconnected from. This is part of the illusion. In truth, there is always a Divine part of us that is always connected; always safe; always secure; always stabile; whole and always expanding.

So, even though life may bring us experiences that cause us to live the illusion of not being something and forgetting our true divine nature, we can always choose to reconnect and remember all that our soul is. This is so much more than we can consciously give words to.

Life will also always bring you to experiences to show you that you are abundant, prosperous, loved, supported, safe, secure, and so much more. You see, it does this partly by showing you people and experiences that are living their own personal heaven on earth life or having the relationship you dream of, the money you wish, and some other desire you have. After all, we are all one as spirit and therefore, if one part of us is experiencing something, then it only makes sense that all of us will experience it too as we remember our true nature and whole self.

Begin to recognize these subtle and obvious, at times, signs from heaven and you too will begin to light up your own heaven on earth in Health, Abundance, Love and the Unity of everything else! As for myself, I am still continuing to learn and expand my true divine nature upon this earth. I believe this is important to everyone to be doing daily in some way, and continue to throughout our earthly life. However, I am in a much better place of feeling safe and secure. That financial pattern and cycle that kept repeating itself and caused me to manifest the eviction notice, is definitely on the way to being broken once and for all of time. I never did get evicted and paid over three months of rent within two weeks of receiving it without any loans or "outside" help.

Ten years later, I'm still living in the place where I was. I have no loans or credit card debt, as I only have a refillable prepaid credit card. This allows me to enjoy the comforts of having credit, without the high interest charges, if you don't pay in full each month. My monthly income takes care of paying all my expenses in full and I am on the way to building a financial nest egg of security and truly living within my means. I am no longer living in the illusion of lack having connected to my true nature as abundant.

I would like to give you some guidance to help you on your journey that my Angels & Guides often have me remind my clients:

1. Love yourself to free yourself of what no longer is serving you.

2. Please keep a positive mindset, even when life's experiences cause you otherwise.

3. Take the time to look for what the universe may be showing or teaching you in your life at the same time. Know that no matter what, everything is going to work out for the highest good of all, after all the universe works for you. You truly are perfect, whole, and complete. You are safe, secure, loved, supported, and so much more. You are always in the perfect place at the perfect time doing the perfect thing according to the universal plan for your journey.

4. Find ways to feel what your wish is to experience more in life. Example: surround yourself with people and things that make you feel happy, abundant, loved, secure, and supported. Remember, life begins with you and with a feeling, then a word, and finally action.

5. In closing, I would like to leave you with the tool that helped me to manifest the funds that were needed to pay the rent and work on improving the quality of my financial security once again. They are a couple of simple mantras that were guided to me by my angelic team.

    - I am a magnet for Abundance and Prosperity. I attract wonderful opportunities to me, and act upon them with beauty, love, grace, and ease for the blessing of all.

    - I accept, I allow, I am receiving now. I relax, I let go, and I am in the flow.

- I am safe, secure, loved, and supported, in known and unknown ways. I am prosperous and abundant, in known and unknown ways.
- I trust, have faith, let go, listen, and follow my soul's guidance.
- I am perfect, whole, and complete, one with everything.
- I now know my life purpose and take divinely guided action to fulfill it each day.
- I send love and gratitude to and for everything.

I would say these statements daily with my hands open and out to the universe, allowing myself to feel the words and energy of the statements as I did so, knowing that things are unfolding in ways I am now beginning to recognize and experience more each day. Throughout the day I would state them out loud, in a whisper and silently, many times. To the point that I had them memorized and I would be going for a walk or doing errands and I would be whispering and repeating them.

I found that by using these statements on a regular basis daily, it helped to keep my mind in the right place and keep myself feeling more abundant, prosperous, and connected to my true divine nature. Try them out for yourself and let me know how it goes for you.

I wish you every success you can imagine in life. May you live a truly abundant heavenly life upon the earth, now and always. May you always know and connect to your true divine nature.

I love and thank you!

Brian

Brian Calhoun is a Heart-Centred International Psychic-Medium who has dedicated his life to bringing high spiritual truths and messages of loving light for the purposes of healing & enlightenment to the world for over fifteen years. He is a Reiki Master, ANGEL THERAPY PRACTITIONER®, Certified Personal Trainer, Chef, Ordained Minister, Spiritual Teacher, Speaker, and International Best-Selling Author. He has released Guided Meditation CDs, published articles, contributed to books, and been a repeat guest on International Radio and Local Television. Raised in the City with the literal Heart of Good – Timmins Ontario, Brian now calls Ottawa, Ontario, Canada his home.

www.angelswithin.ca

www.facebook.com/angelswithin

Michelle Scarborough

17
The Energy of Money

I have never been driven by money. This may sound like a funny thing for someone to say who works in the financial industry, where everything is driven by the exchange of money to make business move. A dollar for a piece of the action, another dollar to pay for a product or service, and so on. At first, I thought that I was not driven by money until I discovered my relationship with it.

Money, or rather the relationship to money, does funny things to people. It makes them feel like kings and queens or poppers and peasants. It makes them donate to others, steal from others, become reclusive or better yet, come together to accomplish great things. Money is energy and the relationship you have to that energy is the key to mastery of your relationship to money.

It is my relationship with the energy of money within me that is directly tied to the results I have in my life. For me, money is tied to my self-worth. The more I feel worthy, the more I am open to receiving and having money in my life. You could say that money is one of the measures to my self-worth. The opposite is true as well. When I feel unworthy, my flow of energy slows right down to a trickle. Take a moment to think about that for yourself. Can you see a connection between the relationship your feelings held within and the energy of money?

As humans, we tend to get caught up in needing more and more money to live life. I know I certainly did and still do from time to time. We are separated from the source within and think that we need some outside source for our money to buy or build things, to amass material or other goods, to have a good life or an even better life. But instead of looking at money, I ask you to look at the energy of it.

- What is that energy intended to do?
- What is your relationship to it?
- Do you barely make your payments each month or do you always

have more than enough?

- Perhaps you believe that you have enough and that you will always be taken care of?

If you want to attract more money into your life, you must first unlock your resistance to it and allow it to flow. Money is energy and it needs to flow freely, much like a river. When you the block the river, you stop that flow. Negative emotions, feeling unworthy, comparing yourself to others, or a taking on a "have-not" attitude are like the stones that are blocking the river. Wherever you place your emotions and focus, you will radiant more of that energy into your life, which in turn attracts experiences that cause you to feel a certain way, and thus forth stop the flow, aka harvest, of your own natural energy.

For me, I have found that whenever I take on the attitude that I am not worthy enough to have money, I block my own flow. I call these my "poppy-pants" moments, and trust me like many of us, I have had an abundance of them. I do my best to remain conscious and aware of when I may be having these moments. When I recognize them, I then take my power back and turn my attention to changing my attitude about myself and my worthiness. I can then accept the situation as it is with love and gratitude, and reopen the flow that perhaps I have closed or slowed down. Once I do this, the energy flows and money follows.

We have all used affirmations and they are very powerful tools to help you. But saying an affirmation without meaning or feeling it will do nothing for you. You must truly believe and feel what you are saying.

If you are going to create and use affirming statements, I encourage you to make sure you believe what you are saying. Rephrase the statements if need be, so that it rings true, and moves the energy in the direction you wish the flow to go. You must find a way to change the way you feel about money while you are saying the affirmations. This will change the intention and help you to open the flow. Everything is interconnected.

I like to say my affirmations after asking Spirit to help. Then I turn my attention inward to make sure I am feeling the truth of what I am affirming.

Let us ask Spirit to help you connect and development the relationship with the source of abundance within, so that you may be more open to receiving, accepting, and allowing the prosperity that is now flowing into your life through the source within. Feel yourself in this flow.

A couple footnotes:

1. *Be open to receiving and believe that abundance is your natural birthright,*

and money is already here. You must believe you are worthy and know that your wish has already been granted.

2. *Don't limit yourself.* If you want an abundance of money flowing in continuously at all times, then ask for it – ask for millions of it to come to you freely and clearly in win-win ways.

3. *Listen.* Creating an abundance of anything is action oriented. You can't just sit back after you asked waiting for it to fall from the sky. Action is required.

4. *Share the Wealth.* As we say, money is energy and to continue the flow of money in your life, you must give as well as receive. Taking care of your needs is an important way of showing the universe that you are one with it all, and in the flow.

Make time daily to check in with your relationship with money by loving and appreciating what you have now. As you nurture your money relationship within, you nurture your available resources within life.

Michelle Scarborough is a Senior Executive in the Finance Industry, has received recognition for her leadership throughout North America, and is a strong supporter of women in Technology & Finance. An entrepreneur and innovator, Michelle sits on several public and private companies that she believes in. She resides in Canada.

michellescarborough@me.com

Maggie Power

18

You Can Rewrite Your Story

Have you ever had the desire to travel and see the world? It seems to be a popular dream for a lot of people, but the thought of traveling never really occurred to me. It always seemed like something other people did, specifically people with money. In my early years, my family really struggled with finances. I remember my parents would say things like, "We don't have a lot of money but we're rich in love." It instilled a sense of pride about being poor and a rejection of such "frivolous" things as vacations to Disneyland.

Besides, I wasn't the adventurous type. I was quiet. Sensitive. A little reserved. That was the story I told myself anyway. Maybe it made it easier to be left behind from a grad trip to Mexico or to decline a wedding invitation on the opposite side of the country. It definitely made it easier to hide from the world. I figured if I never went for it, I couldn't disappoint anyone, including myself. So I stayed in my comfort zone... until the Universe and my angels decided to show me it was not so comfortable after all.

They say when the student is ready, the teacher appears. This is but one of those stories.

"R" was unlike any other person I had known before. She had a lifestyle that was totally unreal to me. She had studied and practiced the healing arts with high-profile experts and master healers all over the world. She had an ever-burning passion for learning and experiencing all life had to offer and took every opportunity to do so. In my eyes, she was a free spirit, dancing to the beat of some etheric drum that only she could hear. I would have been happy to catch but an echo of such a drum; to learn the secret to living in such a rich and joyous way.

When I met her I had just opened a small wellness spa in St. John's, Newfoundland. Previous to that I had been living in Ottawa and had begun learning about energy healing while I worked as an esthetician. My focus was always on the wellness (as opposed to the cosmetic) aspect of spa treatments, so it seemed only natural that I would gravitate toward the world of healing. An Ottawa-area teacher helped me get my bearings in that world via healing sessions and workshops that he offered. Soon after I had begun my official healing journey, the opportunity to open a spa in my hometown came up, so back to The Rock I went.

"R" came to see me for a manicure after a long trip back from New Zealand where she had been studying with the local shaman. Over the manicure table we discovered our mutual interest in energy healing; as I buffed and polished her nails, she told me all about the positive impact a manicure could have on the human energy system. I was fascinated. I had to learn more!

I booked a healing session with her and began to see her regularly and attended most of her workshops. It was not something I was used to spending money on but my rising curiosity was stronger than any common sense I had about living within my means. Plus I was finally learning to trust my intuition and it was telling me the best was yet to come.

She must have sensed something in me – potential, maybe? And so my mentorship began. I also started my transition from spa owner to full-time energy healer. There were many highs and lows during this period, but having a connection to angels helped me stay somewhat centered. I became certified in healing modalities that worked with angels as well, which deepened my connection to them. My own healing practice was growing too, slowly but surely. I was feeling pretty good about my work and the strides I had taken to get myself out there.

Yet deep down, I knew that I was still playing small. In a way, I was hiding behind my mentor, like a baby bird afraid to leave the nest. I still had fears about being seen, which was a reflection of my self-worth, which was connected to my lack mentality. I was still turning down bigger opportunities for expansion and using money (or lack of it) as an excuse. My business was growing, yes, but it wasn't bringing in any more than enough to cover expenses. I still depended on my husband to pay the bills. I so wanted to fly, but I was too scared to take any major leaps, even though I was getting too big for the nest.

When the student is not quite getting the lesson, sometimes the Universe will send in a tutor.

I had heard of an angel workshop being held in town by a woman who was visiting from England. "R" and I went together. That's when I met "G", a stunning goddess of a woman, who channeled the vibration of angels through her voice. She also traveled the world to share her unique style of healing, which included music and movement. I was excited to be shown by the Universe that living a life of adventure and abundance can come in different forms.

The workshop was beautiful and as we learned the story of how the angels had guided our lovely facilitator to use her voice for healing, my own urge to sing during healing sessions (which had been happening for several months) made sense! After the workshop, I knew the next step for me was to ask her if she would teach me how to sing with the angels too. I had always loved singing, but would never do it in front of anyone, and this seemed like a bold choice to make, but again, I was learning to trust my intuition when it came to these things.

She agreed to teach me and when she returned to England, we began my lessons via Skype. I was using an old desktop computer that I had inherited from my brother, and it would shut down in the middle of a lesson more often than I would have liked, but I carried on. I was aware that normally, I would feel embarrassed or ashamed that I couldn't afford the latest and greatest technology, but I was truly grateful for the gift of having access to any kind of computer at all. Besides, I felt like something exciting was just around the corner, so I wasn't going to let anything distract me from the momentum I had gained.

A few months after I had begun studying the healing art of angelic singing, my new tutor told me of a weekend retreat she was holding a few months from then at the Chalice Well in Glastonbury, England. "R" had stayed in touch with her and was going to be there as well. I had heard many of her travel plans, but this was the first time that I felt a real longing to go. I told her so, and she said, "Yes! Come with me!"

My brain automatically came up with the usual list of excuses: no money, not a traveler, not for me, etc. I'd probably say, "No," like I always did, but the reply that actually came out of my mouth was, "I'll think about it."

Did I just hear myself correctly? Those four words gave me the space to step back and look at the situation a little differently than I normally would. What was happening? Was I opening up to a possibility? Were the years and months of mentorships leading up to some kind of major breakthrough? I felt a wave of excitement; then it turned into a tsunami of anxiety-inducing questions: If I said yes, how would I afford it? I'd never gone to an overnight retreat before, let alone left my safe and cozy home to fly across the Atlantic Ocean to go to one! I'd never been outside the country. I didn't even have a passport! I trusted my teachers, but the fear of the unknown was in my face right now, and I wasn't yet 100 per cent trusting in myself. But oh, that ache in my heart for wanting to go...

I thought about it for several days. I contemplated about how the Universe had brought these two incredible women into my life, both of whom followed their hearts and said YES to life. I remembered the spiritual teaching analogy that we are all mirrors for each other. Each person in our lives reflects what we see in ourselves, or what we could be. I thought about how my old belief that "I wasn't like them" had done nothing but keep me small. And separate. Hadn't I learned the true meaning of oneness? Was I not made of the same stuff as "people with money who travel" and therefore had the same potential?

That year in February I was assisting at a day retreat that was in honor of the goddess Brigid. Before the participants arrived, I had a quiet moment to myself and I decided to let the angels give me a sign that I was meant to go to England that spring. In one of the ceremonies we were to choose a pashmina from "R's" travels, and drape it over another participant's shoulders as a symbol of support, like to cloak of Brigid. I was told that the one my partner had chosen for me was from no other place than... Glastonbury! That was my sign from the angels!

"Woohoo! Now what, angels?" I thought.

"Get a passport," I heard them reply.

So I had finally decided - I would go to England in the spring! I felt good, and only a little nervous, but kept reminding myself that I had left it up to the angels and the Universe to figure out the "hows" and my only job now was to get excited and keep following the signs. That's when the magic really started to happen.

In the next few weeks, I booked more clients than usual and had an unexpected increase in my credit limit, which was exactly the amount I needed for the airfare. When I told Georgie of my decision, she said I could stay for a while after the retreat at her place and we could do some further lessons together in person. Wonderful! Yes! My husband helped me with the passport application and other little details. I told my dad about the whole situation, and as a huge supporter of my spiritual work, he generously donated his travel points to me (and booked the ticket), so now I had spending money. Woohoo! I was in awe of the whole process.

I went to England that spring and had one of the most powerful and life-changing experiences of my life. For now I will just say that it's another story for another time.

I had a chance to reflect on the whole experience on the plane ride home. I had done it! I had taken a leap and learned to trust – in the Universe and in myself. My teachers had been living examples of what's possible when you believed in yourself and your dreams. And I, too, had followed my heart and said YES to life. And of course, I couldn't have done it without my angels' guidance as well!

Life really is naturally abundant. No matter what your limiting thoughts and beliefs, you can always change them to ones that work for you and your heart's deepest desires. I encourage you to open your journal to a new page, grab a pen, and start writing your new story without holding back or playing small. You can do it – I'm proof of that!

And the fun has only just begun.

Maggie Power, or as she is known by many, Magalie, is an Energy Healer, Spiritual Teacher, and a believer in the transformative power of love. In her healing practice, she creates a safe and nurturing space for her clients to allow the magnificence of their own being to be known by them. Maggie is very passionate about empowering others and her sessions, music, writing, meditations, and affirmations are intended to do just that. She encourages others to connect with their inner child and cultivate their creative energy to bring joy and magic into their everyday lives.

www.maggiepower.ca

www.facebook.com/magalieshines

Marie-Hélène Fortin

19
Out of Despair Came Prosperity

I had always believed myself to be a spiritual person. At a young age, I was following my inner guidance; not truly knowing where it came from. I don't think I was aware of the love, protection, and guidance my angels brought into my life. I am now aware that they know what we need and how to bring it forth. Let me share with you how one of the hardest times of my life ended up being filled with so many examples of true abundance.

Life has brought me through multiple traumas and different life challenges. The toll they took on me eventually became too much and in late 2015 signs of severe anxiety began to show up. I remember the night of my first panic attack, and it just went downhill from there. I was told that I was suffering from Obsessive Compulsive Disorder and Post Traumatic Stress Disorder.

I could not sleep for many weeks. My physical health declined rapidly. I felt fear ALL the time. My head felt like it was going to explode with all the OCD thoughts. It really is hard to explain, and for anyone to truly understand, unless you have lived with these disorders. Simply put, there was no break in the negative and fearful thoughts; you are bombarded every minute of the day and night with them. It was a reality that I had never imagined possible and, to me, was absolute hell. The pain was too much to bear.

I remember the day my husband came home in the middle of a terrible episode and I told him I could not do this anymore; that I wanted to leave this planet. Somewhere from within something gave me the courage to say that to him.

Looking back I am forever grateful for the Angelic Intervention because that is what it was. It was a loving push from my angels who knew it was not my time to leave. Our angels can foresee how magical and prosperous our lives can be. They can guide and lead us. They know our purpose, what we are capable of, which lessons are needed to be learned, and exactly what we need and when.

I had a purpose to fulfill here on earth. The hardest time of my life would become the greatest gift of my life as I learned the many abundant ways that I was being supported by the angels with blessing after blessing.

When I speak of abundance, it encompasses so much. It is more than just financial or material. It is the opportunities, people, resources, connections, and answered prayers that come in magical and miraculous ways. The abundance of help that came my way and the multiple shapes and forms it appeared in was (and still is) miraculous and magical.

Let me back you up to 2014 when I realized that I was a healer. I knew that my life purpose was that of a lightworker who would bring healing, light, and love to the world. At that time I was just starting to understand what it meant for me.

My first course that I was called to take would result in my spiritual counseling and healing certification. The course was held in California and while calculating the cost of the whole trip I started to worry. I did not have the money but I just knew I was meant to be there and made the decision to say a sacred yes from my heart. I did not know how it would all unfold, but I trusted it would work out.

A few weeks later, I received an email from my boss letting me know I was to receive a bonus for the year, which was the exact amount I needed for my trip. That was my first lesson in abundance. We have to make a commitment from our heart first; then have faith and trust that we will be given the resources to fulfill that commitment.

From there, I went on to educate myself in different healing modalities that served to fuel my passion to be a healer. I had decided in my heart that one day I would have my own healing business and I started to work towards that goal.

In late 2015, I was ready to "press play" on my business as I liked to say. But the Universe had other plans. While the Universe had heard my prayer of wanting to have a healing practice it was not going to answer in exactly the way "I" had envisioned it. What was about to unfold was the way the Divine knew was for my highest good, and that is a precious gift in itself.

My desire to step into my healer's shoes meant I would have to heal myself first. The following year would prove to be the biggest healing journey of my life. I did not know how I would get through it, but I trusted I would with the help of my angels.

This brings me to what were my second and third lessons in abundance. Lesson two was learning to ask for help from the angels. This was followed closely by lesson three which was to learn that when we receive guidance, we must take action!

I first asked my angels to bring me a team of healers. I also asked for help finding the funds as I was unable to work. I received abundant guidance from my celestial friends after praying for help. And of course it needed me to take action and trust in the guidance.

First a friend recommended a wonderful psychotherapist who was perfect for me; gentle, knowledgeable, and most of all very spiritual!

She, in turn, mentioned this wonderful man who was conducting a trial on individuals suffering from PTSD using his holistic approach of Neuro-Structural Activation. On top of being guided to work with Doctor "T" and his partner "K", I was told that because it was a trial, it was free! If I had gone to them just a few weeks later I would have had to pay as they had found enough people.

Next, a wonderful being came into my life with his four-legged friends. My angels had left me a trail of guidance to locate him. I had seen an interview on television once and was intrigued. I had come across them online when looking for somewhere to take simple riding lessons months before. I had noticed at the time that they used horses to help people suffering from mental illnesses and PTSD but at that time I did not know I was suffering from OCD and PTSD myself.

The connection was finally made months later when I felt the urge to drop in without notice. After meeting "R", I really wanted to work with him but was not sure how I would be able to pay. Later that day, I was telling my father about this place and right away he generously offered to support me by paying.

And there I had it; my dream team that I had asked my angels to help me find!

The Universe was also showing its support and taking care of me through my relationships with the most loving, understanding, and caring souls. Many established relationships became stronger and more meaningful. While some new people who had gone through similar challenges started to appear. I had the perfect set-up around me to be able to heal.

My husband who saw, heard, and experienced this journey day in and day out was right there by my side; supporting me financially, emotionally, and in many other ways. Without him, I would have not been able to get through it. I am forever grateful to him and to the Universe for having brought us together. Beautiful opportunities also came my way and helped me discover and expand on existing passions I had never taken time to explore. For example I have always loved nature, flowers, and animals. I have always had animals since I was a child.

The next step in my healing journey was to slowly reintegrate myself into "normal" life. I was guided by my angels to do this through volunteering to help animals. The signs were clear and it unfolded so fast and fluidly, which is often a way of knowing the universe is supporting and providing for you. I remember getting an email from my husband with only a link about a wild bird sanctuary. I barely paused before emailing the person in charge. A short time later, I met with her and was so excited about this new opportunity.

When I came out of the meeting I took a short walk on a trail nearby and stopped in a clearing. I put some bird seed in my hand and had a dozen little chickadees eating out of my hand within moments! Looking back on that moment now I think they were there to show gratitude for the work I was about to do. I started the very next day!

Being around these breathtaking beings helped me heal. The energy exchange was immense and brought me so much. I took this passion for nature's creatures and trained to be able to offer Reiki to animals as part of my healing practice. What a dream come true...to take a love I have had since I was a child and make it a part of my life purpose.

The opportunities I was receiving from the divine had no price. What I was experiencing was more than recovery and healing. I was recovering my true self. What a beautiful blessing this was. Truly, what has more value than being able to discover who you are in all your truth and, as a ripple effect, to realize more about your life purpose?

Recovering my true self meant and brought so much to me. One of the things it meant was that I could step into my healer's shoes but for that I needed to gather tools.

My healing journey was my school. It was not an easy way to learn and felt more like boot camp! But the Universe knew it was how I would best learn. I would find the perfect tools to make me the healer that I was meant to be so I could go on to help others with the wisdom of so many life experiences. What better way to gain experience than to become your very best first client yourself. I learned so much...in one year I learned what felt like 10 years' worth of lessons about self-care, compassion, truth, inner-strength, resilience, love, spirituality, and much more.

My psychic abilities not only started to come back but actually became stronger than ever before. I learned how to harmonize the heart and the intellect; when to ask my mind to take a back seat and to let my heart guide me.

The biggest lesson was what I learned about fear. My year was like a dissection of fear in so many ways; I learned to appreciate and be grateful for fear. By doing so, it did not rule my life anymore. I am not saying I don't feel fear. Oh no, believe me it is still there. But to acquire knowledge about fear was a HUGE present. I could have easily chosen to see it as a negative experience. And although it was, in all honesty, the hardest thing I ever went through it also was the most gratifying experience. It has been filled with so much knowledge, skills, awareness, and comprehension of an emotion that nowadays seem to rule so many people on earth.

Heaven has showered me in creative ways with many gifts and blessings during my healing journey. It continues to provide for me in so many ways to support my growth and expansion as a soul on earth.

I am forever grateful and thankful for all the abundance from up above.

Marie-Hélène Fortin is an Energy Healer, Psychic, Medium, and Angel Intuitive™. She has done much healing, from multiple traumas to various life challenges, in her life. These "teachers" have given her an empathic depth in her sessions, assisting clients in their therapy. One soul a time, Marie-Hélène holds space for others to align to their Truth (body, mind & spirit). With a natural affinity to nature and its creatures, helping people heal is another huge part of her mission. Owner of Leading Light, her certifications include Usui Reiki, Animal Reiki, Crystal Healing & Angel Intuitive™

www.leadinglight.ca

www.facebook.com/LeadingLightHealing

Michelle Mayer

20
Abundance is Destiny

SPOILED is my vision of abundance. What is abundance to you?

We are destined to be abundant in at least one part of our lives, and in truth in every part, at every moment of every day. It is our life's calling and what is intended for all of us. We are all here for a reason; find your reason, your why, and see how far you can go.

Abundance can mean so many different things to different people. You can be abundant in love, health, relationships, family, work, money, just to name a few. To me, abundance means ALL the possibilities in the world today. We can create, build, and undertake anything from the comfort of our own homes. We are able to reach millions of people with the click of a button, right from our computers. Compare this to the past, where you were not able to even think of such a blessing. THAT is abundance, giving us the opportunity for endless possibilities.

We have been quite blessed and spoiled in life. Let me share a story on abundance with you. I was sitting in my living room, back in 2006, when an idea to start an Animal Rescue came to me, which I jotted down to consider. At the time, many people in my life asked me about the idea as they couldn't understand why I would even consider this any further. Questions were raised about the dogs peeing in the house, providing care for the dogs, veterinary costs, and more all came forth through these well-meaning friends and family members. To me I wasn't worried about all this; I said that I would be well supported by donations to help me with costs, that I would provide training for the dogs, and make some home renovations to help with maintaining and caring for the animals. They just couldn't see it, but I knew my "why" and that was to save lives! Everything else was secondary and I knew that there were people who would join my quest and help. I felt it in my gut as my intuition was strong.

I knew that my destiny was to help save these precious little beings from death row. Helping to rehabilitate and train the dogs that came from "abusive homes" or "puppy mills" was my calling. I was really looking forward to the experience and challenges that came with it all, and I am still excited to this day.

I would not let others spoil my fun. I began my quest on the internet, posting for donations, crates, food, and all the items that I needed to start up. I researched the pounds in the surrounding areas to be able to pick-up my first few rescued canines. I love animals. My mission and priority was to rescue these particular ones from the pounds, other shelters, and such.

Challenge begun, I worked on getting the company incorporated, a website with the mission, adoption details, and everything that was needed in order for my newly found rescue to prosper. It was definitely something that took time to do before the official opening on April 24th, 2007.

Like any business when you first start, the shelter began slowly. With the knowledge that many businesses will either make it or close within the first two years, I kept pushing on by getting our name out there through flyers, free ads, setting up tables at every event, or partaking in parades. Slowly we continued to progress despite it being challenging at times or having to deal with people's negativity. Persistence was my friend and I just kept moving forward to get my dreams to become a reality. If this was doable for me, a volunteer for this charity, without an income, then let's agree that it is certainly possible for you to amount to anything you set your mind towards.

In the last ten years, the rescue shelter and I have been through our ups and downs, but overall it was a great challenge at times like anything in life. We just need to accept the good or bad, keep our vision in mind, pushing forward and standing tall.

January 1st, 2009 was one of our hardest periods. While out celebrating the start of the new year and my birthday, I returned after midnight to find myself homeless after a fire broke out, taking with it my home, all my belongings, and the worse yet, all our rescues and shelters belongings. I was in shock and devastated at the turn of events, standing out on the streets on one of the coldest winter nights of the year. While the firemen and policemen were all standing by and helping out with the disaster, all I could think was that my life was over along with the shelter. Now what? Where would I live? How are we going to get through this? Everything was lost, certainly we can't continue – can we?

That is exactly what we did, all because of the generosity of strangers. If people wouldn't have stepped up to help, I'm not sure that the shelter would be in existence today. Once the news of the fire hit the media, the abundance of support came in. There was so much to do to get back up and running, and all we wanted was to get on with our lives. It was because of all the public sponsorship that the shelter continued on. Without the

Compiled by Brian Calhoun

loving supportive emails, the motivational words, visits with donations or just a hug when I was in tears, I can't say what would have happened. But everyone helped us to push forward and work through the hardship. I felt so blessed to have witnessed the amount of greatness and amazing people in this world, stepping up to help a cause that they felt worthy of assistance. It showed me that there is definitely an abundance of good and greatness in the world, despite that the media tends to focus on the negative.

It was unbelievable how many amazing individuals came by with donations, not just for the shelter, but for my daughter and myself. People showed up with a kitchen table, chairs, sofas, appliances, bedroom furniture, bedding, clothing, and so much for us and the shelter, including dog crates and tons of other needed supplies. And it wasn't just everyday people, coming out to donate, volunteer, or to help with the renovations, but organizations came forth with building materials, vetting supplies, and onward.

It was this abundance of assistance that motivated us to rebuild both our lives and the animal rescue shelter. Thankfully we had been lucky the previous year when we were given a modular home, which was on my property, as this was now where we could live and continue on with the mission. We took what was essentially just a shell, studs and siding and with the public's help, we made it livable. This was outside of the plans we had when we got it, which was to turn it into a permanent shelter for the rescues that would be separate from my home. So there we were with the abundance of volunteers each weekend putting up drywall, connecting water, sewer, installing a new roof, and everything that would make it habitable in a matter of months.

We continued to receive such an abundance of dog food, treats, beds, and other donations for the rescues during the renovations, we filled a second trailer to the roof. It was so plentiful that we could pay the generosity forward by sharing with multiple other rescues, helping them in the process, and saving even more precious lives. Before we knew it, we managed to get back on our feet and back to our mission of rescuing those that needed us most, our beloved canines. It was all thanks to people just like YOU, the wonderful and amazing public.

We feel so abundant with all the time, energy, and resources that the public continues to bring to our farm to help the rescues out. Whether it is feeding, bathing, walking, or something else every weekend, especially during the summer months, the farm is a flurry of activity. Everyone enjoys spending time with the dogs, enjoying our beautiful trails in the woods, and helping out. We are always amazed when children are so generous by asking to have their birthday gifts given as food donations for our rescued canines; children truly are our future.

Our rescue is saving many animal friends and this was all just the beginning of the abundance that we saw throughout the years. The shelter has been transformed to a foster home environment and our modular home re-vamped as a speciality store in order to help raise funds for our fur-babies we call rescues. Donations keep coming in daily with many items to sell and supplies for our four-legged friends. This is enabling us to accommodate for major surgeries costing thousands of dollars, such as eye removal or leg amputations, not including the regular vet care such as spay/neuter, needles, and the list goes on.

Without even realizing it at the time, I was the one creating all this abundance. By loving this company and the dogs so much, I was sending out good vibes to the universe and amazing things just happened. Friends and family members today are not only part of the saving of rescues, but always state that we are truly lucky and spoiled. This is so true. Whatever it is that is needed, it's always provided through organizations or individuals. Permanent homes are easily found for our rescues, and new volunteers or foster homes appear freely after hearing of us. Some of our clients even bring us Ice Cappuccinos and donuts on the weekends (my addiction - Ha! Ha! Ha!); gas gift cards for the volunteer drivers picking up rescued canines from hours away; too many abundant things to list.

Today, having researched and understanding the law of attraction, I am conscious that because of my focus, I attracted all this amazing abundance in support, resources, and outstanding people. I was calling forward the law of attraction just by loving what I did and believing that there are other people like me, wanting to help these little souls. All this from one young single mother starting this in her living room, sharing her house with ten to fifteen small dogs to a group of over fifty volunteers working together in a donated modular home where over thirty to forty different little spirits live every month; loving life, enjoying the attention, running, and playing.

Today, it is easier to manifest things we want and we always get huge discounts on items we need to purchase for the rescue and personally. There is a reason for that – we are sending the right vibes out to the universe and it is answering. Ask and you shall receive, believe and it will be given!

Try it for yourselves. Think positive, ask with love, determination, and belief that you are receiving and then see the changes in your life. Do not let anyone tell you otherwise; keep your head high and believe. In the end, all that matters or is of importance is what you think; not what others say or think. Love, believe, and you will see changes, day after day, once you let go of negativity, anger, and worry.

Anger is a big thing. It is not healthy and is unnecessary. Take a deep breath, think of something that makes you laugh, and release the anger. We're sure you can find something funny that has happened in your life. We all have special entertaining and hilarious moments.

Life is very short. You never know when your time is up. Enjoy every moment, be positive, and have fun!

We wish to give thanks in advance to everyone for your support throughout the years past and those to come. We send you BIG hugs and kisses from our rescued canines.

Michelle Mayer is a single mother of a wonderful daughter who is in her second year of University. She feels so blessed to have been able to pay for her daughter's tuition without any help. Michelle created the Navan Animal Rescue Corporation, a non-profit charity, in 2007. She currently works for the federal government and is an Independent Brand Partner at Nerium International, learning the science behind anti-aging. Michelle volunteers as an animal trainer and veterinary technician. She enjoys spending time with her daughter in Cuba visiting many close friends, and is an outstanding caregiver, animal lover, and entrepreneur.

www.narc-charity.ca

Instagram: narc_rescue_nerium

Bonnie Scarborough

21

Have Faith, Dear One

In 1980, I became very ill. I went to many doctors who all said that I was dying but they did not know why. They said I was like a puppet on a string who could die at any minute and that I should get my affairs in order. I was thirty-nine years old with two young children, my husband and I had just bought a lovely new family home in the country, and this was not news I wanted to hear.

I had fought back from two near-death experiences earlier in my life; I believed in miracles and in both of those instances my miracle of continued life came true. I did not believe the doctors this time either in my heart, knowing that this was just another lesson in my journey. I have learned through experience that life doesn't always give you what you ask for but it always gives you what you need. And so I surrendered to what I call Divine Blessed Energy – the healing energy and love of Spirit and Mother-Father God in order to heal once more.

Over the next two years I stayed at home. I spent about 80% of that time in bed while the Guides and Angels worked their magic on my physical and spiritual bodies, sending blessed energy and healing guidance. During those two years, I went out five times, one of which was when I was told to buy a Lasso Apso puppy. I was guided to a certain pet store where I found a six-ounce female mini who became my healing companion for nearly eighteen years.

Healing vibrations continued to be sent to me while I received many other messages from Spirit. As I tapped into this energy, I found myself opening up and transforming darkness into light and sickness into health, though the faith and belief that I was healing. "Faith, tolerance, and understand, first of myself," were but a few of the messages I heard. This was one of the lessons I had to learn, some might say the hard way. However, in my opinion it was also an enlightenment in unconditional love for all, and for myself as well.

There were many dramatic changes through this process of healing. My diet changed as I found myself able to only eat a baked or boiled potato with nothing on it for six months, and my weight dropped to fifty-five pounds! Then I added color to my diet, starting with a carrot! Slowly, I found myself including more whole foods, and I became a vegetarian, which I still am.

I had to learn the art of loving myself exactly the way I was. Looking in the mirror – I laughed, I cried, I was angry – but I was determined to cherish myself. So, I started where I felt I could, which was loving my earlobes and day by day, I began to appreciate a new body part until I loved all of me.

Throughout even the darkest moments, Spirit, our Angels and Guides are always with us. At one point, during this latest experience, I was feeling very alone and depressed, when suddenly the roof blew off the house, and in poured the most beautiful Angelic Music filling me with a sense of peace and inner serenity. This divine gift was from the Angels, which I can still hear within me today and am filled once again with infinite gratitude.

I was guided to become a healer, using the unique gifts that I have been given, to work with individuals around the world. I have been in service for more than thirty years, working with clients' individual and higher selves as I bring the Divine Healing Energy to them. As a Master Herbalist, A Bodytalk Practitioner, and a Specialist in the use of Flower Essences and Essential Oils, I help a person's energy body, mind, and spirit tune into the natural healing energies available. I truly feel blessed to be in service for my clientele, who come from all walks of life and have been working with me and their guides, many since the beginning of my practice. I know that had I not gone through my illnesses and near death experiences, I would not be here now telling this story and doing what I love, which is helping people.

In closing, I would like to ask that you take time to love and appreciate what has unfolded in your life, for each moment is both a mystery and a miracle. The message I would like to leave you with is one that I still carry with me today: "Discover the real purpose for being here; then have the courage and faith to act upon it. When you discover your reason while following the divine guidance, you will expand your abundance in life."

Go about each day with the divine truth held in mind and heart that "We are all blessed." This simple truth can be truly life-changing in itself.

Bonnie Scarborough is a Divine Energy worker, Master Herbalist, BodyTalk Practitioner, and Specialist in the use of Flower Essences & Essential Oils who is guided by Spirit to combine the use of the various modalities for the clients' highest good. She has been practicing for over thirty years in Alberta, Canada.

bonniescarborough@me.com

Ivana Risianova

22

The Adventures of Discovering My Passions

When I finished college, I still had no clue what I wanted to do for a living. University was not the path for me as I didn't want to study something and realize later on that I didn't like it. So, I went off on an adventure of traveling the world seeking for what I would enjoy.

First off was a stop in England where I learned the English language to be able to communicate better around the world. I worked as an au-pair, which was only temporary, as I traveled. Sometimes, I would have extra jobs, but they were short in duration (seasonal) and never truly fulfilled me. After a few years, I eventually found myself in Ibiza where I stayed for five years.

I needed a change and thus my next move was to Barcelona where I signed up for a photography course, which was my new passion. I wanted to improve my skills and then work as a Photographer. However, when my course was finished, my father passed away and I wanted to go home to see my mom. At the time, I didn't have a lot of money as I only worked part-time, so I looked for a job before I went home. I got hired with a Rental Company and thought this would help for a couple months once I came back from visiting my mom in Slovakia. At least I would have a steady income. This turned out to be the longest job that I held. My boss was very cool, my office was beautiful and modern, and the job was never boring as I got to travel via scooter to complete the check-ins at the apartments. Every day was different.

The business was growing at a crazy speed, but it was a young company that was still getting everything organized. I often had crazy long hours and so I would prepare my lunch at home which allowed me to eat healthier. At the end of the day, I would be exhausted, eating my prepared lunch while sitting on my bed.

I soon found myself promoted as a second Manager of the Check-in Department. This meant a lot of hours and responsibilities, including many exigent clients I would deal with. I found myself having lots of tension in my neck and shoulders while I started to gain weight around my hips from sitting many hours at my desk. The money was good but my soul was not satisfied. I realized that this was not what I wanted to do for the rest of my life and decided that I would look for a way to go back to Ibiza. I would find something that would keep me in shape, and something that I would truly enjoy.

I loved ballroom dancing since an early age and was active in the field for ten years. I even represented Slovakia in European and World Championships, which allowed me to travel across Europe while I was young. I thought this would be something that would keep me fit so I would teach dancing again once I re-established myself in the industry.

I found a dance school and a dance partner. We then started to seriously train throughout the week for three hours a day. We were preparing for our first competition when my partner said he was leaving to open up his own dance school. I thought my dream was over as I was dumped, but I was not going to give up so easily. I would find a new partner. Here I was, twenty-eight years old at the time, and most people were likely to be ready to get married, start a family, and settle down. They weren't willing to start training for competition like I was.

I considered moving abroad so my next adventure was traveling to look for a new partner in England, Italy, and Holland. I found one that I connected with the most, but as I was returning from Holland, I felt something telling me to not to go for this. I felt an internal "No" within me. I still wanted to dance so I thought perhaps I could bring a partner to Barcelona. I then found someone from Kazakhstan, but it was going to be complicated to bring him over just to see if we could form a dance partnership.

When I was thinking about the next step, I thought of Pilates. You don't need a partner for this and I had loved it when I tried it in the gym before. I found out in a book that I bought that there were Pilate studios and there was even a school that taught the Authentic Pilates Method in Barcelona.

After visiting and trying one of their classes, I floated as I walked out. Suddenly, life was truly beautiful. The studio's class was completely different than the one at the gym. I felt refreshed, renewed, and happy. I truly was glowing and smiling as I walked along the street. The Pilates innovator was right, it was like an internal shower for the whole body. This is what I was to learn and share with all the people I knew back in Ibiza. I had found my answer I had been seeking.

I didn't know how I would pay for the course but knew this was what I wanted to do rather sitting in an office, coordinating staff and dealing with demanding clients who had just checked-in and were then calling on the phone wanting Wi-Fi codes. I was able to get credit from my bank and away I went learning.

As I was finishing my course, I was invited to teach in Madrid. They promised me I could teach twenty hours a week, so I thought this is a great experience for me to learn and see another functioning studio in action; not to mention that the owners were Osteopaths which would only enhance my knowledge.

I started my teaching career and I soon realized that I wanted to have my own studio in Ibiza one day. One of my students said, "Oh, I love Ibiza. I did my Military service there." It warmed my heart knowing that someone actual knew of my beautiful island that I had been dreaming about for the past five years. He said that his wife worked for a charity that helped women who wanted; start their own businesses and asked if I wanted talk with her. The next day I was speaking with his wife and we were making a business plan together.

My time at the Madrid studio was coming to an end and I was invited to Barcelona. I was also not enjoying the Madrid Studio as the owners were giving me less hours and I felt wrongly treated. I know today that I had to go to Madrid in order to meet my friend's wife who helped me find the finances to begin my business.

I am so grateful that I was in the right place at the right time and met the right people as I recently called the Madrid office where my friend's wife worked, and although they don't help with finances anymore, they still provide legal assistance. Without their help, I wouldn't be living my passion and having my business that will be completely paid off as of this year.

It is a true pleasure, that feeds my soul, to be able to help people strengthen their bodies and overcome the tensions and pain held within through this amazing method that has been around for over ninety years. As I write this, I am planning to start Pilate retreats on the magical island of Ibiza. I feel so blessed to share this remarkable method.

Sometimes it feels like I am my own doctor because if I feel my knees are sore after assisting clients the day before, I can use the skills I teach others and the pain is gone immediately. I feel tension or pain in other parts of my body if I don't train on a regular basis because life is keeping me busy. I know what exercises help loosen me up quickly. It truly is magic.

Pilates is an authentic workout that also prevents injuries. It was created for men, by a man, back in the 1940's when there were no gyms and it was uncommon to see women exercising. It's quite incredible how it has evolved, and today people think Pilates is for women.

It is truly unfortunate that many people come to me, desperate with pain and tensions held so deeply, as a last resort before surgery. Most of them are amazed with the change in their bodies in just a few classes; many avoiding surgery all together thanks to their continued practice of Pilates.

If only this was part of a basic education, our society would be standing up differently, walking taller, feeling better, and having more confidence. My goal is to help as many people heal, love, and destress their bodies through the power of my passion, Pilates, as I can.

My next adventures included meditation.

My friend was constantly talking about the meditations she was doing with someone from England. She ranted about how her healing had completely changed her relationship with her mother. I thought it was interesting and wondered, "What is meditation?" I had been talking with, and questioning, my friend and someone else who knew of this lady from England who said, "Why don't you come and see for yourself what it is all about." I went and was truly amazed by the beautiful energy I felt throughout the moments.

With this all being new to me, I found it a bit strange when channeling was taking place. This is to be expected especially for those of us who can be sceptic about things. I thought if she was faking it, she was doing an extremely great job! I knew deep down that she wasn't; she was the real deal. So, I booked a private healing session with her after the group meditation. The experience with her and the Angels started me on the next part of my adventure – going within to connect with my soul.

During my Christmas break, I completed a silent Vipassana retreat, which was truly the biggest gift I could give myself. It was hard work at times, especially when it would bring up old wounds that I held subconsciously. However, once I overcame and released them, it was like I was hugged by a giant beautiful Angel while I was filled with a love and energy. That experience has brought me to a new level of looking at and understanding situations from my past and present while in a different light.

I believe everyone should complete a retreat like this as it acts like a reset for the body, mind, and soul. My passion is to share Pilates and its amazing benefits, that have changed my body and life completely, with the world while incorporating the nourishing soul techniques I have learned along the way. I believe that taking care of my body and my inner being is just as important as brushing my teeth. In fact, it is essential to my well-being, especially with all the distractions of social media, television, chemicals found in foods, and the biggest disease of this era, stress.

I now realize that it is by going within to connect with our souls that nurtures our expansion and learning. Everything is connected and we are one in body, mind, and soul.

Thank you to all my amazing teachers, my life adventure, and to the universe. I am truly grateful for everything in my life.

Ivana Risianova is a Romana Pilates Certified Teacher and owner of Pure Pilates Ibiza where the original authentic equipment from EEUU is utilized in the classes. She has an established base of many happy local clients and world renowned celebrities. Born and raised in Slovakia, Ivana now calls Ibiza, Spain home after traveling to explore and find her true passion, learning new languages, and living in different countries. Ivana has a mission to share Pilates and its amazing benefits with the world. Life is a university where she continues to learn, grow, and experience all her soul guides her to.

http://www.purepilatesibiza.com/

Cheryl Sinfield

Creating a Life with Passion and Purpose

My journey with the Faeries started in early 2007, when my father was very ill. My father was an electrical contractor, and was still wiring houses the month before he died. While my father was still here, my time away from worrying about him was drawing. Everything I was drawing was faeries and dragons, especially dragons.

After my father left this realm, I was surrounded by people that were creating faery houses. They were using Chinese lanterns as the form of the house and then embellishing them. As an artist with a Bachelor of Fine Arts from Queen's University, my medium, is sculpture. After seeing their faery houses, I started making my own version of what a faery house looks like.

My first faery house was wrapped wire that looked like twigs or branches and the walls were made of cloth autumn leaves. The wire was formed into a shape of a ball and the leaves were sewn onto the wire. There was an opening left for the door, for the faeries to enter. The floor was Spanish moss or green dried moss.

After making this faery house, it got me thinking about what a faery door would look like too. My first faery door was strips of wood wired together. It had a little door handle that would be for a drawer. It had a huge medallion on it that used to be a piece of jewellery. My husband even helped me put a door jamb on it, so it opened and closed too.

I believe the Faery realm has been trying to contact me for a very long time, even before 2007. In 1995, I was drawing these faces in a sketch book. They were male faces. One had leaves growing out of his face and the other was a side profile of a man with pointy ears. I found out twelve years later, when I started to listen to the spirit world through psychic readings, that I was channeling faery-spirits guides from other realms.

This leaf man or Green Man is my spirit guide, as well as a protector. His name is Isaac. As said, he looks like the Green Man, with Pan Legs and cloven feet. He has faery wings and a tail too. I found out what his body looked like from a good friend who reads tea leaves. During the tea leaf reading there was an outline of him as described with me floating on a cloud behind him in the bottom of my tea cup. I had faery wings too!

The sketch of the pointed ear man is the same guide as Isaac. He ended up in a painting which was made up of three canvases, called a triptych. His energy was a Centaur, named the Sexy Centaur.

The drawing of Isaac became a portrait of the Green Man. I feel this was a huge turning point in my life, the Faeries became my passion and life purpose. I wanted to spread the word about Faeries.

Back to my faery houses and doors, with the knowledge of these two mythical creators coming through my drawings, I believe all my faery houses and doors I create are channeled through me to this realm (earth). Every one of my one-of-a-kind faery houses and doors is for someone in this realm. I do not think people are conscious of this either. My Faery art is a dream come true! It is incredible that I can incorporate my two passions and life purpose together – my art and the Faery Realm.

When I go to art shows and festivals to show and sell my faery art, I never get tired of telling people why I make faery houses and doors, as well as telling them how my life purpose birthed. I love telling the abundance of people the story about my father's illness and how I thank him every day for bringing them into my life. People are always interested in my art and what to do with it too.

I share with them the purpose for a Faery house is a magical home for the faeries to feel welcome when they visit the earth realm. The house lets the faeries know who believes in them and who welcomes them into this realm too. I also let people know that a faery door is a magical door that the faeries can pass through to come and go from the faery realm to the earth realm. And when they get home with their faery art, it will direct them where it need to live in their home because it is a magical object.

The faery realm and my passion with art, has brought to me and my family a faith that has drawn us to an earth-nature based faith. We believe that everything is magic. We see the magic in everything and everything we do.

When the faeries began to be part of my life, my research took me to very well-known people who channel the Angels. One particular person has been told that faeries are part of the Angel realm. They are very close to the earth and help and protect our animals and earth.

When someone does purchase one of my faery house or door, it is a good way to start to connect with these beautiful earth angels; it lets them also know you believe. Know that you don't necessarily need to own a faery house, door, or even fully believe in order to connect with the faery realm.

Like anything, there is the good and the bad. The faeries have good and bad faeries. To attract only good faeries, set the intention by saying in your home, "Only good faeries are welcomed here, no one is welcome with negative or bad intentions."

Another way to connect with the faeries is to leave them small gifts, thimble of honey, mead, shiny objects like stones, crystals, or pennies and unwrapped candies. Faeries are a lot like humans – they have an ego and will judge you; unlike Angels, which see us as divine beings, no matter what. Faeries will see that you are trying to connect with them and they will give you little tasks or tests to see how you react to a certain situation. My tests were picking up pieces of garbage; they may want to see how you treat animals and the environment.

The turning point for me when they accepted me was on a summer day when my family came home from work and school to see this spider on the kitchen floor. The spider at the time chose to have live baby spiders in the middle of the kitchen floor while we were bringing our bags and lunch pails in after a busy day. Instead of stomping on them, the family joined forces. My son, the animal and insect lover, picked up mommy spider and took her outside and we swept up the babies and took them outside.

I am not the only one in the family who believes in the elemental kingdom. Like truly does attract like in life, and we sure do have an abundance of Elemental, Nature, and Mother Earth connections together. Knowing what I know, we definitely choice to incarnate together to live a life on passion and purpose, each in our own way.

I believe my husband is an incarnated Green Man. He is my protector in this realm, as Isaac is my protector in the spirit realm. My husband has always been the one who finds my lost things that the faeries take for a little while. He has introduced me to a tree in our back woods near our house that has become our very good friend to the family. The tree dwarfs all the other trees around it and has an old stone fence beside it. His name is Cornelius, or Corny for short. We think he is an ash tree. We go see Corny through all the seasons. We build faery houses at his trunk. We give him gifts too. One of my favorite things to do with Corny is meld with him. When things get too crazy, I go see him. He grounds me, and brings everything back into perspective.

I have been told I am incarnate faery on this earth realm...I am physically petite and my personality is usually always happy and mischievous like a faery. In the past year, I have even cut my hair in a pixie cut from my long hair which is more faery like too.

My son is tall like an elf and he has always been passionate with animals, reptiles, and insects. He loves to draw and make origami.

And last but not least, my daughter is like her mother, petite and has long hair. She loves to draw too. She is the first person in the family to tell people that we are unique in our nature-based faith and passions with nature and Mother Earth.

I have created faery houses and doors for almost ten years now. Along with the doors and houses, I have created faceless faery sculptures too. They are made of sticks, wire, leaves, and material. And a new addition is faery portals, as they are a meditation tool. They give us a glimpse into of the faery realm which is a gift from the faeries. My artwork has changed in the past year. I have taken up fibre art with yarn and branches, weaving the yarn onto the branches. I have also been sewing symbols onto burlap and canvas as well. The symbols are related to nature based faiths.

I have always signed my artwork as Ce Ce. My nieces and nephews when they were young could not say my name Cheryl, so they ended up calling me Ce Ce. My faery name is Faery Ce Ce and through the years has expanded to Elemental Ce Ce, which includes all the elements of nature: Earth, Air, Fire, Water, and Spirit.

Through my ten years' journey with the Faeries, I have gotten my message and artwork distributed to their proper owners by going to art shows, festivals, and craft shows. One of these festivals I created myself. It is called FaeryFest, in Perth, Ontario, Canada. It has been a great place for me to get my artwork out there. It has also brought like-minded people together, who believe in the Faeries. FaeryFest has been going since 2010 and there have been five festivals so far. It has grown from thirteen exhibitors to over fifty exhibitors showcasing their art, crafts, and passions to the faery population. It has inspired many people and given them a safe place to come and dress up with faery wings and costumes to really show their true colors!

I have been a very fortunate faery, as I have been able to able to discover my passions with art and the faeries while incorporating them into something that inspires people. With the help of the Elementals, especially the Faeries, I feel I am so very blessed in so many abundant ways.

In closing, I encourage each of you to take time to sit with the elements in a natural setting and call upon the Nature Angels. Let them know you would like to invite them into your life with love to develop a deeper connection with our friends, the Elemental Kingdom. Ask them how you can help them, and then listen to the guidance you receive. As you help them with love, you can be sure they will be grateful for your assistance and show you it in an abundance of ways from unexpected houseguests to an abundance of love, laughter, and other life gifts.

Don't be surprised if you find your keys turning up in mysterious places or other mischievous signs once you welcome home the Faery Kingdom with love and kindness.

Cheryl Sinfield is a Queen's University graduate of Bachelor of Fine Arts, a Reflexologist, and is certified in Aesthetics. Her journey started in 2007 with the Faeryfest Realm, which transformed her life's purpose. She creates one-of-a-kind faery houses and doors and is the founder of FaeryFest in Perth, Ontario since 2010. Cheryl lives just outside of Perth with her supporting and loving husband, their two teenagers, and their cat, Poppy.

https://www.facebook.com/cheryl.sinfield

http://bit.ly/2lM4mhm

Michelle Scarborough

24

Creating Abundance

Is it your intention to create abundance in your life?

Do you feel you try but don't succeed?

Ask and it does not come?

It is your God-given right to have heaven on earth and to create abundance for yourself and others wherever you go. This is the life well lived. So, how do you create abundance?

Let's begin by covering the Philosophical component of the abundance equation quickly.

First understand that Spirit is within you, God is within you. If that is so then you have the power to create your world and all of that love and abundance you so desire. But here is the catch. You must create it with love; with kindness for self and others; for the betterment of yourself, others, and the earth, and where no harm comes. Only then are you in alignment with God. You see, God does not want harm for you, any one of his creations, or the earth. As such, only love and right alignment to self and Spirit will create it.

Think of everything in terms of vibration and energy. The energy of God within is the same energy within everything. Therefore, if God is within you, and is connected to everything through the vibrational energy, you must truly be connected and one with the energy of abundance within on some level. Your true nature is one of abundance, love, appreciation, health, and all the good of heaven. Seriously!

Now for the Practical Component – how do we do this?

Here are five simple steps to help you manifest all of the abundance in your life.

- Forgiveness
- Love
- Create

- Let go
- Allow

Forgiveness

Let's start with forgiving yourself and others for not believing that you have abundance in your life now. Forgive where you are. You are exactly where you need to be in this moment. Forgiving releases any negative energy that will get in the way of your loving manifesting of abundance. Let us also say that forgiveness of others is not about them or the experience. It is about freeing yourself so that you can be more heart-centred and manifest with love.

Love

Think about something that you would like to have; something that makes your heart happy when you think about it. Imagine what your life would be like if you had it right now. As you think about it, feel it and feel love for it. Think of love as a power source that gives life to your creation. So, take the time to love and appreciate it fully until you feel that you are one with your creation.

Create

Visualize what you desire. I always do this through meditation but it doesn't have to be. If you have trouble visualizing, there are lots of options such as vision boards. The internet is a fabulous place to find pictures that you can use to help your process.

Think of visualization as a game to push your limits of thinking of what that abundance looks like for you. Go big and create a picture that is wonderful, loving, and fun! Be clear and ask for that picture to come to you now. Think of visualization as a way to connect with your inner child and to imagine your life. There is no right or wrong way to visualize, so relax and have fun with it.

I always like to ask my angels and guides to bring my visualization forth now for my highest good, the good of others, and the good of the earth.

Let Go

Once you have this vision of abundance for you clear, and you have asked to receive, let go.

Let go of all of your expectations around what it should or could look like. Let go of all of the ways in which it will show up and when. Let go of how badly you want it to appear now, this minute. Let go and bring in the feeling of knowing that it is already here.

This is a hard one because if you are like me you want to control the agenda and the outcome. Well that isn't the way this works. Let go and Let God is the message here, so perhaps ask your angels to help you to let go and surrender to the higher power that is your Godself.

Let go also of any fear that you have around the expectation of this abundance coming to you. If you have trouble letting go, write it out, work it out physically – do something that helps you to release the death grip you have on what you are trying to bring in.

Just let go and allow the universe to take over the reins.

Allow

Sit back now and allow.

This is the best part (outside of visualizing that is). Be open to receiving now all the abundance, love, and light that you asked for; allow it to come to you in all of the ways you need. Look for signs of it coming into your life and be grateful when it appears. Practice allowing.

This is another tough one for me because I like to control the agenda. Meditation and physical activity (whatever it might be for you) helps get us out of our head and into our heart and the feeling of allowing. When you are in this space, it helps you to surrender to the moment, which in turns allows energy to flow as required.

We are conditioned to control everything, to follow steps and processes, and to live in this very highly regimented world governed by the few. It is time to open to live the life that you are meant to live – an abundant life filled with love, laughter, and pure joy.

Go live life fully now! Let your true nature shine!

Michelle Scarborough is a Senior Executive in the Finance Industry, has received recognition for her leadership throughout North America, and is a strong supporter of women in Technology & Finance. An entrepreneur and innovator, Michelle sits on several public and private companies that she believes in. She resides in Canada.

michellescarborough@me.com

Georgie Deyn

Angels of Abundance

25

If I ask the Angels of Abundance to help me get rich, will they?

Are they like a genie from a magic lamp bringing untold riches?

These are some of the questions I get asked when talking about the Abundance Angels at my workshops.

It doesn't quite work like that but they have a very important role. They don't just help with money and prosperity. The Angels of Abundance wish for us to understand what abundance is. They asked me to share this with you on the subject.

"Abundance is a supply that comes from a trust in your own Divinity. You are a Divine creator. You can use your Divine gifts and talents to have an abundance of friends, opportunities, love, health, and wealth. Focus on your Divine light and shine it out brightly."

This story is about how I turned my life around by understanding that principle.

Yes, we can ask the angels to help us win the lottery but would that really make us happy? Would we find true friends? True love? Be guided to take amazing opportunities? Or be healthy and whole, if all we cared about was money?

We work with the Angels of Abundance as a team. Their role is to help us remember and connect with our Divine Self or I AM Presence. To put it simply, we all have an Angelic-self, which sees everything from a positive perspective, with eyes of love, harmony, and abundance. In fact, our I AM Presence only knows itself as one with everything, including Abundance.

When you can cease the chatter from your ego-self, which dwells in the realms of fear and only connect with your Angelic-self, you will become a co-creator of lavish abundance in many forms. When you are merged with the highest vibration of yourself, you cease emitting stress and discord and begin to shower yourself and others with harmonic blessings. Your inner state of perfection and peace will be reflected around you in your outer world. As you raise your vibration and radiate bliss, grace, and abundance, you cannot help but bless those around you

This all began to fall into place for me when I began to hear the following key phrase:

Ask, Believe, Trust, and Receive.

Ask, Believe, Trust, and Receive.

Ask, Believe, Trust, and Receive.

I kept hearing the words over and over again in my mind.

The angels and my Angelic-self were trying to guide me and help me with my concerns. I had been so stuck and terribly unfulfilled in my life. I knew there was something missing, not just financially but deep in my heart. I knew there was something that I needed to allow into my life but I was blocking it. Deep down inside my core I felt unworthy, even of the angels' love.

There I was telling others to ask the angels for guidance. Was I doing it? Of course not, I just wanted to help everyone else, because everyone else was so much more worthy of the angels love and abundance than me. I was so stubborn; I refused to ask for direction because I was too scared to listen to their words.

We have free will, and if I didn't ask I wouldn't receive advice or guidance. I would safely stay stuck and unfulfilled. Nothing would change – a much SAFER option.

It was also easier to listen to psychics, clairvoyants, and card readers than to listen to my own heart and the voice of my Angelic-self; which was telling me that I had outgrown my dance school. It was indeed time to move on and focus on my work with the angels but my inner critic and ego told me, "Who do you think you are? You're no one special. There are hundreds of angelic healers out there far better than you." True, there are a lot of healers out there but there are also a lot of people that need healing. I was one of them for heaven's sake.

So, I took a moment to ask the following questions: *"Okay, Angels please show me my way forward, my unique selling point! What have I got inside me that I can share with the world? Please show me what to do. Please give me some guidance and prove it is coming from you and not my ego."*

Now I have to say, I was not always making time to meditate. I was connecting with the angels to help others, as I said, but I didn't really give them chance to guide and talk to me. One particular day, they certainly made me stop and listen to them.

It was during a visit to Ibiza where I was scheduled to give healing sessions and a talk about angels at a charity-healing day. Everyone there was giving their time and gifts for free. It was during this trip that my healing work was about to change. As my client lay on the couch, I realized that there was no healing coming through. I was connected to the angels but the light was not flowing through me. What was going on? I had done all my usual prayers and preparations; it had been about five minutes and still no healing light. Why were they not working with me?

"Please angels, what's happening? Where are you?" I silently asked in my mind.

"Sing, sing in the chakras, trust us and be guided by us child. We are with you."

I started at the base chakra with the tone "Oo" and worked my way up to the crown with the tone "I."

At the end of the session I waited rather eagerly and nervously for the client's response. I felt like she had been a bit of a guinea pig as I had never done anything like this before. I remember her words quite clearly. She said, "I did not feel a thing at the beginning of the session but when you started to sing, wow, I've never felt anything so powerful or amazing. It felt like I was flying with the angels and was taken to a healing sanctuary. I want to go back there."

That was the beginning of Angelic Harmony Therapy, a celestial sound healing modality that I developed with the guidance of the Angels and now certify other practitioners in.

I did as they asked and continued my healing work with a combination of all the techniques they had shared with me. Bit by bit, I was guided as to which Angel would sing into which chakra and the framework of Angelic Harmony Therapy began to take shape.

I attended festivals and began to share Angelic Harmony Therapy as a group healing. Step-by-step the angels guided me to create the manual which included self-healing techniques which I use on myself daily. Healer, heal thyself! Too many healers forget to help themselves; an important blessing from this beautiful gift that I had been given, was that of self-help.

I'm not going to tell you that I have made lots of money but I am earning money from my teaching, healing, and music. I am not part of a big marketing campaign either. Those hardcore, heavy sell, sign up, and I promise to get you a six-figure turnover leave me cold and turn me off completely. I knew that was not the way forward for me. It really did not resonate. So, once more I asked the Angels of Abundance.

"Please show me the way to reach those I can help with my gift that you have given me."

Not long after asking, believing, and trusting, I received a message about this beautiful book, which I was drawn to be part of and privileged to be accepted. I was then guided to sit and meditate whilst singing my soul song, from my heart. So, this is where I can help you now.

The Angels of Abundance would like to share the meditation with you too. Read it through, maybe record it on your phone, and listen to it every morning when you wake and at night before you sleep. You too will be given opportunities, gifts, and blessings in many abundant forms.

Abundance Meditation

Bring your attention to your heart, feel the love within.

Send that love down into the earth and make an intention to send your blessings into the womb of the Mother, where you shall blend your love together as one.

Breathe in and up the healing white mist. Feel it travel up into your body and out of your crown, cascading all around you, forming a cocoon of bliss.

Now once more, connect to your heart and feel its capacity for love. Send that love out from your crown and up to the celestial realms where once more you will blend with the Light of the Divine Creator and intending to embody your Angelic-self.

Notice how you feel as you do this.

Your Angelic-self helps you to see life through the eyes of love, harmony, bliss, and grace. Notice the light of love welling in your third eye, like a spiral of purest vibration waiting to be transmitted out into the cosmos.

Now, as you send out this light, see it touching the hearts and minds of all it reaches, awakening their connection to the abundant supply of their Angelic-self.

With this beautiful vision in process now sing your tones of love from your soul, your soul song; which contains bliss, grace, and angelic harmony. There is no right or wrong way to do this, you simply intend to sing from your soul and allow your Angelic-self to guide sweet vowel tones from your heart. You may well be surprised as to how divine your voice sounds, when you allow the pure vibration of love to be channeled through you.

Now see your vision increase in light and expand with love as you expect abundance for all. Bless this vision with unconditional love.

Notice how those you have touched with the light are beginning to sing their soul song, as they too send out spirals of the purest frequencies to the cosmos.

Within your vision beams of light intersect and as they do, orbs of abundance in the form of peace, joy, love, and blessings appear at the points of intersection.

Each orb begins to grow and expand; soon these orbs surround everyone in these purest frequencies, diminishing all lower vibrations in its path.

Now bring your attention back to your heart and feel how it has expanded, with light, bliss, harmony, love, and grace. Anchor those feelings into the womb of Mother Earth and say "thank you" to all those souls whom have connected with you.

I recommend that you try this meditation at the start of a new moon and continue until you feel that you and your Angelic-self are one, twin flame in holy union.

May this chapter's blessings bring into your life the divine abundance that waiting for you and rightfully yours to receive.

Remember to take time each day to "Ask, Believe, Trust and Receive."

Bless you all.

Georgie G. Deyn is a Singer, Healer, Teacher, and Channel of Love in its purest forms. She works with the Light and Sound of the Highest Realms, including the Archangels, Seraphim, and that of the Divine. She has been inspired to channel Angelic Harmony Therapy, a celestial sound healing, into fruition by the light. Since 1999, Georgie has worked with groups and individuals of all ages to help them connect to their most Divine selves. She brings healing and inspiration through the messages, meditation, music, and movement from her angels, guides, and Divine Feminine collective consciousness to all.

www.angelicharmonytherapy.com

https://www.youtube.com/user/AngelicHarmonyHeals

Regina Wright

26

Mahsi Choo: A Northern Thank You!

At the beginning of a new millennium and new century, I received a phone call that would change my life. The chair of the District Education Council and former chief of the Gwich'in First Nation called to talk to me about accepting a position at the K-12 school in his community. I had been offered a position tutoring English to students who had difficulty getting the credits in English they needed to graduate as well as teaching career and personal development. My husband had been principal of the school the previous year, wanted to return for another year, and wanted me to go with him.

For the past three years, I had been traveling around the province of Newfoundland and Labrador delivering two four-week programs I had created – one for adults and one for youth at risk, as well as offering workshops to corporate clients. I had studied and incorporated attracting abundance into my workshops using tools like goal setting, affirmations, and vision boards; I had manifested many wonderful things into my life! I loved my work, where I lived, my circle of friends, etc. I did not want to travel to the unknown at the other end of the country. I was about to surrender and trust the universe!

However, deep down I knew I was been called to adventure! My soul needed to leave the familiar in order to embrace the new and fully awaken. I wrote in a journal every day when I lived in the north – it was a way for me to process what was happening. As I prepared to write this chapter, I read what I had written during my year in the Beaufort Delta. I was surprised at how difficult I had found many of the experiences and that I still needed to release some of the energy – it has been very healing.

Preparing for the Journey

A month before I was to leave, preparations began for the move north. I thought more than likely it would be for a year; however, it was closer to ten years between the Northwest and Yukon Territories. As we were planning on renting our house, I went about going through each room and clearing out anything I did not wish to keep or take with me. I put personal items I wanted to keep in a few plastic bins and stored them in one small closet. Hundreds of books, university assignments, and business attire made their way to thrift stores or the dump. I felt the process of shedding the old had really begun.

The night before we left, we dined with friends at our favorite restaurant downtown and afterwards strolled along the waterfront where many people had gathered to see the replica of the Norse ship that was in port as part of the 1000-year celebration of Norse settlement in Newfoundland. As we mingled among the crowd and listened to familiar music, it dawned on me that I would be at the airport very early in the morning for my journey to my new home leaving all that was familiar behind.

The Journey and Settling into My New Home and Job

After an early morning flight to Edmonton via Toronto, we spent the night at a hotel near the airport to rest after the business of the last few days. The next morning, we flew to Inuvik and drove down the Dempster Highway to Fort McPherson. We did not have our vehicle and an RCMP officer and his family who were on the plane with us offered us a ride. We traveled about an hour and a half before crossing the mighty Mackenzie River at Tsiigehtchic on ferry and then travel another forty minutes before we came to the hamlet.

After travelling over 10,000 kilometers, we had arrived! Fort McPherson is a community of approximately 950, the majority being of Gwich'in ancestry. The roads in town were not paved and the houses looked rather shabby compared to those down south – they did not have basements and most were open around the bottom. Our house was not on the main road but on a piece of land overlooking the Peel River with the stunning vista of the Richardson Mountains in the background. Standing facing the mountains, I felt a chill go through me. I felt the spirit of the mountains – they were alive! I knew I would be connecting to them often during my time here.

Over the next few days I explored the community and school and on the second weekend we were invited to travel south on the Dempster Highway one hundred and eighty-two kilometers to Eagle Plains for Sunday brunch. A short distance from town we crossed the Peel River on a cable ferry and began our journey south.

The scenery was breathtakingly beautiful with the hills on sides of the road covered with foliage of brilliant reds and purples with the Richardson creating a perfect frame. We stopped at the border to the Yukon to take a few photographs and little did I know that in less than a year the Yukon would become my home for eight years!

Compiled by Brian Calhoun

A short while later, we stopped at the Arctic Circle for some photos and felt rather strange to stand next to a sign that said "Welcome to the Arctic Circle" as I had traveled south to get there! We continued on to Eagle Plains and enjoyed our bunch.

On the way back we stopped a couple of times to have a little hike while keeping an eye out for wildlife. I did not see any caribou, grizzly bears, or arctic wolves, but a gopher that seemed to be posing for photos! On the second hike, I stayed closer to the vehicle while my husband and his friend went a little further. A lone eagle circled in bright blue sky above and I felt it was a sign for me to look at things from a higher perspective.

I took every opportunity to get to know the community and its people. I attended the feasts that were held regularly to celebrate special occasions. The Gwich'in make beautiful crafts and I learned how make a medicine pouch with traditional beadwork. I loved to talk to the Gwich'in language teachers and learned several words that I would use as often as I could.

I loved talking to the elders and eagerly soaked up all they told me about the traditional ways of life. As an aromatherapist, one area that was of particular interest to me was the use of plants for medicine. I was told that with the arrival of missionaries this knowledge and practice was discouraged and went underground, but is making a comeback. The elders told me how important it was to have respect for the land and when harvesting to do so away from roads and communities, to take only what you need, and make offerings and say prayers. Being taken out on the land and connecting to the spirit of the various plants was truly one of the most powerful experiences of my life.

Working in a K-12 school was a new experience as my teaching had been at college level. There was a massive learning curve and I worked long hours preparing for classes and correcting work. I was very tired for the first few months but gradually settled into the routine of school life and at the end of two terms was enjoying it. Then at the start of the third term I ended up taking over the grade three class because of a set of tragic circumstances in the community. This was an extremely difficult period for me but by the end of the school year, I had a beautiful relationship with the class and felt like I was indeed their teacher.

Winter and Summer Solstice

Christmas vacation had arrived and for the first time in four months I did not have schoolwork to do and I could relax! Early on the morning of Winter Solstice I prepared a flask of coffee, dressed in extra layers, and headed out to perform a personal ceremony. We were weeks into the twenty-four-hour period of darkness and by this time, I had become used to the lack of sunlight.

As I slowly walked along the path below our house, the northern lights seemed brighter and more colourful than usual with florescent ribbons of greens, blues, pinks, and yellows shimmering across the sky. It is said that an unborn child can see the incandescence from the womb and I felt that I was about to experience a rebirth. I found a place to sit facing the mountains and took my walking stick and drew a large circle in the snow. The silence was deafening and the only movement was in the aurora borealis overhead; it was as if time stood still. I felt at one with the land, the mountains, and indeed the whole universe.

On Summer Solstice, once again I headed out very early in the morning to perform a personal ceremony. This time we had been in a period of twenty-four-hour light for a few weeks. I sat facing the river and mountains and felt the powerful energy of the sun. I would be leaving the community in just over a week and part of me felt very sad. I had grown so much over the last several months. I had reconnected to the natural world and to my own life force. I had learned to walk "the beauty way."

Time to say Goodbye

As I conclude this chapter, I opened sacred space and gathered several items gifted to us during the year and placed them on a special cloth with beautiful embroidey of roses and the words "God Bless Chris and Regina" lovingly made by the school secretary. As I type this, I am wearing moccasins made for me as well as a necklace of crystals and stones gathered from places important to me in the Northwest and Yukon Territories and I am vibrating with their energy. This morning I found a small publication about the history of the Gwich'in people of Fort McPherson with notes written to us by the staff at Chief Julius School. They mentioned our contribution to the children and community and how thankful they were and we would always be welcome there.

Over the last several days as I reflected on my time in this place of contrasts, I knew I could only share a small portion of the experiences from the year I spent above the Arctic Circle. I remember being told that only about ten percent of Canadians visit the Arctic once in their lifetime. I know how fortunate I am to have lived in such an amazing place with truly beautiful people who opened their hearts to us. I came to really appreciate ordinary things like a fresh apple that were not easily obtained as well deep spiritual experiences that made my soul sing.

I believe gratitude and abundance are connected and I started a practice of consciously giving thanks every day as soon as I arrived in Fort McPherson and continue this daily practice.

My life is incredibly rich in so many ways. My divine soul had awakened under the northern lights and midnight sun! My passion and purpose had been ignited and I now help people find and ignite theirs.

Mahsi Choo! (Big thank you in Gwich'in).

Regina Wright is a modern-day shaman and soul coach weaving together the transformational practices of ceremony, ritual, shamanic journeying, and sacred creation to uncover energetic blockages and limiting beliefs to awaken the inner light and beauty of her clients. She has traveled extensively and studied with many of the world's top spiritual teachers and healers as well as traditional medicine men and woman. Regina is a life-long learner and holds degrees in English literature, business, and education. She lives in the beautiful city of St. John's, Newfoundland coaching clients, leading workshops, retreats, and women's empowerment circles.

www.reginamwright.com

www.facebook.com/moderndayshaman

Compiled by Brian Calhoun

HALO
LOVE

Angie Carter

27
The Healing Power of Love

Sometimes tragedy strikes and there is nothing you can do except learn to live with it; but sometimes tragedies lead you to beautiful destinations. There is a rare kind of love that exists that is so beautiful and powerful, it has the ability to heal the deepest of wounds.

I was a single mother trying to survive when every parents' worst nightmare became my reality. On the morning of June 28, 2014, my nineteen-month-old daughter, Isabella, didn't wake up! I was in disbelief and the next day I went into shock and stopped breathing. I saw the infamous bright white light and instantly felt Bella's presence. I begged her to take me with her. She reassured me that she would always be with me but explained that I couldn't stay with her because her brother, Hudson, needed me more. I woke up in the hospital with a new awareness. Bella kept her promise and I have felt her presence ever since.

Bella began communicating with me immediately following her transition to the spirit world, but the realization of these events didn't become clear until a month later following a session with a Medium. He confirmed that I had spoken with Bella and continued to feel her presence. He validated that my connection to her was real and informed me that Bella had a plan for me. She had become my guide and would be helping me from the other side.

Bella told the Medium that I would soon meet the man I would spend the rest of my life with. She called him her "Dream Daddy" and said she was leading him to me. She described him as everything she could have hoped for in a father, and he would be even more for me. This man would understand me and would have suffered a loss similar to mine; he would be able to relate to the emotional pain I was experiencing. The Medium said I would know beyond any doubt that he was the one and we would both know Bella guided him to me.

About a week after that conversation, my best friend contacted me about something shocking that happened; she was visited by my daughter and wrote a message for me. Details included the man I would marry and a description of our wedding day. She saw a teacher, books, and said he would be picking me up for our first date. My friend has since discovered her gift as a medium and has been relaying messages to me from Bella ever since.

We live in a small town, the type of town where everyone knows everyone. I knew who he was but we had never met or spoken. I knew him as my eighth-grade teacher's son, and he was once very good friends with my sister and brother-in-law. He is a teacher at my son's school and was the Special Education teacher at the time, the person I surely would have interviewed had one of his students been a client of mine. These are only a few of the many ways we could have met but didn't. We had been to many of the same events yet our paths had never crossed.

It began as an innocent comment on a Facebook post and turned into an in-depth conversation about life, death, and everything in between. As my best friend predicted, Tom, a teacher, picked me up for our first date and showed up with books for my son. As I was waiting for him to arrive, I knew in my heart I was about to meet the man I would one day marry.

He took me to the finest restaurant in town, yet I don't remember a single detail about the meal. We were too busy talking to eat and our waitress kept asking if there was something wrong with the food. We left in time to see the second half the concert we also went to, and then he drove me home. We kept talking until the early hours of the morning.

Tom kissed me that night and after he kissed me, I felt something fall. I looked down and saw that my bracelet had fallen off; it wasn't broken but somehow the clasp came undone on its own! This was the first sign Bella sent us.

The next night, I was feeling emotional after putting photos of Bella up throughout my house and when Tom, another friend, and myself sat down, we were in awe of a beautiful rainbow that filled the TV screen, which was turned off. Signs like this became an everyday occurrence and I believe it was Bella's way of making her presence known.

From the moment we met, Tom felt very familiar to me and we are both certain that we have lived many lives together. Tom felt Bella's presence long before we even spoke. One month to the day after Bella's transition, Tom suffered a heart attack. He was sent to a hospital out of town and although he was physically alone, he felt comforted by a presence that was with him. He felt as though this presence, or energy, was taking care of him. He eventually realized it was Bella and he continues to feel her energy today.

We discovered that Tom was able to feel Bella's energy at the beginning of our relationship when she would make her presence known to us often. It became sort of a game and we would see if we felt her in the same place. She would normally be sitting on my lap or beside me. Tom would feel all around me trying to find where she was. We would feel her in the same place every single time, which confirmed, what we were feeling was real.

We took a Reiki course together and although Tom was playing around with energy before this, he learned how to use energy more effectively to help me through my most vulnerable moments. He would place his hands over my chest when grief would intrude and help ease my pain. He learned how to feel my chakras and he was able to balance the energy centers in my body, which helped ease my anxiety. In the early days of our relationship, the waves of grief were strong and unbearable; Tom was always there to help me through these moments. One evening, when I discovered the clay mold of Bella's foot was shattered, raw grief returned instantly. Shock took over and I stopped breathing again. Tom helped me through that moment by using energy; he was able to calm me and once my throat relaxed, I was able to breathe again.

The pain of child loss is not something anyone can understand unless they have experienced it. Tom has two children who are alive and well, but around the time we met, a temporary separation from one of his sons allowed him the ability to understand my emotional pain. We experienced similar heartache at the same time and helped each other cope. Tom knows what it's like to be separated from his child and he now understands my heartache as much as anyone can without experiencing the death of a child. This level of understanding allowed him to quickly become my safe place.

Our first Christmas together was difficult for us both. After numerous unanswered phone calls, we drove many hours to attempt to pick up his son to bring him home with us for the holidays. We came home empty-handed. I woke up on Christmas morning and felt dead inside. We helped each other through the day and I asked Tom to help me find a way to change the meaning of Christmas. I hoped that by associating a different meaning with the date, it would help me cope with the pain of celebrating Christmas without Bella. We prayed for the situation with his son to resolve. Thankfully, after several trips, I was finally able to meet him. Due to the distance, we don't see him as often as we would like, but we make the most of every moment with him.

Tom and I have spoken with a few mediums. Our first experience was during a family session in our living room. This medium informed us that we had a daughter on her way to us and said she would be coming in July. A few months later, we went to see a world renowned medium who told us that Bella was wanting to break through once again. She told us to go home and make a baby!

Two weeks later, I went to Maui for a week on my own with the purpose of healing. Tom wasn't with me physically but he continued to hold my hand from a distance through the process. If not for his support, I wouldn't have had the courage to go. On my trip, I met many people who helped me on my healing journey including some well-known spiritual leaders. On Maui, I was finally able to succumb to my emotional pain; I grieved as I was finally able to let go. I was also able to forgive myself for not being a perfect parent and accepted this new connection I had with Bella.

Upon my return home from Maui, we planned a gathering for Bella's first "Angel-versary." I choose to refer to it as such because to me, she is now my guardian angel. It was a beautiful celebration of the memories we made with Bella and we sent pink balloons to her in the sky. Two weeks later, on July 13, I found out I was pregnant!

My relationship with Bella changed once I became pregnant. Her presence has still remained, but I haven't felt as connected to her as I was prior to this. She let us know that she is watching over her baby sister by making an appearance in her sister's ultrasound photo. When the photo is turned sideways, a face is visible behind our baby's head. By looking at a photo of Bella beside the ultrasound photo, it is clear that the face is hers.

Tom remembered what I told him about wanting the meaning of Christmas to change. He succeeded on the morning of our second Christmas together. He proposed to me in our living room in the presence of our family. We haven't set a date yet but I can't wait to become his wife!

Our beautiful baby girl, Aria Isabella, is now five months old. We refer to her as our rainbow baby, a gift following the storm of loss. She was created in pure love and radiates this through her happy disposition. We have been informed that Bella is Aria's guide and her energy surrounds her sister. Aria is her unique self, although she is very similar to Bella in many ways. I appreciate every moment with her and she fills my broken heart with joy.

Supporting someone through grief is not easy, but Tom chose to be with me through this process. His love held me up through my grief and his ongoing support keeps me together. The power of his love helped me heal from the tragic loss of my daughter, and I firmly believe this is why Bella sent him to me. The pain of losing Bella isn't something that will ever go away, but my grief no longer controls me. Love knows no boundaries, and although Tom never met Bella, they have an inexplicable bond beyond anything physical. Bella remains an important part of our family and we will always include her in all that we do.

Love is a powerful force, limitless in its abilities. It extends beyond what our senses can reach and touches every cell in our bodies. True love is pure and selfless, gentle and kind. It is the greatest gift we can give to another.

Compiled by Brian Calhoun

We are proof that love heals!

Angie Carter is a grieving mother and inspirational writer who began her penmanship as a way to cope with the sudden loss of her nineteen-month-old daughter, Bella. Her blog *"A Mother's Journey Through Grief"* is dedicated to Bella's memory. Angie's writing offers perspectives and encouragement to parents worldwide. The strength she was able to find during her traumatic life experiences have been an inspiration to many. She has deeply touched others with her understanding of life after death. Angie resides in Larder Lake, Ontario, Canada with her partner Tom, her son Hudson, and daughter Aria.

www.angiecarter.ca

www.facebook.com/angie.carter81

Jamieson Wolf

28

The Love Tree

I dreamed of love.

I yearned for it, desired it, ached for it. I wanted a love that was unconditional with a person that would love all of me. The only problem was, I didn't have very much luck with men. The men that I was drawn towards were all the same in one way: they tried to change me to fit their vision of what I should be.

In 2013, I was diagnosed with Multiple Sclerosis. I knew that finding love, or letting it find me, would be all the more difficult now. How could I let someone love me when I couldn't even love myself? I was uncomfortable in my body and what it had become. How could I be open with someone and show them all of myself when I didn't even want to look at myself in the mirror?

I knew that I needed to change my outlook on life and how I viewed myself. So, I started doing everything I could to enrich my spirit. I attended Tarot courses, Reiki workshops, Crystal Healing seminars. However, the most important workshop I took part in was on manifestation. This workshop was all about manifesting the future and the life that I wanted.

I learned about Emotional Freedom Techniques and tapping to bring about a change in me and in my Spirit. At first, I thought that this couldn't possibly work but after a few classes, I started to notice a change, mostly in what I thought I was worth.

I was going on dates, despite how afraid I was. I was putting myself out there, letting myself be seen. Yet every date that I went on was disastrous in its own way. One man was still in love with an ex-boyfriend; one man let his heart problems stop him from truly living. Another couldn't handle the fact that I had Multiple Sclerosis. Yet another man was dealing with his own kind of depression and couldn't understand how I could be happy and thankful with a disease.

On February 14th, I was looking forward to a second date with a man when he sent a text canceling the outing. As I sat there looking at the text, a change came over me. I had been so focused on finding someone else to love me when I should have been focusing on loving myself. I was so intent on proving to someone else why I was worth of their love when I should have been working on nurturing the love I felt for myself.

All those men I had gone on dates with had taught me valuable lessons as well. They demonstrated to me what I didn't want in a significant other; what I didn't need in my life. I had spent so much of my time with men who couldn't love me completely because they didn't love themselves.

I resolved to change that. After my Valentines date fell through, I took myself out to dinner and got myself a present – a fancy watch – to remind myself that time moves forward, one second after another. I should do the same, one step at a time. I got a couple of romantic comedies and a bottle of wine and that night resolved to love myself completely, every part of myself. I knew that it would not be easy, but it would be part of the journey that I was on.

In March, I received an email from a man that I had been corresponding with. We had started talking earlier in the month, just an email or two back and forth, and then he told me that he was busy with work and would email me when he was free. I thought I would never hear from him again. Imagine my surprise when he emailed me later in the month and asked if I was free for coffee. I decided to be completely up front with him about having Multiple Sclerosis and Cerebral Palsy. Part of loving myself was about being able to accept all of me and be to honest about what I carried within me. He responded with an email that still floors me:

Thanks for telling me up front. It tells me a lot about the type of person you are. I know the world can be very judgemental about any perceived weakness or difference, but thankfully not everyone is like that.

I knew I had to meet him. We had agreed to meet for coffee, but I still wasn't sure I wanted to go. I was afraid – terrified of being rejected, scared of being completely myself and possibly being rejected. It was my mother who put me on the right path.

"You're always talking about wanting love, about being open to it. So now you have a chance at love, and you're going to turn away?"

"It's not love, it's just a coffee date."

"Well, love has to start somewhere. Go on the date and see what happens."

With my heart somewhere in my throat, I went to meet him at a local coffee shop. As I was ordering my coffee, I heard my name and turned around. There he was, his head framed by a halo of light. I think I fell in love with him right then.

Now, three years later, we are about to get married and start the next chapter of our lives together and I couldn't be happier.

The seed was planted when I began to love all of myself. The seed was given water when I was honest about who I was and what I deserved from another man. The seed was given nourishment when I decided to trust in Sprit and be brave enough to be open to love. It was given sunshine when I met him and let him love me in return.

The seed grew into a tree that reaches towards the sky and the clouds. It thrives on the love we have for one another.

Jamieson Wolf is a Number One Best-Selling author of over forty books. He is also an accomplished artist and storyteller. When not telling tales or creating art, Jamieson is a Tarot consultant helping others find clarity in their own lives.

www.jamiesonwolf.com

Sharon Hickinbotham

29

Love

Do I believe in Love? True love at first sight; Love that makes your whole world spin; your troubles melt away like ice cream on a hot day; body tremble with overwhelming feelings of love, compassion, and magic when you are hugged real tight followed by a gentle passionate kiss?

The answer is simple, YES, I do believe in love. The love between my partner and myself, after eight years, still leaves me breathless. The connection I feel cannot describe the feelings of love that I have for him. When I gaze deep into his eyes, it is almost like I am hypnotized, unable to blink or turn away. It's in those precious moments of love shared where our soul speaks to each other without needing words. I'm so proud of the life we have created together. He is everything I love in a man, special to me in every way. In many ways, the love he has shown towards me has saved me in ways by bringing my walls down, one by one, which I created to protect myself from being hurt again.

It takes inner courage, trust, faith, and hope to look past the pain of your past and the things you've gone through starting from birth; to be able open up to trust someone new into your heart and to believe that you will not go through that pain again.

If I said love was easy, that would be a lie. Loving someone is easy, but as each person has their own personality or beliefs, it takes two to make it work and last forever. Our faith, love, and believing in each other – that's real love. Loving the highs and lows is what makes us the person we are.

Don't live your life like a movie with fantasies and follow in the footsteps of your family beliefs. Meet true love in person, face to face starting with yourself. If you don't love yourself, how will anyone be able to love you 100 %? Love between two people isn't just sparks flying, it is being in each other's arms, holding hands, and being lovey-dovey filled with kisses. Maybe it's a choice. If you love yourself and your life, you give yourself a chance to be loved in return, and to receive the love one deserves.

True love is a decision, taking a chance on someone, and giving of yourself fully. Don't worry about receiving anything in return, or wonder if they will hurt you. Just enjoy the story between you both, the chapters of your lives together. If love is going to last or even begin, that is out of your hands. You can't control love, or make it happen.

Love is a feeling. The love shared between my partner and myself, in the many different ways, that's true unconditional love to me. Give yourself a chance to let your inner love shine from within you, first allowing that light to overflow shining outward for others to see, and then to be loved in return.

It's amazing after all these years together with my partner how he talks straight to my heart without even saying a word. His smile and the truth in his eyes tell me how much he loves me. Our story has just begun. I believe in you, I believe in our love, yin and yang, we balance each other. Salt and pepper, we go together. I wrote this about my partner, Chopper, who loves all of me, both the good and the bad, through the highs and lows.

River of Love

Thoughts I think, keep me warm,
Let's give a friendship a chance.
I speak from the heart, River of Love
I speak from the heart, Your Love is life,
I love you like a river of love.
Take me in your arms, Keep me warm,
Let's give our Love a chance.
Let the river flow, Hold me tight, and never let me go,
You're my ROCK................Strong,
I'm your FLOWER............Sweet,
You're my heart, you're my soul, stay with me forever,
It's the only real thing I really know is true.

There is so many different meanings to the word Love. It's not just about being in love, or being intimate with another. You, yourself need to love and that starts with loving yourself. Love yourself first and be loved by allowing another person or animal to love you back. The most important thing is to love who you are and how far you have come through all life's challenges or struggles. Love never dies, it's always within us; sometimes it takes a simple reminder of love's gentle touch, seeing or feeling to remind you or reignite the love you have within yourself to not give up hope within this thing we call life.

Compiled by Brian Calhoun

Love is all around us, not just within people, but in the animals, nature, the flowers, the trees, the beautiful lakes, rivers, waterfalls, mountains, even in the moon and the sun, wind, and rain. If you are open to receiving love, you will see and find love has been around you all along; in the infinite love of the universe's love and light. It's an added blessing to have another human being to share your intimate love with and all the adventures living life brings. Till death do us part, and even after death of the body the spirit lives on.

Love is a funny thing and often a lot of people take it for granted, like when someone passes away. We say all the things we loved about them, but we forget to tell them more often while they are still alive and breathing. Tell the ones you care about deeply that you love and appreciate them for all that they do; make time in your schedule to enjoy each other's company. If you have drifted apart use that time to reconnect; perhaps is it your partner, your Mum and Dad, or even a brother or sister, maybe a friend. Who haven't you told lately or in quite a while that you simply love them?

Love is an emotion of strong affection and personal attachment. It can dissolve your worries and ease your anxiousness or fear in a heartbeat. A loving relationship begins at one of our most vulnerable times, our birth, as you are welcomed into the world with open arms and hearts; not everyone is fortunate enough of this beautiful welcoming for many different reasons.

Our story began with the love of our birth as our mothers hold us, as she calms all our fears from this strange new environment out of the once safe, warm womb in our mother's tummy. This is how a healthy attachment of love begins, grows, and shapes our lives forever.

For the less fortunate whose lives started in foster homes, abandoned, or living in an orphanage because mums were perhaps at the time emotional – due to depression, breakups from their spouse, mental illness, drugs, alcohol, or sexual abuse. The world may seem not to be a safe and loving one in which the adults can be trusted or depended upon. This alters our experience of love because of how we first came to be in this world. We all want love and to experience love.

You can experience love from another, as we human beings feel for another, to enable us to share the love connection between two persons. Some people love their material belongings or things that are very valuable or sentimental to them. Love can also be attached to the food we prepare or eat, much like when we eat a delicious meal and say, "I loved that meal." Or you can just simply Love yourself and who you are, here and now.

For many people the word LOVE can mean so many different things, as it's not just about being in love. It all starts with us and how much love we have for ourselves. This in turn allows love to heal every area of our lives from the sadness, anger, fear, stress, and worry as love casts out fear.

Change your thoughts and this will create change in your life; positive creates more positive as does negative attract more negative. Holding positive thoughts create positive feelings, allowing you to experience life that will have a more positive outcome in every area, thus building you up. Holding negative thoughts will have the opposite effect, much like when we over think or try to control events or situations. Feeding these toxic thoughts or lies in your head will make your whole body ache and become sick in the pit of your stomach, trying to destroy and pulling you down.

There is no greater journey than love. Do what you love and tell yourself, "I am Lovable and I am worthy of receiving love," and then watch the many miracles of love transform your life. Not just with other people, but everything around us including nature, strangers you meet, the cashier at supermarket, a stray animal, everywhere. Love is everywhere if your heart and eyes are open to receiving.

Being an animal lover, I still am blown away at the loving affection and heart of my animals when I need it most. The love and affection cheer me up with the many different ways they do. Sometimes my two dogs and my cat, as they are all great friends, do really silly things that change my mindset and I just laugh and smile, which then pulls me back into the positive love energy again, smiling, and of course feeling loved. Or the gentle understanding of my ginger cat, Angel.

One particular day when I was upset and thinking I was all alone in my struggles and that no one understood what I am going through, Angel did the unexpected and jumped up onto the bed. She then sat there just staring into my eyes; her paw reached out and touched my falling tear that was running down my cheek. In that moment, it changed my thoughts instantly. I knew she understood me without any words spoken but by feeling, compassion, and soul. She had empathy towards me and was comforting me.

In that moment, I knew I wasn't alone and it reminded me of my Mum's advice. She always says that when I am down, "Just go sit with the animals and let them comfort you." I really understand it fully now and I often allow the love of my animals to pick me up, filled with their unconditional love for me that they have, and I love them so much like my children.

So for me, I do love myself, my struggles, mistakes, and strengths as they are what makes me who I am today. I love my family, my partner, my animals, and the life I have. I love my life. I am grateful each day for all I have in and around my life, as many others aren't so lucky and live in poor conditions, or don't even have a place to call home to feel safe, clothing to wear, or food to eat.

I don't know your story, but I will tell you something true that you are very loved and worthy of love. You can be lonely but you are never alone in this world. Just look around you, in your daily routine and see what love is around you that you never saw before.

Love truly heals all wounds. Love heals, uplifts, blesses and connects us all.

Blessings of Love to You

Sharon Hickinbotham is an Angel Intuitive Reader who has the ability to connect with your Departed Loved Ones and is an International Best-Selling Co-Author who has contributed to multiple books. Her passion is to inspire others to follow their heart and soul. An Animal and Nature Lover, Sharon is a caring and sensitive empath whose abilities and love for helping others and nature drives her life purpose. Like a Semicolon used in writing (;) she is the writer, the sentence is the sentence and her story isn't over.

http://www.facebook.com/PurpleReign444

shar.hicken81@gmail.com

Julie L. Dudley

30

Creating Your Love Masterpiece

Most of us have loved, and felt lost or helpless within matters of the heart. We seem to know who or what we don't want based on past experiences. Every relationship brings its own lessons and has its own flow. And no two couples will follow the same map. The map is yours to create with the one you love. The truth is, love can be as perplexing or as magical as you make it.

The fairies encourage us to see relationships as fun and less about work. Switching your perspective to seeing love as an endless adventure and path of discovery is a great step.

I'd like to share nine ways you can get started on creating your own love masterpiece, inspired by the fairies. These can be applied to existing relationships or blooming friendships.

1. Nature

   Bring nature into the relationship. There are endless ways of doing this. It can be by buying a plant or taking up gardening together. You can take nature walks, swim, or ski with your partner. Planning a vacation can be a great way to explore, leaving any worries behind you. The point is to connect through the energy of nature in fun ways.

2. Connection

   By looking deep into each other's eyes, you can see and feel things so profoundly. Holding hands is another way to unite your two heart energies as one. Explore the many possibilities to connect as we all connect differently.

   Keep your heart chakra healthy by meditating daily. You can try the following heart connecting exercise with your partner:

   Sitting across from one another (in a peaceful setting) legs crossed, facing one another, breathe in and out, and clear your minds. Focus on your heart space.

When you feel peaceful and full of love, envision sending that love to your partner, in whatever way feels right for you. It can be by sending light from your heart chakra to theirs.

When you're both done (you will feel it) open your eyes and seal it with a kiss.

3. Authenticity - Being authentic makes life so much easier.

   Speak your truth about your likes and dislikes right from the beginning of a relationship. When one is speaking their truth even though it may not always be received from the place of love, it nurtures a sense of trust and respect with your partner.

   Your words should match your actions through and through. If you are saying one thing and doing another, or your body language is saying something else, your integrity may be called into question. It's equally important to keep your promises and maintain an open dialogue if anything shifts over time.

4. Rituals

   By creating weekly, monthly, or seasonal rituals to do together, you have things to look forward to and excitement is important, in order to maintain a lasting relationship.

   It can be as simple as a movie night or trip to a museum. You can make decorations together, run a marathon, or something you do exclusively together. As long as it's something both people enjoy doing and look forward to.

   Keep date nights alive and on your schedules. Most importantly, have fun along the way.

5. Understanding

   No two people think or feel things in the same way, so it's a good idea to try to see things from their point of view. At times, we think something shouldn't hurt someone's feelings, but sadly that doesn't mean it won't.

   Here's a simple exercise to try when you feel confused about how he or she is feeling:

   In a quiet space, close your eyes and take three deep breaths. Picture yourself dis-identifying from your ego, your thoughts, and feelings. When your mind is clear, think of the other person and ask for clarity on the situation. If you would like you can ask to see things through their eyes.

When you feel you have better understanding, gently come back to the awareness of your personal energy or space and open your eyes.

It's great to feel at one with somebody but you're still separate entities. Opening your heart and developing the ability to be empathic towards another is something to strive for.

6. Nurture

    What you eat is so very important; who prepares it even more so. But cooking healthy meals together and putting love into them is a special gesture. By simply savoring food with your loved one, you deepen your connection.

    There are countless ways to nurture someone and the relationship. Foot rubs, massages, making a special gift are a few examples. Remember to keep it simple and fun.

7. Playfulness

    It's so easy to be playful at the beginning of a relationship. By dancing together, laughing and flirting, or even tickling each other, you release stress and worries. It's also a nice gesture to surprise one another in unexpected ways. Think of the many times you just found yourself having fun when dating and how it uplifted you.

8. Appreciation

    We should always remember to appreciate the time we get to spend with the one we love. Any heartfelt gestures made should also be acknowledged and appreciated. Show gratitude to the creator for all the blessings that come along with the relationship.

9. Union

    A relationship requires uniting together as a team. It involves mutual respect and trust. It's important to show support in his or her projects and dreams even if that involves stepping outside of your ego. Be willing to meet each other halfway as it may be sometimes necessary. More importantly, by doing so it shows how much you love another to put their needs first sometimes.

Love can get messy, and you need to be up for the challenges. The rewards are innumerable and if you remember to maintain a deep connection, open mind, and open heart, with a willingness to grow, it can be the masterpiece of a lifetime.

I wish you plentiful love and blessings on your journey with your love masterpiece.

Julie L. Dudley is a Reiki Master-Teacher and IET Practitioner who offer sessions and classes in the Gatineau/Ottawa area. She is a Certified Fairylogist and Realm Reader. Julie offers Angel Card Readings and is a clairvoyant with over twenty years' experience working with Tarot Cards, Rune stones, and Crystals.

www.Mystiquedreams.com

Quin Van Hagen

31

The Transforming Power of Love

June 15th, 2015 is a day I remember like it was yesterday. That was the day that I left the Bahamas to move to Ottawa, Ontario, Canada. On the way to the airport, I was filled with joy knowing that I was finally leaving the country I grew up in and desperately wanted to escape from. At the time my relationship with my mother was certainly not the best. We ended up getting into a shouting match on the car ride to the airport where my feelings of joy quickly switched to feelings of anger.

I was enraged at how she always wanted to control the way I lived my life, and how she would tell me what to do for my future. This wasn't the first time we had our disagreements. These emotional outbursts and feelings came down to me feeling misunderstood. My family just never understood me in general. I felt like there was nothing that I could do or say to them to help them to understand who I was and who I wanted to become.

For the majority of my childhood, as an empath, I always had such deep feelings for everything. Everyone knew me as being very sensitive. This gift of feeling others emotions as my own felt like a curse. Overtime, it felt like I was being conditioned to bury these feelings within me and to just live life with momentary feelings of joy and love; becoming forced to be the person my peers, family, and society wanted me to be.

For me that was never enough. I needed more in my life; something that would give me a great and everlasting sense of joy and love; something that made being alive magnificent and glorious; something that would give me a feeling of purpose and belonging. For my whole life, I lived in a state of wishing for more love, joy, acceptance, and freedom. This game of searching for an external factor that would give me the feelings I longed for was overall, exhausting.

In April 2016, this all changed and I had what most people would refer to as a Spiritual Awakening during a meditation. This awakening led me to realize that there was no reason for me to ever search for something outside of myself to give me more of what I desired because within me was everything. The awakening also led me to the understanding what I was always searching for was self-love. Through this experience, I was guided to learn to love and accept myself for who I am in the moment, without judgement. I learned that I could completely accept all my flaws and imperfections.

This created ripples in the entire universe that I now loved myself, and my whole reality reflected that. The feelings of resentment I had towards my mother and family quickly subsided and I now adore and cherish my family very much.

Along the journey, I also realized that the external world is simply a reflection of my internal one; both positive and negative; both unconscious and conscious. It taught me that whatever the cycle we keep repeating in life with people, such as running into individuals that kept us at a distance, mean, or cold, are simply reflections of the vibrational frequency we are emitting.

So, if these people were treating me this way, perhaps I needed to make some inner shifts myself and start loving, appreciating, and accepting myself as I am now. After all, if we truly accepted, loved, and appreciated ourselves, it would be no surprise that the people we would encounter and befriend will have enormous self-love and acceptance for who they are themselves. It just makes sense; the outer world is a reflection of the inner world. As the universal spiritual law of attraction states, we attract what we are on all levels of consciousness and being in life.

When I started doing this by telling myself how much I loved myself and everything every single day, it seemed like every person I met was super nice to me and caring, even if they had never met me before. Everything in life now seems as it is falling into place according to divine order, with the result of bringing eternal joy and love into my life, more than I could ever have thought possible.

The majority of my life, mainly primary and middle school, I always stood out since I was so sensitive. In school it almost felt like I was bullied and mistreated. Now when I reflect to those moments of my life, with my new found perspective, I definitely had a strong lack of self-love and did not think very highly of myself growing up. Perhaps it was true that I was mistreated in school, but in truth I feel that my world was a reflection of where I was within at that time in life. This also led me to attracting many unhealthy relationships in my life, from romantic relations to many intense rocky friendships with people.

After my awakening, I discovered my true eternal nature and developed the knowledge that we are all literally love. This is because the universe and everything encompassing it is love and light at the very core. I told myself, I will no longer attract people into my life who do not serve my own expansion and who do not love and accept me as I am, simply because these relationships do not serve LOVE. I love and respect myself enough to walk away from anything in my life that does not expand the feelings of love within, through, or around me further.

I now take the time daily to connect to my inner core being through deep meditation. In fact, this is where I discovered the transforming power of love.

The more love you have for yourself and the more love you give out into the world, the more love you will receive. After all, what you give out must come back. It is one of the universal spiritual laws known as the law of circulation. Love truly has the power to transform everything and anything in our lives, if one chooses to serve and step into the power of their true nature. Love is continually expanding and you will feel this expansion in all areas of life as much as possible. To me, what people call God, Source, Spirit or Divine, amongst many other names, at it's core, is just LOVE.

The moment that you start to love yourself, the more love can instantly transform who you are and everything around you. I am still learning and growing every day, but I now look at everything and everyone through the eyes of love. I know that everything and everyone, at the core, is truly the eternal abundant love of the universe. I am so grateful and blessed to know we have a creator who made the universe out of love.

Love is the strongest, most transforming and healing power of the universe. Love can heal and mend all. Love is something we all truly live and strive to have as much as possible in our lives. Love is the answer that everyone is looking for. Wouldn't you want to feel and see the love in everything? It all starts with learning to love yourself as you are. It starts with learning to connect with your wholeness and remembering your true divine nature.

Most people have been romantically in love with someone at some point in their lives, so I would like you to take a moment to imagine those moments when you have been in love with someone where it always feels somewhat like an obsession. Now remember how you felt in those moments.

You probably felt complete bliss for that person, like you were flying around on the clouds all day fantasizing how happy, ecstatic, and whole this person made you feel. We all know romantic love can be very intense. I have been truly in love with two women in my life thus far and certainly know how powerful the feeling of being in love is. Now imagine that feeling of being in love and extend it to yourself and to all things.

Take time to do this daily, and you will feel what I felt in a deep meditation experience listening to music that was produced in the 432-hertz frequency, which brought me into a deeper state of consciousness. In this state, what was an hour-long meditation flew by, feeling more like ten minutes. After this meditation, I could not stop crying uncontrollably for two hours. I realized that I had connected to my true essence, my true divine nature for only a moment in the meditation, but it left me having uncontrollable tears of joy for an extended length.

I felt that in the meditation, I was also releasing all the pain and energy I had buried and supressed inside me during my childhood years. I believe through the releasing of these tears of joy, I was healing myself on a deep core level as I felt the immense eternal love surround me and within me. All I remember telling myself, this feeling in this moment, it is the true nature of all. This meditation and the emotional release I had, has allowed me to feel love and everything much deeper which to me is certainly a blessing. I believe we all here to feel and to experience. Meditation and connecting to my true nature through self-love has allowed me to feel that much more, and for that I am ever grateful.

Time is something to me that is also an illusion that comes with this physical reality. I mention time because time is not truly linear as we think of it. The past, present, and future all happen simultaneously now. All we truly have is the present. It is called the present for a reason, it is our GIFT. I may only be currently nineteen years old, but the amount I have changed as a person in the past six months of my life, has shown me that time cannot exist linearly. I accredit all of this to learning to love and accept myself completely, here and now. This allowed me to remember my true divine nature – an eternal energy of love and light.

The moment that you decide that you are going to stop believing the thoughts in your head about what's wrong with you and start accepting the thoughts that tell you what's amazing and right about you, is the moment you will start to automatically start to feel more self-love. My suggestion is to every day make sure you are doing what you love and living your passions. If you start to do this, you will find that you will not be worrying about anything because the universe will automatically take care of all your needs as you believe. Respect and love yourself enough to walk away from anything that does not serve your expansion and the eternal feeling of love which is your divine birthright.

To me, we live in a perfect divine universe that is constantly expanding. When you decide to constantly grow and expand yourself every moment with it, stepping into the natural flow of the universe, love will flow through you instantly and expansively.

I am now in the process of moving back to the Bahamas as my heart and soul is guiding me there. With my few found perspective on life, The Bahamas is exactly where I want to be.

I want to remind everyone who reads this that you are perfect, whole, and complete. At the core, you are love. Start loving yourself more by meditating, doing what you love and anything that makes your heart sing, and watch the transforming power of love magically change your entire existence right before your eyes.

Quin Van Hagen is a Reiki Master currently living and working in New Providence, Bahamas. He is currently in the process of completing his Bachelors in Metaphysical Sciences at the University of Metaphysics and will have become an ordained metaphysical minister by the end of the program. He hopes to live and inspire all to live on earth with the highest love and joy. He encourages everyone to live in unity and harmony with one another and the planet.

https://www.facebook.com/quinevh

https://www.instagram.com/quinvh/

Nicole Black

32
The Day I Learned to Love Myself

I caught a glimpse of your very pretty face in the mirror and I wondered why I didn't notice you sooner; wondering why hadn't I fallen in love with you sooner? Why did I never notice how unique you are?

"I'm sorry," I whispered. I don't say those words often. For this though, I truly was.

When I was a teenager, I hated myself because I was short and had curly brown hair. Why couldn't I be tall? Why couldn't I be thinner or prettier? But, prettier to whom?

At forty, I finally realized that I didn't want to be tall or super skinny. And I vowed that I wouldn't let my daughter ever look in the mirror and see anything other than the beautiful human being that was in there looking back at her. In many ways, it was my daughter who made me realize that true beauty comes from within.

All of the self-deprecating talk and behavior that I had employed when talking to and about myself needed to go away. It was a layer that I was used to seeing in myself and so very used to hiding behind. It was a crutch of sorts that would no longer serve a purpose in my life, if I could get ahead of it. After all, I had tried to work on my marriage, but even with the best of intentions we had gone through too many trials and tribulations. We recognized that it would be easier to part ways while we could still remain civil to one another. I beat myself up over that for a long time. Maybe if I had tried harder, maybe if I just weighed twenty pounds less, maybe if I was taller, then things would have worked out.

The truth is that things did work out. They didn't work out the way I expected them to or certainly the way I planned for them to, but they worked out. And it wasn't my place to judge how it happened. It was my place to love and accept myself exactly the way I am because I am perfectly imperfect in all of my flaws. We all are. There is a light that shines brightly inside each one of us. The trick is to find that light and really let it out.

For me, my moment of clarity came when I was all alone and feeling hopeless. I felt a despair so deep in my bones I wasn't sure if I was going to be able to come back from it. How could I face this world? I had failed at so many things. I had failed at my marriage, which was the final straw for me. I knew that I needed to dig deep and remembered back to when I was a cheerleader. My favorite cheer came back to me, "Big Blue. Dig In. Go. Fight. Win." And I dug in deeper. Digging in deeper doesn't mean that everything is always puppy dogs, rainbows, and butterflies for me. My life is far from perfect but I no longer need to see things as perfect. I only know that I need to believe in myself and trust that everything will be okay. And it is okay, it really is.

We are all perfectly flawed in our imperfections, yet, we try to hide behind external factors. Whether it is how much we weigh, what we wear, whether or not we use chemical injections to make ourselves appear younger, tighter, thinner, or taller, there are so many standards for beauty that are out there. As a young girl, my grandmother would tell me that it didn't matter what I looked like on the outside. Of course "I was pretty" she would reassure me. "It's what's inside that counts," she would often whisper in my ear. And she was right all along.

Life doesn't always turn out the way we plan it to. Sometimes even with the best of intentions, things tend to go array. I had no idea that my dad's passing would lead me down the path it did, a path where I ended up as a divorcee, a single parent, and after having put my everything into my former spouse's business, I realized that somewhere along the path I had lost myself and I needed to get me back. I needed to go back to work on myself and for myself. I promised myself that I would never give up on my dreams again or sacrifice my sense of self. I have a daughter and I want her to see me as a strong and independent woman who can pick herself up when she falls down.

Here I was alone at a friend's house. I had no idea I was about to recognize how strong I really am and I can't pinpoint exactly what happened that day, but when I woke up I knew something was different. A relationship I was in was ending and I knew that it had nothing to do with what I looked like or how much I weighed. It had everything to do with me growing up and realizing that I deserve all of the best things that this life has to offer. The relationship that ended that day was the one where all of the negative self-talk died.

I always say that I wouldn't change anything in my life. Everything hasn't happened for a reason, but it's happened and I can't change it. So, no, I wouldn't go back and change anything. There is one thing I would do. I would love myself more, and sooner. And I wouldn't wait so long to learn to love myself. And to realize that there is no need today, tomorrow, or pretty much ever to be insecure about anything. Try it and don't like it?

No worries. You tried. We don't have to be perfect at everything but we can never stop trying.

Nicole Black is a certified Rolfer™ Massage Therapist, and writer. She lives in southern California with her daughter and when Nicole isn't writing, she enjoys traveling to distant lands, Pilates, and chasing butterflies.

www.NicoleBlack.com

Tracey Nguyen

33
Awakening to Authenticity

We awaken to consciousness when we have suffered emotionally enough and where the pain of staying the same becomes greater than the pain to change. It is this catalyst when our ego begins to shatter open, the voice within begins to scream louder, revealing the layers of our onion for us to peel back, layer by layer, which can leave us open, raw, and vulnerable. It is in this space that we begin to build our authentic foundation in our truth.

I wanted to write about this topic because it's one that many people have been confused on due to many varied teachings from the personal development gurus and spiritual teachers. Some will advise you to transcend your emotions, some say the ego is evil, others say surround yourself only with light and love, change your thoughts, and the list goes on.

Positivity and high vibes seem "all the rage." "Negative people" and "bad energy" were even things that I resisted in the beginning of my journey. For some of us, we even have a "Spiritual Ego." For a while I found myself judging others for not being spiritually awake, which made me feel lonely and hurt. In the beginning, when we awaken, the transition has our ego telling us that we do not belong and that we are separate.

My inner shifts began with self-compassion and the courage to feel what was really going on inside, which brought up a lot of pain. It was also an invitation into spiritual ecstasy with a new way of being. I found myself immersed into different spiritual practices such as Meditation, Yoga, Life Coaching, Crystals, Reiki, Angels, Guides, Dream Work, Chanting, and more. In all of this, I found myself lost and questioned, "Who am I supposed to be, with all these gurus, paths, and goals?" At first, I would always preach about being compassionate, empathic, and this kind of "awakened" person, denying my shadow self. My Spiritual Ego was at work.

The Law of Attraction became the new fad on my way to live life, especially in regard to abundance. In the beginning, I was an amateur in thinking that I could attract anything I wanted. I soon discovered that you attract what you are, not what you want. I wanted to be a spiritual millionaire without really understanding within what this truly meant. I became reckless with how I would regard money because I thought it would appear like magic.

I also tried life coaching for a bit because I really thought I was in a position to guide people how to live their lives, even when I didn't even know how to guide my own. These things that I wanted to be became a projection of what I wanted myself at the time.

There are a few of us who fall into the personal growth trap of trying to change our mindsets, trying to make all this money, to create this vision, or to achieve these dreams. Although this is great, for me, in starting out, I was delusional and running from my healing. Having goals and vision boarding are good tools, however, sometimes we don't know that it is really the feeling we are after, not actually what we make it appear to be. I think the feeling we are all after, is similar: *To feel loved, happy, and fulfilled in life.*

If I claimed to be all these great things, then, why was I still ruthlessly searching for something in personal development? After many years, I realized that personal growth really means learning to love who you are, what you do, and serving others.

Looking at all the Motivational, Inspiration and Confident Speakers, Authors, and Coaches, I found myself wanting to be like them. There was a certain piece though that I knew I was missing from all that.

Surrounding myself with positive people made sense too. But in some ways, the resistance to my family and close friends who triggered me, also felt like something was off. I learned that when I have a strong emotional charge or resistance to something or someone, that it could be my shadow. In fact, Mother Theresa's saying, *"If you want to change the world, go love your family,"* points us in the right direction.

For a couple years on my path, I did not even want to admit to myself that I was not okay with myself in my stillness or that the way I felt about myself wasn't so great. I was coming from a place of lack, pain, and low self-esteem. I heavily projected my desires onto "my dreams." At the time, I had no idea because my ego was so clever at thinking I could find my peace and happiness through my goals and dreams. I am sure you have heard that saying "Once everything falls into place, I'll feel peace." The spiritual truth is "Find your peace, and then everything will fall into place."

By the third year of being "awake," I began to find my peace toward self-acceptance, in the light and shadow parts of myself. Prior to that, when I was running and distracting myself from my own issues, I found myself sick with autoimmune disorders. I had no choice but to detox my mind, body, and soul. Little did I know, at the time, that my illness was an invitation to love myself.

There was so much anxiety, repressed anger, and other negative emotions within me, it took almost a year of various therapy work in order to learn to let go, layer by layer, and to allow myself to feel the pain to become clearer in my soul. The thing about pain is that it demands to be felt. I spent months feeling my shadow or disowned parts that were triggered by my relationships to people and things and were trying to rise to the surface to be integrated.

I have found that if we are feeling terrible all of a sudden or have waves or sadness and despair, that it is best to sit with it to feel and heal it. Fear and pain are just platforms for faith, love, and soul expansion. The road to authenticity commands us to feel the fear, the pain, emotions, and to be fully present in all our experiences, both positive and negative. Much of the time, we resist our fears or pain, and do not fully grant permission to allow it into our experience. If we take the time to allow it to come to the surface, to accept and feel it, we are then giving ourselves permission to let it go and to clear the energy. However, if we resist it, it will continue to follow us like a heavy shadow.

As much as I tried to distract myself or escape through positivity and spiritual fanaticism, I finally understood what I have longed for and continue to work toward, which is the wholeness in the authentic self. Without allowing the fragments of the past pain, held within our memories, to come up to be cleared and integrated, we continue to live and project in our shadows. Therefore, we cannot be fully present and alive.

Many people in the self-help world always say, "Just love and be yourself," and for the longest time, I didn't even know what that meant. It's such a complex unravelling of layers that simply saying love yourself doesn't cut it. It is imperative to be honest and vulnerable with how you actually feel with yourself. Having a strong sense of self, through knowing one's truest values cultivated from our vulnerability, invites in fulfillment and wholeness.

We all long for our darkness to merge with our light, and not have it as a repressed memory or pain but as a contrasting friend which lends to our dual spectrum of human emotions.

I believe we desire to feel everything in being human, but popular culture has made feeling sad, angry, or hurt a bad thing. In many teachings, there is only high vibes and positive emotions, but I have always found that there was an element to that teaching that was unfulfilling and inauthentic to me. If I'm feeling horrible, the last thing I want to do is to deny how I feel and pretend or affirm to be positive. We live in a world of duality where the sensation of pain feeling of fear exists to appreciate pleasure and love. Non-judgement and non-resistance to all of our feelings lead to emotional and personal freedom.

In the awakening, we learn that deep victimhood has many layers and can penetrate in so many facets of our lives. Playing small, keeping our voices quiet, and using varying degrees of blame or justifications on people and situations need to be peeled away in this process.

Sometimes, I still catch myself and wonder, why this "terrible" experience is happening to me? But I always remind myself that it is these circumstances that bring up old hurts to be released and cleared so that we can expand. The universe is always looking out for us, and it is important to not take the "negative" experience too literally. For example: a bad fight with your partner, that has caused you pain, is something you attracted to heal and release in your subconscious.

Presence with our pain and allowing all the emotions is the key to healing, emotional freedom, and authenticity. There is no serving anyone to continuously blame anyone for how we turned out. It is imperative to give yourself the full permission to feel pain and to completely surrender to all of it. I believe that non-resistance and the art of allowing are the most powerful personal practices we can commit to regardless of our spiritual faith or religion. Your inner voice will become clearer with stronger faith, as you clear your repressed emotions. I believe this is also the process of resurrecting your soul.

Whatever your shadows are, your personality and soul self longs to be fully integrated on earth together. It just didn't make sense to me to just be spirit without enjoying the human senses and desires. When you are fully integrated, you'll have a wholeness that when you do dream with goals, that they are from your whole self and not just the part of you that projects your desires because of lack.

As for forgiveness, it is not about forgiving others, but it is more about asking God to forgive thyself instead. The power is put back into our hands when we take the responsibility to ask for forgiveness and to know whatever experiences we were and are having, it is what we have called in to help us grow. If "bad" things are happening to you, it is just old programs playing out and the pain surfacing is for our soul's expansion. Stepping into knowing that being fully responsible with all that happens to you, is your path to personal freedom, for it is your karma in eternal history to even have had those painful experiences.

We all want that kind of love from our parental figures we need to thrive in our present, yet many of us fail to understand they too wanted the very same thing, which can be a huge block to forgiveness with our inner childhood issues. When one takes the time to love the present moment, they are no longer held back by the perceived lack of love in the past. I didn't fully understand this in the heart at first until applying it to my parents. We are all children of God and to truly learn to forgive ourselves and one another is to understand this first.

Awakening to Authenticity is a return to your truest self. "Unlearning" what doesn't serve you in your personality traits and merging with your soul self: this is the pathway to a fulfilling life that you don't necessarily dream of, but allow yourself to be awakened to.

I invite you to fully feel and allow it, to break down your barriers of resistance and to surrender to who you really are.

Tracey Nguyen is a holistic RN and Emotional Counselor. In her MN degree, she specialized in mental health, therapeutic communication, and her subsequent training in Mindfulness, Therapeutic Touch, Reiki, Yoga and Gestalt Methodology. She has worked deeply with healing the emotional body, the inner child, several physical ailments, and has transformed personal relationships with her family members, friends, and reunited with her twin soul. She believes that awakening to our authenticity requires the willingness to be vulnerable, the courage to feel pain, and shining the light of awareness on all the shadow parts of ourselves.

www.traceynguyen.com

Jennifer Dahl-Kowalski

34

Speaking from the Heart

My mother and I have always had a strong relationship built on love, support, and open communication. When a serious matter arose in our family, we were honest about how we felt and would acknowledge what the other had to say. My mother would listen to my viewpoint and would take the time to explain the situation in greater detail, allowing me the opportunity to understand the larger picture. She taught me that my voice matters and that I should never be ashamed about how I feel.

I can still remember the feeling of being heard and accepted as a child when she gave me a thoughtful greeting card because she wanted to apologize for something she had said or done. She was always aspiring to be a better parent and was not afraid to admit defeat. By demonstrating through her actions that a parent can be vulnerable at times too, she taught me that it was okay to admit when you have made a mistake. I never felt like there was any shame in being honest with my feelings and striving to do better next time. Through cultivating this open dialogue, I learned that vulnerability represents a strength of character because it implies that you take responsibility for your actions and that you hold yourself accountable to your standards.

As open communication was a large part of my mother's parenting style, it was also a large part of her life. She always spoke her mind and never held back on expressing her opinions on important matters with others. There were times when I admired this about her but other times I found myself feeling embarrassed by her direct objections to controversial issues. When she expressed her beliefs around individuals who disagreed, I could feel them judging and criticizing her appearance, her words, and her intelligence in their heads. My immediate response to their negative assumptions about my mother would be to defend and justify her behavior.

I often wondered why she felt the need to express her opinions around people who disagreed. Would she not prefer to spend her time and energy talking to like-minded individuals? It appeared as though the critics she conversed with were already stuck in their ways and cared little of what she had to say. They would rather make jokes about her than be open to hearing another point of view. I despised having to sit there and watch while they snickered at her. At times, I wished she would stop talking completely because I thought that their silent assaults would cease if she remained quiet. In many cases, instead of being on her side, I found myself judging her aggressive stance and her outspoken personality.

I also observed while growing up that most people were content with the status quo and spent their time enjoying the comforts that their lives afforded them. This was in stark contrast to how my mother viewed her role in the world. She insisted that society was not doing their fair share of taking care of the world for future generations to come. She was an activist who believed in protecting the environment and preached about the necessity to recycle, reuse, and reduce before it was trendy. She also did not believe that persons with disabilities were given enough respect and advocated for equal rights in the community.

She became extremely active in the Multiple Sclerosis community when I was young. She had MS herself and felt that it was her mission to ensure that persons with disabilities were given the same access to public facilities and transportation as every other citizen. She advocated that they were given access to all public washrooms by ensuring that each one was equipped with a washroom stall fit for a wheelchair. She also fought for them to have access to all city sidewalks by curbing each street block and all public transportation by creating a space for a wheelchair on each bus and each light rail transit line. In addition to her advocacy work, she assisted in the promotion of these initiatives and even had her picture taken in a wheelchair stall on a light rail transit line.

Through pursuing her far-reaching initiatives, she often rubbed people the wrong way. They would react defensively and would find multiple reasons why her ideas were unrealistic and not possible at that time. As a child, I saw how others were provoked by her strong will and walked away upset after speaking with her. I began to get the sense that she liked to create problems where there were none to begin with. I wanted her to stop raising her issues because I did not like seeing how others were negatively affected by what she had to say. Again, I felt embarrassed and annoyed by her persistence to foster change. Despite my protest, she was not fazed by my or other people's opinions and she continued to move forward towards her goals.

As I grew older, I chose to stay neutral on many subjects. I wanted to remain open to hearing a myriad of viewpoints and I wanted to fully understand where each side was coming from. When it came time to developing an opinion, however, I found it difficult. I would choose a standpoint that I thought made sense only to find myself debating the other side in my head. Thus, I tended to flip-flop on what I believed and did not hold strong values of my own.

Even though I tried to remain impartial, changing my mind often came across as hypocritical and I found others were irritated by my inability to form a position. Friends had difficulty following what I had to say because I never stood for anything. I could easily feel one way about a subject one day only to change my mind about it the following day. I resisted making any type of strong stance because I did not want to follow in my mother's footsteps of being ridiculed and judged. I also did not want to be seen by others as demanding and difficult.

During my mid-30s, I hired a coach that noticed my deeply felt resistances towards my mother's outspoken personality and guided me to acknowledge that these resistances were affecting my ability to be seen and to rise to my full potential. By choosing to judge my mother on her candidness as a child, I limited my own ability to speak up as an adult. Furthermore, she explained that I was projecting my own insecurities of being liked and accepted by others onto my mother. The truth was that I had a deep-rooted fear of being unlikeable. I wanted to please everybody but instead I ended up pleasing no one.

And through all of this, I discovered that my soul had been the casualty. I was betraying my soul's desire to express itself. I had chosen to ignore what my inner guide was telling me because I valued other people's opinions over my own. I worried more about what other people thought than how I would feel. Thus, my relationship with my soul was falling apart.

I decided it was time to start putting me first. It was time to start using my voice and speak from my heart. As my mother once taught me, my voice mattered. It was not important if what I said mattered to anyone else; it was important because it mattered to me. And it was more significant to me than any fear of being judged or criticized. I was ready to confront my fear and move past the resistances that held me back for so long. And I felt it was essential that I start by revisiting how I viewed my mother as a child. I was willing to see her in a new light.

I visualized my mother when I was eight years old. I scanned through old memories of her in my mind and suddenly thought about the way some of her friends use to compliment her on how assertive and unapologetic she was when she stood up for what she believed. I saw the joy in their eyes when they looked at my mother. I felt the admiration they had for her, wishing they could be more courageous themselves. And I realized that I had been blocking these memories from my past because they contradicted the discomfort I felt when people judged her. I was not seeing the whole picture.

I began to consider how fortunate I was to live in a household where important issues such as the protection of our environment and equal rights for all was discussed regularly at the dinner table. I also felt grateful that I had a mother who taught me about her beliefs by acting on them. She taught me that one person could make a difference. While growing up, I had the honor of witnessing my mother change the lives of many persons with disabilities by increasing the amount of accessibility they had to public transportation and washroom facilities. And she did it despite what anyone else said. She had made a huge impact and I had neglected to see that.

After seeing my mother with fresh eyes, I began to see myself in a new light. I started to tune into what I believed and felt an inner acceptance for it. Even though it was uncomfortable, I began to stand on my own two feet and speak my truth. I felt alone in what I had to say but I sensed it was right because it came from my heart. I realized that this was what it felt like to be empowered. This is what it felt like to love yourself. My soul felt alive and I was ready to take on the world.

Jennifer Dahl-Kowalski became conscious of her gifts following an unexplainable illness in 2013. With no clear diagnosis, she ventured into unchartered territories and searched within to uncover her own innate healing abilities. Through utilizing the power of thought, tuning into her intuition, and mastering her sensitivities to energy, she was liberated from her sickness. Dedicated to sharing her wisdom, she helps others release anxiety, stress, and childhood traumas by breaking through old patterns and offering powerful practices that lead to a life with meaning. Jennifer currently resides in Canada as an intuitive coach, certified energy therapist, public speaker, and author.

www.ignite0your0light0.com

www.facebook.com/ignite0your0light0

Valerie Cameron

35

Animal Speak

Have you ever noticed that we are being triggered or confronted by signs or synchronicities when we are been challenged. It may come from a client, a random person at a grocery store, and of course most commonly is our own family members or even our pets. For me, I have really noticed that the wild animals and birds in nature such as crows, hawks, coyotes, deer, moose, and many more come to me when I'm in an emotional circumstance or situation that requires my attention.

My very first experience with animals was when I was living in a small northern community. I was going out for walks every day because I really felt in tune with nature and I always felt its calming effect. At the time I was asking God, the universe, source, whatever you may call it for some answers to certain emotions that I was feeling. This was a very important period for me in my life as I was trying to find who I was.

My first occurrence came in the form of attracting dogs. It was my husband who brought the first dog home during a very frigid winter that year, with temperatures reaching -35 to -40 Celsius. He was a small type of house dog and I was surprised to see that he was wandering the streets.

Over the next two years, I ended up helping four other dogs. The second last one that came to me on one of my walks had been injured, so I brought her home to help her heal. It turned out she was pregnant and I knew that I could not give her away until after the pups were born. It was during this time that I realized that all the dogs that I had been attracting were messengers for me. I just didn't know what it was at the moment. I named this particular dog Brownie; she had twelve pups but only nine survived, and I managed to find homes for seven of them.

On my last trip, I knew that I had to take Brownie and the last two pups to the Humane Society. My heart was broken. I could not understand why I was attracting these dogs, yet having to find homes for them in the end. Every time I did, it felt like my heart was being ripped out. It was during this trip that the message was brought to me.

I had decided that I wanted to take a different route and missed my turn off as it had been years since I had used this way. So I had stopped and pulled over to the side the road. I was crying and very upset when I happened to look over at Brownie. As I started petting her, I realized that the message given to me wasn't about me abandoning the dogs by finding them good homes; it was me that had the abandonment issues.

I was totally in shock; I never realized that I was harboring these feelings within myself. I felt going through this experience helped me to have a greater understanding of the connection of the two seemingly separate issues.

My next journey was with Red Tailed Hawks. My husband and I were on a road trip at the time and I was gazing out my window at the beauty of the landscape. Over a period of time, I had seen four different hawks: the first one was sitting in the trees with blackbirds diving at it; the second hawk I saw was flying, and there were blackbirds flying and diving at it; the third one I noticed was just sitting in a tree peaceful; and the fourth hawk was coasting and flying freely above the landscape.

It had dawned on me in that moment they were giving me a synchronized message.

- The first two hawks were showing me that it doesn't matter what comes at you in life, even with all our obstacles and challenges, we can still find balance.
- The third was showing me that in stillness I could find peace within myself.
- As for the fourth hawk, one can rise above anything, not getting caught up in the drama of life and it also revealed to me that I can see things from a different perspective.

Considering what I was experiencing in my life at the time, this was the perfect message for me personally.

In conclusion, it is important to be aware of the subtle signs that the universe may be showing us through the various messengers that show up in our lives. When we begin to do so, we will see that the messages are truly perfect for what we are going through or in answer to our request for guidance. It just happens that sometimes it's through nature's messengers, the animal kingdom.

Do know that the universe loves you so much that it will continue to keep sending you messengers to repeat the message to you until you finally get what is being said. Once acknowledged, the universe then can take note that you received the message and will move on answering your other concerns through the natural messengers in your life and in the world.

Love yourself to become conscious today.

Valerie Cameron is a Certified Life Soul Coach and Reiki Master-Teacher in Alberta, Canada. She has been an entrepreneur for over forty years, and it is through this and her abilities as an Intuitive Psychic and Spiritual Medium that she is able to compassionately assist those who ask for guidance.

www.earth-balance-healing.com

Natalie Bélair

My Soul Journey:
De-Rooting My Authentic Seeds Authenticity

I am truly honored and grateful to have been given this opportunity to share my story with you. As I connect heart to heart, soul to soul with you, we become one. I now connect deep within my heart and soul, giving myself the right to exist and permission to feel my emotions to be seen and to be heard, without judgements.

You have been guided here today at this very present moment to hear this beautifully powerful message. It is one of self-love, self-acceptance, self-worth, self-healing, and the appreciation of my identity as I surpass some deep-rooted seeds of my fears of being judged, compared, rejected or labeled. Today I make a conscious choice to replace that fear by choosing myself and taking charge of my thoughts as well as my emotions by accepting them, giving them love and importance, then surrendering them to the universe. As I surrender, I surpass my challenges and succeed.

I am a survivor of various types of abuse and toxic relationships. As a child, I was verbally and sexually abused which led to physical, emotional, and psychological abuse in my two marriages.

In 2009, after giving birth to my fourth child, I had postpartum depression that was untreated and turned into Post-Traumatic Stress Depression (PTSD). Against my will, I was medicated for my PTSD and eventually became addicted, feeling lost, and alone. I lost my identity and my passion for life. I did not know how to exist, nor did I want to exist, which led me to attempt suicide with the medication. I blacked out, was revived, and woke up at the hospital. As the days went by, my relationship with my second husband accelerated to a non-existing relationship.

On January 1st, 2012, I had a rude awakening when my husband called the ambulance to send me to the hospital. I was told that I was not to return to the house as I was no longer welcomed there. I was left homeless, with no clothes, no money, no food, and no kids. Shortly after that, I felt completely disconnected, vulnerable, and had a second suicide attempt. When I was in the hospital the only thing that kept me going was my faith. I asked myself this question: "Do you want to live Natalie?" My answer was, "Yes...Yes, I do want to live!"

Unconsciously, I knew I had a purpose in life, but did not know what. That alone gave me the strength and courage to keep going and to keep fighting to live. I went back to his house, picked up my car, some of my clothes, and pictures of my kids. I didn't have a place to live so I even slept in my car during a minus forty-degree blizzard. Eventually, I connected with my social worker who kindly told me to call a local women's shelter.

I continued to pursue my journey as I bounced from shelter to shelter, house to house. I send my blessings and deepest gratitude to the beautiful souls at the women's shelter, who were like angels sent on my path. They embraced me with opened hearts and served unconditionally, twenty-four hours a day for my five month stay. With their guidance and support, they helped me to keep going where I found myself again. Thank you for being a constant source of strength, for picking us up off the ground when we lost hope, and for continuing to encourage us when desperately needed to see the light. Without you, all the beautiful soul lights may dim to darkness.

It was while in the shelter that I was able to start to take my power back and reconnect with myself by meditating faithfully every day. I resumed using my healing crystals to reconnect with my soul and higher self. I felt my identity slowly coming back to the beat of my own rhythm. A short time later, I registered with local groups which helped me understand who I really was, and why I was going through these patterns of toxic relationships and abuse.

Doubt began to creep in as I started to question, "What was wrong with me?" Seriously. The only common denominator in all my relationships was "ME" ...Huh...sigh...Am I the toxic person?

I continued to move forward, got settled into my own place, and repeatedly questioned, "Why I was feeling that way?" I googled and looked up, "Why I felt energy? Why I heard things? I learned about Angels and Guides. I was looking for answers. "Why am I the black sheep?" I did not know of any family members or friends who had my experiences.

Confused, I was determined to find like-minded souls on the internet. After two years of researching my interests and passions, I clearly asked my guides to "please, connect me with like-minded souls here in town." And, they did.

The next day, I connected with a spiritual group that did energy healing and learned about the significance of karma and clearing it, forgiveness practices, and even the importance of learning to open my heart further. All so that I could become a better and unconditional servant with the purity of my heart. I then noticed it was easier for me to forgive everyone, except myself. Ouff. Not so easy, and an even greater challenge!

After a while, I felt a strong need to go even deeper within myself to have a better understanding of my deep-rooted seeds; as well as a massive need to express my words and emotions. I felt the urge to go into nature and scream with all the power of my lungs, to let out my anger and frustrations, as I still felt a need to be heard and loved. I questioned myself, "When will I be good enough? How much forgiveness practices do I need? When will it be good enough? Am I that bad of a person that I need so many hours daily of forgiveness practice? What is it exactly that I do need? What am I looking for? Again, why am I still not happy?" Seriously. Sigh…I then heard, "Emotions!"

"Emotions?" I asked with a puzzled look on my face. Oh! I need to express and understand where my emotions come from. Shortly after, I was guided to take a two year course called, "Vivre en Relation," (Living in Relationships). I then decided to fully invest myself in how to better live in relationships, how to set my limits, and how to respect my boundaries. I found myself in my element, being extremely passionate of healing, understanding, and de-rooting my emotions in my most important relationships. My relationship with my Authentic Self. WOW, this is what I needed! I heard the calling from my soul. Finally, I had found what I was looking for!

Learning to embrace my authentic self by accepting who I am was my most important investment. I found myself judging and blaming everyone along my path but mostly judging myself. Now, I understand why I found it so difficult to forgive myself. I had an "AHA" moment.

It wasn't the souls on my path that were toxic, I was the one abusing myself all this time. I had to take responsibility for giving them my power for thirty-eight years of my life, as I was staying in the energy and forgetting who I was because I felt the need to serve and save everyone. I completely lost my identity. I also let everyone else's fears, emotions, beliefs, and judgments affect me so deeply that my unconscious mind led me to these patterns and experiences.

As I continued to flourish and grow on my spiritual journey, I explored my inner self by reaching deeper into my soul. This brought up deep rooted emotional, childhood, or trauma seeds that were planted in this or in previous lifetimes. These deeply rooted seeds had been trapped in my physical body and anchored there, which created blockages.

As I am intuitively guided by Heaven's Team, I release these seeds and ask for forgiveness for myself and my ancestors. I unanchored these seeds from my physical body. Through the spherical bodies, such as DNA and RNA, cells, and spaces between cells, those seeds are then energetically released through the energy body and then to the universe. From there my physical, mental, emotional, and spiritual body magically transforms my energy to something different; I feel that energetic clearing and release. Next, I plant a seed Full of Divine Love, Light, Forgiveness, and Compassion and let this beautiful seed flourish. By doing so, I embrace my inner child; a celebration and freedom of being ME!

I now see myself with a different pair of eyes and with a positive outlook. In every relationship I encounter, I now see them as my mirror and I use my tools and my intuitive healing gifts that I learned along the journey, to embrace and recognize my authentic self.

I can honestly say that at this present moment, I am truly happy and grateful as I embrace my "Identity." I am proud to recognize and listen to my intuition and to nourish my needs. By choosing and respecting myself, I feel joyful! I hear my words and feel my deepest love. That is a "Divine Miracle!"

I am proud today and filled with gratitude, as I confront my fears and surpass my challenges. I am finally on the path of fulfilling my dreams!

I now would like to take this opportunity to invite you to ask yourself:

- Are you being your Authentic Self?
- Are you respecting your Identity?
- What is your Life Purpose?
- What are your Dreams?
- What emotions are stopping you to make your Dreams a Reality?

I would also remind you to always remember, that, YOU are Your Own Master!

To continue to express my deepest gratitude and bless you further, I am offering you a Divine Healing Hands Soul Healing Blessing for Self-Love right now.

Please take 3 deep breaths, connect with the Divine and say:

"My name is_____ and I am open to receiving this blessing for Self-Love, as appropriate."

Now close your eyes for five to ten minutes and simply enjoy by letting yourself receive in gratitude.

In closing, I would like to give my gratitude to my Heaven's Team, all the Teachers along my journey, Countless Bowdowns to the Divine with continuous love and gratitude flowing to all.

I am forever grateful!

In Love & Light,

Natalie Bélair

Natalie Bélair was born and raised in Timmins, Ontario and currently lives in Ottawa. She is a mother of four children and Owner of Angelic Changes. She is a Certified Intuitive Energy & Soul Healer, a Spiritual Teacher, Soul Communicator, Inspirational Speaker, Reiki, and Access Consciousness Bars Practitioner. She uses Divine Frequency & vibration of her "Soul Song" to remove Soul, Mind, and Body Blockages to transform all aspects of living, both in the present and past lifetimes. Her mission in life is to be an Unconditional servant, spreading Love, Peace, Harmony and to Shine her Light as brightly as possible.

www.angelicchanges.com

www.facebook.com/IntuitiveEnergySoulHealing

i

Fiona Louise

Love Continues On

I believe that the deceased do indeed live on, not just in our memories, nor as wishful thinking, but rather as universal energy which we can tap into whenever we have the need. Our deceased loved ones do hear our thoughts, and are beside us when we need them: to comfort, lend encouragement, and support us through life's journey.

But I didn't always think this way. For a long time the pain of their leaving stayed with me and it hurt to think about them. When my brother, aged twenty-one, left this world through his own hands, I felt so much guilt, shame, blame, disappointment, and anger. I was eighteen and looked up to him, and his abrupt departure left me broken. I felt abandoned by him. I felt very alone, and frankly, miserable.

When I was twenty-one, a medium told me that my anger held back his spiritual progression, and I needed to forgive him – which made me feel more guilty and angry! My inner turmoil extracted its toll emotionally, mentally, physically, and spiritually. It took me about a decade to come to terms with his leaving, to forgive him, and myself, and also to remember him and talk about him, without pain. But as my grief dissolved, I remembered the good times and the happy memories.

A huge weight lifted off me when I connected with my brother's spirit through a deck of oracle cards created for the purpose of communicating with passed loved ones. Through the cards, my brother told me that his death happened the way it was meant to and he was no longer suffering. He also explained that his spiritual journey continues as he learns and heals, and that whenever I need him, I can call on him. My brother also said that he would have preferred to voice his love for me when he was living – something we never said to each other in words, but knew in our hearts. The messages gave me the peace I needed to finally heal my broken heart.

Grandad C passed away in his sleep when I was in my early teens. After many years of looking after my grandma who had ill health, his body just wore out. When I thought about him as the years passed, the concept that perhaps he would have lived longer, if we'd helped more, stayed with me. So it was a pleasant surprise when I received the message from him that bodily limitations no longer apply and he is renewed!

Over the years through psychics I either purposefully went to, or who literally stopped me at the gym, I would receive messages from my Grandad C and Grandma J. Often, they would tell me to believe in myself, and that the world is my oyster (meaning you have the ability and the freedom to do exactly what you want). They said they would always support me and offer guidance. So when connecting with them through the oracle cards, I wasn't surprised when Grandad C said that he would always lovingly guide me and Grandma J is with me whenever I need her.

When a good friend died in an accident, the unexpectedness of it shocked me to my core, and I still had a lot of issues to resolve regarding our failed relationship. It happened soon after my health collapse and at the time it felt like one more blow I just couldn't take. I felt disconnected because I had moved overseas and couldn't attend his funeral. Yet, despite this, I saw him again in a vivid dream in which he laughed and joked just as he always did, as the life and soul of the party!

The cards revealed that he does indeed visit me in my dreams, and that it is him who sends butterflies to me when I'm in the garden. He requested that instead of mulling over the aspects of our relationship that didn't work, I just recall the happy moments we created together, and when I do, he'll be right next to me remembering with me. My darling friend also told me that he loves and supports me, and as I did for him in life, he is now protecting me so that we both fulfil our purpose.

One of the biggest lessons I learned through receiving messages from some of my deceased loved ones is that holding onto pain, shame, guilt, and grief is futile. Our loved ones want us to live happy, healthy, loving lives, remembering the good times and letting the rest go. The timing of their departure is part of a bigger plan that we may not see yet or fully understand. When we release all the negative toxic thoughts and emotions, we will heal. The spiritual truth is that our loved ones are free of earthly pain and ego worries, and are now enveloped in a beautiful, eternal, pure love from Source, and they want us to feel it too.

Through my spiritual growth, I have learned that we are unconditionally loved by Source and we can open up and tap into that love whenever we want to. Source will never give up on us, and will always help. All we have to do is ask. Our loved ones do reflect on their lives after their passing, and through the infinite Divine love, they are healed and want to share that pure love with us. They are only a thought away, and will be with us throughout our lives. We will reunite with them when it is our time to return to Source, and what a blissful day that will be!

By sharing my experiences with you I hope, that if you are holding onto grief, you can now let it go. Grieving does take time, but holding onto negativity does more harm than good. If you are missing your loved one, my wish for you is that you now find peace, knowing they are with you, always.

Fiona Louise is a writer, student, natural therapist and blogger of both fiction and non-fiction. She has co-authored three International Best-Selling books. With a background in marketing and management in the science and property industries, Fiona left the corporate world to heal from auto-immune disorders, learn natural therapies, and write. Re-evaluating her life in order to heal put Fiona back on the spiritual path which she now shares with others. She facilitates creative workshops locally as she sees a need for people to unwind from hectic lifestyles, de-stress, and have fun! Fiona is currently studying Educational Psychology.

http://www.fiona-louise.com

Sharon Hickinbotham

38

Everything Happens for a Reason

To be a published Author is a huge achievement for me. It's a dream I've had which is now a reality, and this is just one of my stories today. Throughout my years growing up, from a teenager to now being an adult, I've written my stories or feelings down as a form of release when I felt I had no-one to talk to. I didn't have any idea that God had a plan for me to confidently share my stories and poems with the world as an Author to help others know they aren't alone in this earthy world by relating to my sharing of heartfelt true stories.

I lost my brother to suicide in January 2014 as everything was falling into place for me, even though at that moment in time I didn't think so as I believed the world around me and everything I'd worked hard to achieve was falling apart. It wasn't until I stopped working, being unable to cope with my anxiety and panic attacks at their peak, that I went into a place of hiding. I was too afraid to live to be happy, so I put many walls up to stay safe and didn't go out anywhere. I felt like I had all these emotions and feelings of grief that I didn't know how to release in order to be able to heal.

One day while everything was quiet with no distractions, I started to write my feelings down in a letter to my soul. With quiet music playing, I started hearing my inner soul and my intuition speaking to me saying, "Write your pain, thoughts, and feelings down. Share your stories to help others who have or may go through the same situation. It may even save a life."

Losing my brother was hard, and still is at times. Sharing my stories with others is worth every word if it helps even one person. I know that my spiritual journey couldn't have grown the way it has if my brother had not left this earthy world. Love never dies. I know this to be true as he is with me every day reminding me with his endless signs of guidance and love to stay strong.

Depression, sadness, mental breakdown, or a mid-life crisis can all tip someone over the edge when they see no way out, give up, and choose to leave their earthly bodies. My family and I weren't even aware of my brother's struggles. Like a card player in a poker game, he concealed his emotions.

He was a hardworking family man, an animal lover, had a love of gardening, and was a practical joker with a sense of humor which made us laugh to tears. He wore a mask hiding what his true emotions and life struggles were. As I write my chapter here, I know he's helping me as I glance over to his photograph and smile having a sense of knowing he is very proud of me for listening to the divine signs to write and share this story.

Through my grieving and healing I wrote the following poem:

Faith Not Fears

Into the darkness we go
Out of the darkness we climb
We walk towards the light
Our heads held high our faith strong
This is where they stay
Kept close to our hearts
We are guided by spirit
Not by fear
We walk by faith
Our love comes alive
Shiny and bright.

The most important thing I've learned from my brother, through his spirit messages to me, is trusting our intuition, which is the way the Angels speak and guide us. It is one of the methods they help us to learn to love oneself and to find balance and harmony in our lives. Love Never Dies and always casts out fear. It is an act of love to reach out to ask for help when needed and not to suffer in silence. You can heal and let go of the mental stress being trapped in fear; let go of worry, despair, and hopelessness. Let the love energy flow through you which will dissolve all negative thoughts and energies. When we learn to love ourselves, we feel the fear and do it anyway. Take time in every situation send love to it. Feel, see, and believe in the power of love, and focus that there is always lots of abundance in life.

I started taking time daily looking into a mirror staring deep into my eyes having a quiet conversation with my soul. This allowed me to open up to the messages from the one person that knows me best and that was my soul. The eyes are the window to one's soul and I found when I tried this for the first time, I felt uncomfortable silly and was even judging what I was seeing within myself. I want to remind you that it is all okay; there is no right or wrong way to do this exercise.

When I was looking into my own eyes, I began to notice the feelings I was experiencing while in the trance. I began asking myself, "Why are you so scared?" I would also tell myself it's okay to cry and be scared, don't be hard on myself. Everything is going to work out. Just believe in myself saying, "I love you." Sometimes I found myself speaking what my fears were, which allowed me to release them from being tucked away. Asking for signs on how to heal reminding myself to be the love that I know is still there.

Writing down what my feelings were, I was able to release them and the healing began, all the while my brother kept telling me to stay strong and encouraged me to share my journey in a book. He told me, "You can do this," and that by me sharing my trials, pain, and happiness, others would be inspired. "Let my words be read," he would tell me.

I was inspired by my own spirit to let love lead the way and thus I wrote a poem which I called Mirror Image.

> *What do I see when I look at you?*
>
> *Deep into the glance within your eyes I see you; the gentle carefree spirit and gentle soul who is loving, kind and freely expresses love to others.*
>
> *People are drawn to you because of your energy,*
>
> *You give advice freely helping many people feel loved to know they aren't alone.*
>
> *Your smile can make all your troubles dissolve when you laugh it's an infectious energy,*
>
> *You listen to others emotions and feel the pain or love from others.*
>
> *Who is this person I love that is looking back at me?*
>
> *It's easy this person is Me, Myself and I.*
>
> *As I'm looking into the mirror I see me*
>
> *Your reflection is the real love that shines for people to see.*
>
> *Love yourself first love heals all barriers.*
>
> *Believe in yourself have faith and most important LOVE YOURSELF.*

Each new day, I feel my brother's Healing Power of Love and guidance, knowing that even though losing him was hard, I wouldn't be writing this today without help from his spiritual messages. Our physical world cannot exist alone without the help from the spiritual world and their loving signs spoken through our intuition, if we listen.

Let me end this chapter with what I wrote when I knew that my stories wouldn't be just kept to myself collecting dust and to be unseen.

Dear Lord, Universe, Angels & Darren

I'm excited that I finally know how to start my book and all of my spiritual path my emotions poems thoughts pain sadness grief or happiness and all I have learned and still learning as I'm going through this personal growth in my spiritual walk.

Please help me Lord to just have fun creating this book of my life and may stress and worry not be a thought as I know this book when completed will help many people and their lives so everything I write will help anyone who is or going through what I have experienced.

Amen xx

Everything that happens to us in life shapes us into the people we are; to teach us what we need to be taught to grow and learn. I believe everything happens for a reason – it's all part of the plan. Grief teaches us like a faithful dog hanging around to teach us and to learn from. There is a Divine order behind everything that happens. Everything in this universe is mathematically precise. There are no accidents. So LIVE, LAUGH, LOVE & BELIEVE. Dream big and follow your heart's desires and dreams.

Signs of Love and healing start with us. I had no idea when I began writing how I was going to get my stories shared. All I knew was that I believed in my heart that the Universe would help to hold my faith and a few months later I was a published author alongside many other authors in a compilation. Before long the universe brought forth a second and now third opportunity to share my stories. One thing I've learned is to hold your faith and believe even if you don't know all the answers or how it all fits together. That's what faith is: trusting in the unknown. Like the wind, you can't see it, you can only feel it. But you know it's there.

I love my brother to the Moon and Stars, to this world and the next. I truly thank him for everything that he taught me during life and in death. I can assure you that love continues on and that there is no reason to fear death. Your loved ones will be with you always and will always be sending you loving signs to let you know that they are okay and still living life. My brother continues to make me laugh as he did in life as his personality did not change at all and he still helps me in the garden that he loved to so much.

My brother has helped me with my anxiety through his brotherly advice which leads me to places of healing like a crystal store, where I awoke to the use of the gifts of mother earth Crystals and how to use them to help in many areas of my life. I have many crystals that I work with often, and each radiates the perfect vibration for what I need it for. If you feel the call to work with crystals listen to your own intuition in choosing the perfect one(s) for you. You can't go wrong as your divine intuition will guide you to which ones you need.

I also use the healing power of Aromatherapy and Herbs such as sage to help keep the energy within my home and myself clear and balanced. Being outside in nature helps to naturally de-stress and help keep me grounded.

I encourage you to be aware of your emotions – all of them – and to not let the negative emotions or thought patterns control your life; let love lead the way. Love begins with you so have a conversation with your soul about what it is that makes you happy, your dreams, or goals in life. You are the only person stopping you from reaching your happiness and dreams.

I encourage you to let go of the self-doubt and judgement; to know that you are loved and you are worthy of love; that you are safe and protected by your Loving Angels always.

Stay strong – you can do it.

Hold your faith and believe in yourself.

It's okay not to know all the answers.

Many blessings of love and healing from me to you.

Sharon Hickinbotham is an Angel Intuitive Reader who has the ability to connect with your Departed Loved Ones and is an International Best-Selling Co-Author who has contributed to multiple books. Her passion is to inspire others to follow their heart and soul. An Animal and Nature Lover, Sharon is a caring and sensitive empath whose abilities and love for helping others and nature drives her life purpose. Like a Semicolon used in writing (;) she is the writer, the sentence is the sentence and her story isn't over.

http://www.facebook.com/PurpleReign444

shar.hicken81@gmail.com

Compiled by Brian Calhoun

HALO

ONENESS THROUGH SPIRIT

Michelle Evans

39

When Spirit Has a Plan

It was probably September when a friend of mine pointed me towards a four-day intensive crystal workshop that was happening the following June. She was going. Did I want to go too? Oh, how I wanted to take part in that! I've always loved rocks and had been collecting crystals for a few years already. I looked up the workshop registration information and watched the online videos. It looked amazing.

I looked into using my airline points to pay for flights; it would cost me over eight hundred dollars and take me days to get across the country and into the USA. I called my mom to see if she wanted to go with me. I had introduced her to crystals a couple years prior and sharing a room would lessen the cost. However, she couldn't afford it. Neither could I really. I had just left my government job and was now self-employed with very little income. To top it all off, the exchange rate really wasn't in my favor. It occurred to me that the responsible thing to do was to ensure I could pay my mortgage for the next few months. I made the decision to pass on the opportunity. I pouted for a while and forgot it had ever been an option.

I carried on my business as a mortgage broker, doing energy treatments and card readings on the side for fun. I had known for years that I was meant to reach a number of people, yet, never knew how to do that. There are so many other people that have more experience than I do. I didn't know where to start or, that I was even capable of such. I'm just me after all and I didn't know that would be enough. I did start coming out of the spiritual closet so to speak, talking openly to more people about the work I did for fun, why I did it, why I loved it, and how it could benefit people.

It was the beginning of May when I made the commitment to myself; I was going to take the teacher level certification in a modality that had changed my life. This was where I was going to start reaching people. Nervous yet excited, my plan was to take my teacher certification in August. I had a trip to Alberta planned for September, and wanted to run a course while I was down there.

It was a Saturday in mid-May when I woke up with the need to make a necklace. This was super strange because I've never been able to make anything without a pattern. When my kids were little I would have the coolest craft ideas in my head, however, the practical application never turned out the way I envisioned. They rarely turned out at all! This need was so strong I had to go downtown to buy materials before I had even finished my first cup of coffee.

The message was that I was supposed to be using crystal beads for the necklace. Living in a very northern city, shopping is limited and finding crystal beads is impossible. I headed down to the store and picked up wire and acrylic beads. I was anxious to see if this picture in my head would actually turn into a wearable product. Spirit never lies. The actual making of the necklace went exactly according to the "plan" in my head! It was beautiful, and I was excited! I was overcome with different design ideas to test next.

The following morning, I woke up to an email saying there were scholarship spots available for the crystal intensive I had been so excited about months before! I swallowed my pride and sent an email back requesting 100% coverage of the registration fee. I promised to myself, the organization, and spirit that if my registration costs were covered, I would make the rest work. I also admitted to spirit how concerned I was about finances and the cost of the trip. My destination was more than 5,700 kilometers away and all the transactions would be in U.S. dollars. I had sent the email and released the rest to spirit.

While I waited, I continued to create and sell my necklace designs. I also called my mom to let her know about the scholarship spots, so she could apply if she really wanted to go. It was Monday afternoon when I got the call that not only would they cover my registration costs, they would also waive the requirement for me to book a room at the hotel. This meant I could share a room with someone, cutting my cost in half! It would be two days later that we would find out my mom was also having her registration covered and I would be able to share her room.

I had already booked and paid for flights to see her in Calgary while attending a mortgage broker event in June. With a little juggling of dates, I was able to use my airline points to book flights across the country for $172.00, a far cry from what I had seen in the fall. We managed to have our flights line up within a half hour of each other, picked up a car, and headed out for the two-hour drive across the border.

Over the next four days, spirit would bombard me with the message, *"You don't need to DO anything to reach and help people. You only need to BE!"*

I would meet members of my soul family, those people that you connect with so deep and instantly that events outside of this lifetime are the only possible reasoning. There would be much laughter, tears, and validations. I connected with crystals and myself on a level that I never knew was possible. I had people that I hadn't even interacted with tell me how much my presence had helped them. The first few times this happened it felt really weird and I wasn't sure what to say. However, after the first half a dozen times I started to understand that "just being me was a powerful thing."

I had a woman I'd never met before give me money to help with the purchase of crystals, because she knew this is what I was supposed to do. I found discounts that "shouldn't have been there," and was given stones by the presenter of the workshop. I heard people talk about my pure beautiful heart with awe in their voices, and I understood why spirit had brought me here. I needed to see the true picture of who I am. *I needed to see myself from others unbiased points of view, and accept that "just being me" was a beautiful, powerful, and healing thing.*

During this time, I also had an unexpected experience with an amazing medium. It would be my paternal grandfather that wanted to speak to me. This was a little overwhelming considering I didn't get the chance to meet him in this lifetime. He and my father didn't have any communication for years before I was born and he passed away when I was very young. He came to me seeking healing for my family. You see, my father and I don't talk. My childhood experiences were very painful and he is not a healthy person for me to around. He is an addict as his father was before him.

My grandfather spoke of intergenerational wounding on that side of my family. He told me that as hard as my father was and although I may never have felt completely loved; my father had improved upon his own experience. He explained that what we truly think often differs from our actions because pride is a very hindering thing. In this moment, I felt sad for all of us for all the things we had to go through and for all the things we had missed out on. The following morning, I would send my father the first "Happy Father's Day" message in more than twenty years.

I felt like I had been beaten with a spiritual two-by-four. My connection was now stronger than ever. *I saw how spirit was with me and taking care of everything!* Spirit made sure I saw my worth and my path by having numerous people point it out. They took care of my finances; I came home with hundreds of dollars' worth of items and only spent $53 of my own money. They cleared the center lane of the bridge I was afraid to drive over; there was literally traffic all around me and not another car in my lane. There were SO many situations I don't have the room to list them all here.

The best thing though, was how they arranged for my mom to be with me. This was a whole new level of healing in our relationship and I had a witness to the events that transpired. I'm not sure anyone would believe me, or I would believe myself, if she wasn't there to substantiate everything.

Upon my return to Calgary, I was given the name of my business and directed to build a website. Of course upon a domain name search, the name was available and spirit made sure I found the most cost effective means of registering it.

My amazingly talented cousin created my logo in trade for a session; saving me I don't even know how much. She was able to have her drawing emit the feeling I was looking for and I cried when I opened the final image.

Next, I had to design business cards and struggled to find a tag line. I knew spirit would tell me if I would just get out of the way. However, I am human and had to fight to come up with something on my own for a while. When I was ready to get out of the way, I retreated to my treatment room and proceeded to do a crystal layout on myself. As soon as my mind was quiet I received the tag line and the most beautiful message to go with it:

"Opening the door to your soul with love."

Your soul is perfect!

Your soul is all knowing, all seeing, and made of unconditional love.

Your soul is the epitome of perfection.

It is only your human self that knows suffering and limitations, that struggles to find answers.

It is only the human that is imperfect.

When we are born into humanity we forget who and what our soul is.

Let's open the door to your soul!

Allow the answers you seek, the healing and comfort you require to be guided by your soul.

A beautiful thing happens when the soul is reunited with humanity!

We begin to realize that we are all perfectly imperfect and loved unconditionally.

I also received my vision, "qualifications," and mission.

I long for a world where we are armed with love rather than fear; a place where people realize we are more alike than we are different.

I believe once I accepted that I am perfectly imperfect and truly loved, I could better accept the imperfections in others and love them for being human the best they can. This changes the way I interact with people and the ripples that flow from those interactions.

Compiled by Brian Calhoun

My mission is to open the door to your soul, help one heart at a time, and watch the loving ripples flow through the world.

This summarized what I had learned and what I longed for in a way only spirit can. This is how I can reach others, help them, and teach them, with crystal work, teaching, and practicing love-based energy work and helping people to connect with their souls.

I believe everyone has this gift. You may not recognize it, know where to start, or realize the potential you have, but it is there, waiting to be discovered.

Michelle Evans is a claircognizant empath. She has experienced many trials in this human life in order to better understand and empathize with you. Michelle had been practicing "in the spiritual closet" for years helping herself, family, and close friends through spirit communication, energy work, crystals and divination tools. Once out of the "closet", she was able to assist numerous people both at home and internationally through distance treatments. Michelle connects with you on a soul level to provide insight, healing, and connection, with love and the best intentions. May the loving ripples spread from you out into the world.

www.rocksolidlove.ca

www.facebook.com/rocksolidlove.ca

Menna Glyn Andrews

40

Imagine, Listen, and Let It Be So

Every year I would go home to Wales from Canada. You see, my roots run deep in my beloved country. I would return to help my sisters take care of my parents and to spend precious time with them.

Preparing for this voyage one particular year, I remember calling the air travel points' agent and telling her that I wanted to go from Ottawa, Canada to Manchester, United Kingdom. She told me that it could be done, but that I would have to spend an entire day and evening in Chicago, to which I responded, "That's alright, I'll just visit my favorite TV host." She wasn't sure how to take my response. As I recall, she eventually let out a giggle.

Everyone nowadays seems to have a bucket list of things that they would like to do. My list had a famous daytime show on it. The host connected with me, as she does with so many. The topics that the show covered always seemed to come at the right time. She asked the questions that were top of mind for me. Despite her humble beginnings, she has made the very most of her life, something I admire. My personal hero and a woman of great service, I had dreamed of seeing her live show or even being on stage with her.

For the next few weeks, when people asked me when I would be going to Wales, I would respond that I was going in May – adding with excitement that I was going through Chicago and how I would be seeing "The Show" en route!

The tale that I was spinning would stop after I had tried in vain to get tickets online. I was even told that it was impossible. I felt rather foolish for even thinking that I had a hope of pulling this off. Dejected, I confessed to an acquaintance over lunch about the "fairy tale" I had been telling people, and felt rather silly. I have often been told how over optimistic I can be; always trying not to lessen my optimism and enthusiasm for life. This in my estimation could have been one of those times. I'll never forget what she said, or more probably, how she said it:

"Just go, Menna, just go."

As her words washed over me, I felt myself lifted by the smile on her face – one of those smiles that is stamped on your brain. I didn't mention the possibility of seeing that show to anyone after that conversation. It was as if the smile had secured that I would just go.

The day had come to leave on my trip. As always, I was a little sad to leave my Canadian family, but overjoyed to think that I would be back in the land of song embraced by parents, siblings, and speaking in Welsh. You see, since arriving in Canada, on what I thought would be a vacation, I married a Canadian and raised my family in Canada. It was a blessed life, however my heart has always remained somewhere in the middle of the Atlantic. It was an early morning flight of just an hour and a half at best. As soon as I arrived in Chicago, I headed to the airline check-in desk and asked if I could leave the airport but have my luggage remain for the evening flight. After that was arranged, I asked a few people for directions on how to get to the television studio. It would involve a train trip, a bus trip, and followed by a bit of a walk.

On the train journey, I spoke with a few people. I told them how I was just passing through and hoped to go to the television studios. There was a conversation with one woman whose niece worked at the studio and even she wasn't able to get her aunt in for well over a year. I wasn't going to let anyone or anything discourage me from trying. Next was the bus journey. On this part of the trip, I saw a woman clutching a brown envelop and somehow, I knew she was going to the same place I was going. Later on, I discovered she was going to see if she could drop off her book manuscript for the TV host to read.

And then I arrived at the studio, it wasn't exactly how I had imagined it. What took my breath away was the line-up of people all waiting to get into the studio. It made me feel rather discouraged and the probability of being able to get in diminished. I went to the front of the line and looked into the door. I pressed my nose to the glass trying to get the attention of the people inside. Eventually the door was opened, I explained how I was on route to Wales, asked whether there was a possibility of a "no show," and that I would be very grateful to be a replacement…I think you can get the picture. I was polite but an aura of enthusiasm circled me.

I spent quite a lot of time enjoying the people in the line, especially hearing their stories of how long they had waited to get a ticket or how far they had come for this day. I felt full of gratitude to be there waiting with them, and felt almost as excited as if I had my own ticket in hand, only to feel doubly fortunate when I found out that this show would be the last taping of the season.

Suddenly, there was a bustle of activity at the front of the line. An official came out to say that they would tape two shows that day. They wanted to see how many of the folk going to the first taping would be able to stay for the second. Immediately, I waved my hands up in the air, desperately trying to gain their attention. Before even getting the chance to speak, I got a response.

"We already know all about YOU, and you'll be there."

In those moments, I realized that a manifestation had happened. I had followed the universes' message. I had surrendered it all, and now here I was about to enter the studio, against all odds, to see my favorite host live! I was full of gratitude, hardly able to believe that this was all happening.

People in the line-up had told me that they would never let me into the studio with my rolly-wheely luggage (my hand luggage). This was still in the back of my mind as I was approached by a tall, beautiful security guard. I had seen her several times on the show. She said firmly, "You'll have to come with me!" My heart took a bit of a jump as she confirmed that bags were not allowed in the studio. My feelings would soon settle as she explained that I would need to have the suitcase x-rayed and then put in their storage while I was in the show.

We walked around the building to the garage. What I took to be the host's cars were there, and a delivery of fresh flowers were lined up on the x-ray machine. I felt part of the action, I was on cloud nine – I was actually there! The beautiful guard leading me had worked for many years at the studio, and had nothing but positive, affirming words on how she enjoyed her work and her life there. I was savoring every moment – a joyful time.

The doors to the studio opened and everyone flooded in. The VIP rows were, as expected, reserved. I didn't care that I was in the "bleachers" at the back. There I sat waiting, feeling a little giddy – something the audience shared with me. I was in a state of bewilderment. How had I managed to be there, looking down at that set? The creamy/yellow leather chairs I was used to seeing only on TV were right here. I wanted to pinch myself.

I glanced down through the back row and, finally, there she was, the woman I have admired for most of my adult life – my hero. She was in a meditative silence; going through what I can only think was a ritual, a prayer, a call to the universe to do her best. I was mesmerized. I was jolted from my thoughts by an announcement. "We are looking for two people to warm the audience for our host. Who will it be?" A woman a couple of seats down from me jumped to her feet.

"Let me through, let me through!" she shouted. As the words dribbled out of her mouth, I thought to myself, "Why not you Menna?" With all my usual reserved behavior behind me, I bolted down to the stage. I had no idea how I would warm the crowd but I was ready to try.

I will never know if the shouting woman that propeled me into action was the other individual sharing the stage – I rather think not. Regardless, I'll always be thankful that her fearlessness had instilled a sense of courage in me. As I stood on the stage, I looked out into the audience and the image of her preparing to come down the aisle is still fresh in my mind. There was a surge of pure energy that launched itself out of me as I shouted, "What are we going to do when our beloved host comes down the aisle? What are we going to do?" I clapped and waved my hands in the air, the audience roared and waved their hands, again and again until the host joined me.

I have had many other examples in my lifetime of events first imagined and I set the intention; then listened, followed my intuition, and managed to manifest situations, abundance, and joy beyond my belief. One day I will share more of these incredible outcomes of a life far richer than even the fantasies of a girl from Criccieth, Gwynedd, North Wales.

How did this all happen in Chicago? How do things fall into place in the most unusual sequence?

I cannot answer these questions. However, I will never forget the phenomenon and in the host's words that she uses often, "What I know for sure," is that we are never alone; there is a power far greater than us, whether we call that God, Spirit, Universe…or another who is at work for us if we chose to listen. The keys are when we have set an intention, have faith in our intuition, and conviction of an outcome; we become one with our dreams and thus they manifest. My hope is that by sharing my experience, you too will be able to manifest your dreams.

I will end by wishing you "Iechyd da," a Welsh salutation of good health and cheer.

Menna Glyn Andrews' (née Williams) first language is Welsh and she continues to have a strong connection with her beloved homeland of the United Kingdom. Menna founded BestSelf Inc., a company that encourages people to become their best self. She has a professional designation in both life coaching and facilitation. As a fundraiser, she has raised millions of dollars for her community and is a passionate advocate for inspiring people to act on their dreams and become their best they can be. Menna is a proud recipient of the Queen's Diamond Jubilee Medal.

Menna_Andrews@sympatico.ca

Melisa Archer

Saved!

Life gets so busy. I had been stuck in the same cycle for months. As a workaholic, I was in my glory, working full-time as a corporate assistant manager and being a district manager for three of my own businesses. Then…**Boom!** I was in a car accident and life as I knew it was over.

It was snowing as I was driving east to one of my businesses. Ten minutes out, I came over a hill, and I could feel something very bad was about to happen. A school bus was stopped, nine cars ahead. The roads were lined with walls of snow.

Out of nowhere, the winds picked up. I was in a WHITE OUT! I was trapped. I turned on my 4 ways. As the feeling of danger grew stronger I prayed, *"Heavenly Father, please keep me safe. Put me in a web of protection."* I moved my focus to my rear-view mirror, pleading "Please NO CARS."

A vehicle came speeding over the hill towards the back of my car. SMASH! I yanked on the steering wheel to avoid hitting the car in front of me. I spun. I was now driving west and had possession of the lane. With nowhere to pull over, I decide to drive to the top of the hill and pull into the school's parking lot to wait for assistance. As I approached the hill, a SUV came into my lane to avoid the pile up that was in front of him. He hit me head on, and my car spun, then hit the driver's side before bouncing away.

I felt a hot honey-like sensation on the back of my neck. What was that? It was quickly dripping now. OMG! It was my blood. Realization quickly set in that my head wouldn't move, only my eyes.

Staring into the rear-view mirror, someone appeared in the backseat! It was a man, mid-thirties, with brown hair wearing a brown suit, white shirt, and brown tie. He says to me, *"Pull ahead NOW, before you can't."* I'm confused, but I did it. I hadn't noticed I was smashed back into oncoming traffic. I'm was now safe, sideways in the lane that started this mess. When I looked back to thank him, the backseat man had disappeared.

I reach for my cell phone and called 911 for an ambulance. Then called my husband, and my business to tell them I was in a car accident. It wasn't long until a guy came and sat in the passenger seat to check on me. He said, *"Sorry, I hit you. I'm a volunteer firefighter."* He kept me talking as I wanted to sleep. When the ambulance attendants arrived, one sat in the backseat working on my head and wrapped it using my heavy sweater.

I was taken to hospital where the intake nurse said I looked okay, and other patients would be taken before me. As a doctor walked by me, the towel fell from my head. The doctor said, *"This is not a Halloween prank."* The hole in my head was so big that the doctor took me right away. He stitched up three layers in my head and closed it with thirteen staples. I was in shock and denial, and wanted to return to work after leaving hospital.

A couple of days later, my best friend drove me to where my car was to collect my belongings. The outside of the car was destroyed. As I inspected the interior of the car, I found blood all over the plastic triangle, which the seat belt gets strung through. This is what went into my head. Had my head split open in another spot, I may have not have survived.

I can see energies, and took pictures of white lines with my cell phone. One of the white lines in the car went from ceiling to floor, wo lines went from the front seat to ceiling, and there were also lines to my airbags and steering wheel. I thought about that. "Hmmm." My air bags did not go off. Had they exploded on me with my head cracked open, I may not be here today. How was that possible? Volunteer firefighters and ambulance attendants had been in and through my car. How could there still be white lines? I was SAVED.

It's odd how head injuries work. The pain and complications set in over the next few days to last years: short-term memory loss, ringing in ears, stuttering, mood swings, dizziness, complete exhaustion, laughing and crying in the same sentence. After two years of endless appointments, I was proud to finally get my life back. A doctor's appointment was made to request a back to work clearance for the corporate store.

My husband took me to the Dominican Republic for my birthday week as we needed a romantic getaway. He had been my caretaker, which had put much stress on our marriage. While in the Dominican, he let me pick any activity for my birthday. Excitedly, I picked horseback riding as I have owned a horse and enjoyed riding. As I mounted the horse, I had an overwhelming feeling that I should get off the horse. After talking myself through the nerves, I would just take it slow.

The horse in front of me kicked my horse. My horse bucked and threw me off onto a rock in the ground. "CRACK". Something broke. This was bad. I used all of my will and strength to get up and drape myself over a short

Dominican man. A fellow Canadian tried to force me to ground saying she is a nurse. I snapped and told her, "BACK OFF!" I asked the nice man to drive me to the hospital. Of course, we are in the middle of nowhere with craters in the road as large as a jeep.

We got to the hospital and within forty-five minutes, I had x-rays done and was headed for CAT scan. Within an hour, the Head of the Hospital and Head Surgeon were by my side. When the doctor told me that I would have to spend the night, I emotionally lost it, verbally accusing them how it was so obvious they could collect insurance money.

This brilliant quiet doctor left the room, quickly returned with two x-rays, and clipped them up into the light board. The doctor pointed and said, "*This first x-ray is of a twenty-year-old boy down the hall. He had been hand gliding and broke his back. He will leave in a wheel chair, never to walk again.*" The doctor went on to explain that the other x-ray was mine. He said, "*It shows that I broke two vertebrates and compressed a disc, and by the grace of God, you can still walk.*" I started to bawl and sob. "*I'm so sorry.*"

Again, I had been in shock, and somehow felt fine for the first few hours. Pain soon set in; hurting even to breathe. The doctor told me that a brace would be required for up to five months, staying on my stomach.

We flew home and went to a Canadian hospital near the airport. Free health care equaled a four-hour wait to see a doctor in Emergency.

Finally, I was taken for x-rays where the doctor asked my husband if it was okay to take my brace off because it was the best way to take the X-Rays! I went into full stress. My husband is now my doctor? Thankfully the doctor in the Dominican Republic had trained my husband about my brace.

The medical staff then left me upright in a wheel chair for hours! When I couldn't take the pain any longer, we asked a nurse for medication. She asked if that is my only reason for being here! Unbelievable. We were told that all the doctors had gone to another hospital because of an emergency, and the nurse didn't know when the doctors would be back, so my husband took me to a hotel where I could lie on my stomach. "How do I not qualify to lay down in a hospital bed?" I wondered.

The next day we started the six-hour drive back to our little home town. Two hours into the drive, we hit black ice and lost control of the SUV. While we were spinning, I prayed, "*Lord keep us safe. Angels be with us.*" I looked over at my husband as he said, "*I'm sorry.*" It felt like the next minute was in slow motion. I shrugged as if to say, "*Okay, this is it.*"

The vehicle spun circles to the shoulder of the road, and then flipped upside down. It was as if the angels caught us and gently let us toboggan down the steep hill on the roof of the SUV. I was now hanging upside down in my body brace. My husband said, *"I think we're alive."* He was able to release his seat belt, and as he was about to kick open the door, a man pulled it open to help us. He had already called 911. I had to be left hanging, as it was too dangerous to be moved without medical help, otherwise I might have ended up paralyzed. My husband looked around to thank the mysterious man, but he was gone.

The ambulance attendants showed up and quickly built up pillow pressure for me to get released onto. However, I had to pull myself on my stomach out of the vehicle and up part of hill to be put on a body board, as it was too dangerous to pull me.

We were now at our third hospital in three days. The doctor in training said to me, *"Can you wiggle your toes?"* I wiggle them. She says, *"You're fine."* I explained to her that my hand was blue from onset of frostbite, and my neck and hips hurt from whip lash and compression from my brace. She said, *"You are released to go now."* Who's training these doctors? Who's in these hospital beds?

My husband and I left the hospital just thirty minutes after arriving. We were still hours south of our home, with no vehicle. I just wanted to lie on my stomach. We call a cab. Again, my husband got us a hotel room and we pick up our luggage from the vehicle impound. The SUV's roof was crushed; however my husband did not have a head impact and he walked away without a scratch or any other issue.

At the time, I did not think to take pictures of inside the vehicle. I wish that I had. I'm curious to know if there would have been the white lines of light present that saved me again.

Months and years of recovery lead me down a different path. I could not accept chronic pain. I did research and flew to Europe, hopeful of their technology and integrated health devices. While using these systems my back cracked back into place. I'm now pain free and off all medications.

I am now a National Trainer for Tesla Wellness Energy. My Mom and Nana told me I was meant to go through all of these injuries to show how well the machine worked to help the body to repair itself. This is what I was meant to do in life and why I was saved.

A few months ago, the man from my rear-view mirror appear again. I asked him who he was, and he said, *"I'm your brother. Mom had miscarried me and I have been with you always."* He was my childhood imaginary friend! He wanted me to tell my mom that he was all right, and not to cry anymore. Then he disappeared.

I called my mom, but she sobbed and couldn't talk about it. I went to see my dad, and he confirmed that they had miscarried when I was two years old.

I can tell you that I have been saved by angels and protected by God. When the storms of this life come, don't forget to pray.

Melisa Archer is the National Trainer for Tesla Wellness Energy. She is dedicated to the wellness of mind, body, and soul certified in: Rejuvenation Facials, Pulsated Electro Magnetic Frequencies, BIO Frequencies, Laser, Reiki level 3, Raindrop Therapy, Vita Flex, Dolphin Neurotism, Healing with Essential Oils, Chemistry of Essential Oils, Sound and Light therapy. Melisa integrates her ability to see and feel energies to better understand her client's needs, and is also eager to train generations on the upcoming movement of electric yoga.

Melisa@TeslaWellnessEnergy.com

www.Electricyoga.ca

Valerie Cameron

42

My Journey Within

Growing up in a family with six children had its challenges as you could imagine; especially since there were only seven years between the oldest and the youngest child. I, being the second youngest, often wondered how my mother was able to do it as she herself was raised an only child.

As a youngster, I was always very inquisitive to the point where I explored how the ringer washer worked, almost losing my thumb in the process and having to have it surgically reattached.

Challenges were a part my life, especially in school as I seemed to be always getting in trouble for whatever my older siblings had done. Isn't it funny how we often get categorized by whatever our other family members do? It was during this time that I lost my identity or a least part of it. I even moved to other schools where my siblings had not been to try to find myself.

I was what you would consider a middle child and I never really fought with my siblings. Looking back, I now realize the role that I played was that of a mediator, being the go-between to try to smooth things over. I wanted everyone to get along and be happy as I never liked confrontations. To look at me, one might have assumed that I was happy, bubbly, outgoing, and so full of life, but that was not the case. Behind that fake smile was a girl who felt broken and was fallen to pieces. I never felt good or smart enough for most of my life. I believed my feelings didn't matter as long as those around me were happy.

One of the ways that I found to escape, and yes this may sound strange, was to sit on the couch and just rock back-and-forth. I would go into a trance, almost like I was in another world. As I got older I turned to dancing, often dreaming of becoming a choreographer dancer on the Dean Martin show. Shhhh! I spent many hours making up routines but eventually stopped, though I don't remember exactly when.

During this time, in my early teens, I started to experience what I would call déjà vu. I'll admit that it scared me because I never understood what was happening. It was like I was re-experiencing something I had done before. I felt too scared to tell anyone because of my upbringing. You see, my grandfather was a Reverend and a scholar who could speak many languages. I loved him very much and didn't want to disappoint him. I followed all the rules and even took my communion, though it didn't feel right. I remember Mom going to tea cup readers and asking us not to say anything, which just confused me more. I thought when I moved from home I would find what I was looking for.

In my twenties, I settled down and things started to change for me again. I began having vivid dreams and visions. I wasn't sure what was happening or what to make of it. I felt there were messages in them that I was not understanding at the time. I decided to go back to church to see if I could find answers there. I even noticed that my young daughter, at the age of three, was very gifted. She seemed to know things she should have never known. I couldn't help her because I didn't understand it all myself, let alone help myself.

During this time, I made the personal choice to leave the dogmatic religious system that I was raised in because I found it wasn't working or helping me. It took many years before I could or would branch into the spiritual realm of self-discovery and identity.

Changes happened after my children grew up and moved out to start their own families. My husband and I sold our business, moved to a small northern community of about 1200 people, and started a new business. Everything was great at first, but like every other time I looked for something outside of myself, it felt as though things weren't working. It was like a part of me was missing and I wasn't even sure what *it* was.

I went through a very deep depression where everything seemed really dark and dismal. It got to the point where everything was just black and white; there was no color in my life. I decided that I was going to end my life and that's when the Voice Within me spoke. When I heard the words "IT IS TIME," I understood immediately what it meant. What I was looking for on the outside was already within. I then realized that I was looking in the wrong place. I knew in that moment it was okay for me to grow and experience in my own way. I was on the path I needed to be on for my own personal evolution.

As I expanded my own awareness of the Universe, through my experiences, I became more balanced and discerning. Low and behold, the dreams and visions came back. I had four of them in two weeks and within a couple months they had all come to pass. This time I took a different approach. I decided to allow the universe to bring to me what it was that I needed to help me.

I came across a book that changed my perspectives on the world and people. It helped me see things as a whole rather than from their individual parts. This brought me greater empathy because I now understand what is going on inside many people, even if they don't see it themselves. I realize that my journey is no different from anyone else's; it is just the story that may be different, that's all.

I realize now, looking through new eyes, my love for life and the compassion I feel for others is how we can be of service for humanity.

Valerie Cameron is a Certified Life Soul Coach and Reiki Master-Teacher in Alberta, Canada. She has been an entrepreneur for over forty years, and it is through this and her abilities as an Intuitive Psychic and Spiritual Medium that she is able to compassionately assist those who ask for guidance.

www.earth-balance-healing.com

Louise Lajeunesse

43
On a Spiritual Journey

An amazing world opens up once someone realizes they are not alone on this earth. Each one of us has a powerful team structure in place; to guide us and help us remain as close as possible to the life path we have chosen to experience. Just this concept in itself is enough to be overwhelming. An amazing life awaits us, when the veil of limitation is lifted, revealing unlimited possibilities, new life concepts, and interconnectivity between all that is.

With the struggle I still face to accept my gifts, my power, and my life purpose, I still question myself as to *"Why me?"* How is it possible that I can channel and bless people with such powerful messages and energy? With more abilities still remaining to be brought to the surface and experienced, it's with an immense sense of gratitude that I welcome this opportunity to be of service to humanity.

Many questions will rise on the journey: *How to start? Am I worthy?* What will people say and think? But the truth is, it's our journey, not theirs. So let's live it to the fullest and enjoy the ride on the wings of the angels.

******

A life filled with Divine blessings is available to all, especially now that we are transitioning into higher dimensions, where all will be revealed in perfect time. A life of freedom, unlimited possibilities, creativity, blessings, and unity is at our doorstep, as we enter this long awaited and announced Golden Age.

If you feel an inner calling towards healing, being of service, finding the truth, or a certainty that more is possible for this life, then the bells are more likely ringing to announce a time of rejoicing for all. As you evolve, through the awakening process, flashbacks from childhood might make you realize how you have gently been nudged in the right direction to trigger your attention towards your Divine Plan. I sure have!

******

I came into this life as a Master to help the earth and its habitants raise their energy, heal, and clear the density of traumas, karma, and past life contracts.

With my father finding his calling at a later age as a healer and clairvoyant, and a mother with a Divine Gift as a Teacher, I now see that it was the perfect environment to accomplish my life mission. With both being highly spiritual people, it gave me a sense of direction to become a powerful healer and teacher myself. It was through the experiences of my childhood that my parents went through with their strength, weaknesses, heartaches, dramas, financial problems, their spiritual experiences, and their knowledge in that area that allowed my own awakening to take place. It truly opened the doors to my chosen destiny. They helped me to understand, accept my life purpose, and shape who I am today.

From a very young age, I felt the profound calling and desire to heal with my hands. My opportunity finally came one day when my dad couldn't attend a Level One Reiki course he was scheduled for. Once I found out this could be my long awaited opportunity to become a healer, I immediately called the person and registered for the course. In the days following the call, I could feel my palm chakras opening, without knowing at the time what was happening. I just couldn't get enough of this newly found knowledge. A few years later, I took level two, which allowed for distance healing. This is when a major accomplishment happened.

A friend who knew about my ability to channel healing energy, called from Colorado Springs in panic. During a routine practice with her skating partner, they tripped and he smashed into the boards, fracturing a rib and puncturing a vital organ. They rushed him to the hospital and were advised that if the organ didn't seal itself, by the evening, he could die. I immediately went to work on him. She called the next morning to inform me that all was well and that he would completely recover. I felt blessed and had a rewarding feeling knowing that one could make such a difference in someone's life. Love energy truly knows no boundaries.

In my forties, a friend highly recommended that I attend some local courses that were being offered by someone she knew due to his integrity level and spiritual knowledge. These sessions were instrumental to my continued Spiritual Awakening and Development. By the end of the next few months of working with this gentleman, I had attained my Reiki Master and Angel Guide Practitioner Certificates.

A new world of exciting possibilities opened up. Having gained access to my channeling abilities and powerful healing tools to raise the vibrations of others while helping them, a new level of confidence took place. I was really enjoying the wonderful messages the Angelic Realm was blessing me with.

My friend and I, having taken the same training, decided to combine our knowledge to provide healing sessions and workshops which we called "Reiki with the Angels." Under angelic guidance, with incoming messages during treatments, an inner joy, sense of complicity, and bliss filled us, while touching patients at a deep cellular and emotional level.

In 2005, I felt called to channel a deck of Angel Cards. The deck would contain thirty-two cards in total with three different colored backgrounds for the writing; eight in blue, eight in yellow, and sixteen in pink. When it came time to separate them, I couldn't arrive at the correct number for each color. I felt discouraged. So, I turned the cards upside down and asked the Angels, "If these cards are meant to be in three different groups with a specific amount, then guide my hands into separating them." Next, I did exactly that very quickly. In a state a shock, the group ended up being exactly, eight, eight, and sixteen. I almost cried in disbelief! The angels truly guided this deck as even until this date, every time I pick up one of these beautiful cards and read the channeled messages received for each one, I feel overwhelmed. A feeling of love and wisdom from them touches me and everyone else deeply, who has had the pleasure to use them for guidance.

Although, the cards have been on hold for over ten years, I now feel ready to share them with the world. At the time, I felt they required a booklet with additional wisdom and guidance, so I've been channeling this information. As I evolved, so have the energy of the cards and the concept for the presentation. I had previously painted the cover, and it no longer seemed appropriate, so it has also evolved. A French deck is almost completed.

******

I continue to grow and experience new things with my Spiritual Development. Three years ago an opportunity was presented to me to help increase my abilities and confident. My brother, who is also a Healer and Clairvoyant, invited me to join his healing group on Thursdays.

During a weekly channeling for the group, I had the pleasure of having the fairy world open up to me. I could feel something small, moving rapidly with impatience, in all directions in front of me. I thought I was dreaming for a moment until I looked up and realized that my brother, Pierre, had seen it as well. Little fairy Cloé waited impatiently to give me a message for the group and was doing her best to attract my attention. Just thinking of her now gives me an inner sense of joy. I often had the pleasure of her company, including while driving, as she sat on top of my steering wheel. Other members of her fairy family have since made themselves known to me, each with their own strength, ability, color, and wisdom.

******

Throughout my journey of self-discovery, I went through a myriad of experiences and revelations. As I struggled with my own little demons, doors started to open, one by one, indicating a milestone and the possibility to access a higher level of knowledge and commitment to the Source. A bright white and golden light always surrounds each one. As I pass through them, a new path presents itself, filled with new possibilities. Majestic tall white beings welcome me on the other side, along with other guides and galactic beings, called to accompany and guide me on the next step of my journey. The night I agreed to submit this chapter for the book, a large dome of bright white light appeared surrounding the most magnificent large and thick golden doors. The size and brightness were breathtaking. I knew then that this was a marking milestone in my evolution.

Over the last two years, a partnership has been formed with four friends that I met in divine ways. When we combine our abilities during group healings, the outcome is very powerful. Each of us know our roles and strengths, and assist with a purity of intention and wisdom at the same time. We are able to immediately detect what no longer serves the recipient both from past and present experiences, and help to transmute any residue energy, often bringing forth the old emotions and memories associated with physical trauma and experiences to be deeply cleansed and purified. The Angels, Archangels, Ascended Masters, and Guides always join in to assist. It's amazing how a chronic or sudden pain can be related to a death, major injury, accident, fear, or loss experienced in a past life. By acknowledging the memory and the cause, the pain often goes away immediately, confirming its release and allowing for new beginnings.

With my teachings, now coming directly from the Divine Source, the sensitivity and connection of my Divine friends allows me to receive powerful feedback and a deeper understanding of the value and impact these new tools have in the release of negativity, physical pains, and transmutation, in all dimensions of time.

My friend constantly suffered from powerful panic attacks most of her life, and while I was assisting in, I suddenly had the realization that she was surrounded by many trapped souls, looking for a way to the Light. What a major realization to be able to give my friend a sense of relief she had been looking for.

As I proceeded in guiding these poor Souls to the light, more seem to come forward! In asking for Divine Help, a beautiful Golden Elevator appeared, guided by two Angels. With the inner knowing this was the tool to help free them, I started to lovingly guide these souls, with love and encouragement towards the elevator, surrounded by a magnificent beam of white light. As the souls hesitantly made their way into it, we could feel the energy of their reunion with the loved ones in Heaven. It was truly overwhelming. When the other souls realized there was no fear to be had, a line of souls suddenly appeared, with no end in sight. It almost appeared like they were coming out of cavern walls. What a true honor and blessing to be able to help these souls pass over.

We realized that this was an important and urgent task that needed to be accomplished quickly, the entire group joined in and we increased the number of elevators. Clearing some areas lasted sometimes for days, and as such, we continue to do this work as we are guided.

With the powerful healing and transmuting tools given to me to assist all that I am in service for during this time of transition, in closing, may you the reader be infused with a positive sense of well-being and serenity. Everyone can be of service.

I urge all to find your calling and with a sense of gratitude in your heart, go on your Divine Path to help bring Heaven on Earth.

Louise Lajeunesse is a certified Angel Guide Practitioner, Reiki Master-Teacher, Spiritual Messenger, and Therapeutic Touch Practitioner who utilizes her vast wisdom and experience gained through her journey to those that she is in service for. People who have been fortunate to cross her path know that her wisdom, light touch, and gentle loving nature is a Divine Grace. Louise is multi-talented beyond the healing realm and it is her diversity that allows her to reach people on many levels. She is a true visionary, powerful Goddess Healer, and hidden gem on our planet with many gifts still being discovered.

www.louiselajeunesse.com

louiselajeunesse444@gmail.com

Ivana Risianova

44

The Silent Journey to the Soul

It had been a while since I first felt called to go on a retreat. However, owning and running my business does not always allow to take two weeks off, let alone two weeks in the middle of summer without some major planning. Most of the retreats that I had been researching were asking me to do just that. I couldn't in good conscience just disappear and leave my business aside during a busy season.

One day, I had been speaking to my friend about my desire to get away for a retreat. She told me of one that she personally highly recommended and went to, in Germany, herself. Best of all, you could choose the dates that suited you and your schedule.

Yes, that is exactly what I needed and I contacted them the same day. After exchanging a couple emails back and forth, I had reserved my place for the 22nd of December. By the next day, I had my ticket all booked and began preparations for my time off in six months.

I had been wanting to avoid the Christmas holidays for a few years as I found that time of year we tend to overeat, drink too much, not move, and put on extra weight, not to mention, it can be a hectic stressful time for many. This was truly not how I wanted to live my life. I needed to get away, and thus I was very excited to go for this retreat. I knew deep within me that this was the best thing for me.

Time soared leading up to my time away, and before I knew it I was on the first of two planes. I started crying, even though I didn't know why, but it felt so right. It truly was quite strange. I was really looking forward to being in silence for two weeks, and here I was crying as I was getting closer to my destination.

Once I arrived at the monastery, a ceremony for me and two other guys was held. We were told how everything there worked and then off we went, each with a timer to complete our first round.

I started with ten minutes of walking followed by ten minutes of sitting meditation. Every day, five additional minutes were added to each routine.

After a few days as I was going quiet within, going deeper and deeper, I found myself releasing all the unnecessary thoughts and allowing them to pass through my head. They sometimes felt like a wave, sometimes big and sometimes small, either far away or close by. Other times there were no waves and all was calm. The stillness, the beautiful quiet peace within felt truly magical – a touch of my own soul, without body, without mind. The silence felt like I was at home.

My first evening that I arrived I had picked up a tea cup, not paying attention to the words on it. Three days later, however, I saw that it said, "FEELING HOME."

To be in silence was becoming normal. It got harder when I got to about thirty-five minutes as I found it very hard to sit still for so long, especially being a Pilate's teacher where it's normal for us to lengthen our spine and entire body in a workout. Sitting cross-legged all that time was absolute torture for me and my body because in Pilates, we align the whole body. Sitting is definitely not part of the Pilate's routine.

Almost every day I cried; little did I know that the big one was still to come. I was in my sitting meditation and couldn't seem to find the right position to stay still in. I looked at my timer and it had only been twenty minutes. That was it, I couldn't do sit anymore!

I started to cry as it seemed like I was putting huge boulders the size of Stonehenge in front of me. They were so big and heavy that I couldn't get over them or move them. I cried a lot thinking, "I can't do this. This is impossible! It's too hard…"

I took a break to go down to have some tea and after I returned to the meditation room, I decided to try again. I wouldn't go home because of that blockage after coming all the way from Spain to be there. I had been waiting for months for this trip, and had traveled on two planes to get there, so I wasn't going to give up so easily.

Back to silence I went.

As I was completing the walking portion of my meditation, tears began to roll down my face and I was taken back to a time twenty years earlier when my drunk father used to say things like, "You won't get anywhere in your life," or "You won't achieve anything and you will be back here soon."

I could feel anxiety building in my heart, but I kept walking as I acknowledge the old wounds. I kept moving, concentrating on each step. Wiping my nose as I walked, tears were flowing down my face. At one point, I thought my insides were going to explode. It felt like I was going to have a panic attack, which did not feel good.

As I started my next sitting round, I went through the breathing exercises and all I could feel was new energy entering my body with each breath. My heart was filling with love and I felt myself expanding from my heart center. My body did not exist – no more pain, no more tears. It was just the magical energy within me and all around me. It was extremely intense in a good way. Truly Magical.

I had been transported somewhere else, in a vibration of love that was so distinct, I could almost cut through it. I think I had been hugged by a huge Angel, perhaps even my father. Then I heard a timer. It was mine. Wow, I did it! Thirty-five minutes had passed.

I felt light, filled with happiness and joy. The huge stones that had been in front of me disappeared and were gone. It truly was the most beautiful meditation in my life. This is how I felt in the healing session that I had with the Angel lady from London.

I must say that I learned some interesting lessons in the two weeks of living in silence and turning my attention within. Each day from 4:00 a.m. to 10:00 p.m., I spent my time meditating and getting to know my own essence.

Upon the ninth day, I received a special exercise to do and off I went to complete it. At this point my rounds were sixty minutes, but nothing had prepared me for the exercise I was to embark upon. I had to go and meditate in my room for twenty-four hours without sleeping. When I first hear this, I laughed and couldn't believe it, but off I went and did exactly that.

The next day, I was given another exercise with the same conditions, and again I completed it. It was truly amazing! I kept my breaks very short this time as the feeling from the vibration was truly magical. The desire to go within was strong and I was connecting with ease.

After the two weeks on my retreat, I came home having found true happiness. Of course, this doesn't last forever without some nurturing. I need to take care of my mind and purify daily; much like I would take care of a plant.

Since coming home from the silent retreat my life truly has changed. I now set the alarm every day earlier to connect to my soul first thing in the morning. At the time of this writing, I'm doing the daily retreat, which requires two hours of meditation every day. I complete one hour in the morning as I wake up, and another hour at the end of the day as I prepare for bed. On the days I take a longer lunch break, I do an extra hour of meditation.

I now personally practice mindful eating without disruptions: no computer, no social media, videos, or music, and I notice that my food tastes so much better. I have also cut down my time on Facebook by using it for business mostly, only checking my messages, and then closing it down.

I now have more compassion for myself and show the world around me how much I love myself. I do so by not eating after lunch, no more wine or beer, and I have reduced my consumption of living creatures. I was almost vegetarian anyways; I do listen to my body more, feed it what it needs, and that includes its monthly request for some organic meat. I am considering reducing that even. No soul needs to die to nourish me. Even more important is the fact that I find if I am eating meat, dairy products, or sugar, I find it very difficult to focus and set into my meditations. I've also noticed that my memory and sleep have improved.

These are just a few of the ways life has shifted for the better for me since the retreat and the reconnecting to my soul. I am sure more wonderful changes are to unfold still, and I am so excited to see where life takes me. I have a wonderful feeling it is just going to keep getting better as I continue to show myself and the world the love and compassion.

In closing, my personal recommendation to everyone is to take some time to love yourself and connect with your soul daily. I suggest taking at a minimum of ten minutes to start with upon waking up. Then expand the amount of time you take as you make room in your life to nurture your true essence daily.

You will find as you regularly start your day with some simple breathing and awareness within you, the quality of your energy, your day, and life will change for the better.

Why not start right now?

Close your eyes and turn your attention within as you become aware of your heart beat along with the rising and falling of your abdomen as you breathe.

Acknowledge any thoughts that come into your mind and just let the pass through your mind and return to your breathing.

Continue to do this for a few moments.

When ready to return to your surroundings, take a moment to give your gratitude for the blessings in your life, seen and unseen, and your divine connection to the soul.

It simply is that easy. Practice this exercise daily and you will begin to notice the silence within the spaces expanding as you nurture your true essence and bring it into your daily life experience.

Compiled by Brian Calhoun

Ivana Risianova is a Romana Pilates Certified Teacher and owner of Pure Pilates Ibiza where the original authentic equipment from EEUU is utilized in the classes. She has an established base of many happy local clients and world renowned celebrities. Born and raised in Slovakia, Ivana now calls Ibiza, Spain home after traveling to explore and find her true passion, learning new languages, and living in different countries. Ivana has a mission to share Pilates and its amazing benefits with the world. Life is a university where she continues to learn, grow, and experience all her soul guides her to.

http://www.purepilatesibiza.com/

Jennifer Dahl-Kowalski
Experiencing the Soul

One morning in early 2013, I woke up with absolutely no desire to move. Heavy bouts of sleepiness swept over my cold, shivering body. My eyes ached when I opened them slightly to turn off my alarm. I slowly leaned over to grab my cell phone on my bedside table and called in sick to work. As I sank back into my mattress and pulled the warm covers over my head, waves of lightheadedness and nausea washed over me. Without giving it a second thought, I fell back into a deep, uninterrupted sleep.

Days passed by and I continued to feel lethargic and weak. I had no interest in leaving my bed for any reason, including going to the bathroom. It took hours to muster up the courage to get up, and in most cases, I had only enough energy to crawl to my destination. Basic hygiene became a distant memory. Showers were done on occasion. On the days when I had to buy groceries, I would spend hours focusing my efforts on taking each step towards the store, a two-block trip, and then had to regain my energy for the long walk home. Frozen food dinners became a mainstay of my diet. As the days rolled into weeks, fear crept upon me as I realized that these symptoms were not disappearing and that something more serious was surfacing.

Over the next several months, I visited many doctors, practitioners, and health specialists searching for an explanation. They each presented me with their long list of proposed illnesses that we began to eliminate one-by-one through a series of health tests. In the end, they all came to the same conclusion: there was nothing wrong and it must be all in my head. Even though I knew this was not the case, I was relieved to know that I did not have any of the listed life-threatening illnesses. However, with no diagnosis, I began to feel lost and confused over what I should do next.

During this time of uncertainty, I fell into a mild depression. I began to ask questions about the meaning of life. *Why do we get up in the morning? Why do we go to work? What is the purpose of life?* There was an emptiness growing inside of me that I could not fill and it felt like a part of me was missing. I no longer felt like myself. With these new thoughts running through my mind, I was suddenly curious about why we do what we do. *Where does motivation, passion, and creativity come from? Why do I ever feel like doing anything?*

One day while at my appointment with my masseuse, I felt moved to open up about a difficult decision I was making concerning my mom. I had not thought about this issue since I fell ill but it resurfaced in my thoughts and I wanted to talk to someone about it. My mom has Multiple Sclerosis and was being taken care of by staff in a nursing residence back home. I had recently moved to another city and was contemplating asking Mom if she wanted to move here too so that she could be closer to her only child. I was hesitant to ask, however, because I knew this move would take a lot of time, effort, and investment, and I was not even sure if I wanted to stay in this new city permanently.

Unaware that my masseuse practiced self-healing techniques, I was startled when she began to ask me a series of questions about various practices I had never heard of while muscle testing. Through her assessment, she determined that a strong affirmation would help guide me to my answer. I had never used affirmations in this way before but I was open and willing to give it a try.

With her guidance on how to phrase my affirmation, I wrote two powerful sentences that proclaimed the emotions I was yearning for in this situation. She recommended that I go home, sit in prayer position, interlink my hands, and repeat the affirmation until I believed it – until its presence was felt by every cell of my being.

Feeling a renewed sense of hope, I went straight home and prepared for this exercise. I turned off the lights and sat on my yoga mat in prayer position. I placed my hands in the mudra position as instructed. I began to say the affirmation out loud repeatedly. As I began to chant, unexpected busts of anger emerged from inside of me. I was angry because I felt unheard and unsupported. I was furious that I had been carrying around a heavy burden for years that was too much to bear. And I was irate because I was tired of worrying about Mom. Tears began to roll down my face and I started to scream the affirmation. I wanted to run away from these negative emotions and never look back but instead I chose to remain where I was and commit to my chant.

Suddenly, I felt a huge sense of relief rise within me and I started to laugh. Strong rushes of love and joy came upon me. I felt my entire being fill up with the most incredible, intense energy I had ever experienced. I was full of light. I felt completely supported and taken care of. And in that moment, I felt something I had forgotten – something that had been missing. I felt myself. My whole self. My soul. I continued to sit on the yoga mat for about an hour holding myself in silence. I was in sheer awe and appreciation over the experience I had just witnessed.

And then I understood. We do what we do because of the positive emotions we feel when we do them. It is these loving emotions that allow us to experience our soul. And we are only aligned with soul when we do what naturally feels good to us.

Jennifer Dahl-Kowalski became conscious of her gifts following an unexplainable illness in 2013. With no clear diagnosis, she ventured into unchartered territories and searched within to uncover her own innate healing abilities. Through utilizing the power of thought, tuning into her intuition, and mastering her sensitivities to energy, she was liberated from her sickness. Dedicated to sharing her wisdom, she helps others release anxiety, stress, and childhood traumas by breaking through old patterns and offering powerful practices that lead to a life with meaning. Jennifer currently resides in Canada as an intuitive coach, certified energy therapist, public speaker, and author.

www.ignite0your0light0.com

www.facebook.com/ignite0your0light0

Melisa Archer

46

Awakening Forgiveness

There I was on top of the world, feeling so accomplished. I had small businesses, and was a corporate assistant manager. My flagship store had just been nominated top retail business by the community, and had only been open for five months. I have an amazing husband that supported my ambitions. Life was good. I mean **really** good. Then in thirty seconds, it wasn't. A car accident changed my life forever.

No longer could I work. Told physically, mentally, and emotionally I required major recoveries. Being an employee, but also an employer, I did not qualify for financial assistance.

In my absence, cash deposits were no longer being made into the bank accounts. Inventory was missing and unaccounted for – a complete financial nightmare! How could people I love and trust do this to me? I wasn't going to die. There would be accountability for these selfish actions, wouldn't there?

A few days after the accident, a colleague who was overseeing my flagship store, called me and demanded that I come urgently to the store. Although I was in no condition to be traveling, I arrived to be ushered to my bank branch. Guided inside the bank, there were papers all drawn up for me to give this person Power of Attorney and access to all of my accounts! I took the pen. Then something inside me made me stop. I was recovering from a brain injury. Why would I want to do this? I demanded to speak to the bank manager. He said that I had called and requested the papers be drawn up. I said, "I would never do that!"

My colleague got very upset and threw a fit, in the bank, on video surveillance. They said, "You need to do this." I stated, "I am not going to die! I would never have you as my Power of Attorney." They stormed out and went to the car. I made it clear to the bank manager to shred the papers, and that my associate would have a deposit only bankcard, as that was the only access I was allowing.

Stress set my recovery back. I hired two forensic accountants and was shocked and in disbelief of the outcome: money and product was missing from multiple stores. I had been taken advantage of, and I got a lawyer. My colleague denied anything was missing. I had no choice but to terminate their access to my business.

My lawyer was amazing! She had proof of my associate refunding onto credit cards, accepting checks from my clients, and asking them to leave blank checks to be filled out later. My lawyer had the complete list of missing inventory while this person oversaw my business.

Before my day in court, my lawyer got lung cancer and passed within two weeks. Someone claiming to be me picked up my evidence box from the lawyer's office. Where do I go from here? Complete emotional devastation! This nightmare just went from a state of being on track to be resolved with justice about to be served, to completely unresolved. I was devastated that my colleague could be so jealous, deceitful, and selfish.

Next, I confronted my colleague, who was a partner at one of the other locations. I showed them the outcome from the financial audit. My colleague admitted that their personal financial pressures led to the lack of deposits. We ended the business partnership. We went to the bank, and I gave them more money. Although we are no longer friends, I actually respected that they admitted their faults.

I prayed about this a lot. I felt like Job, from the bible, who had everything taken away from him at one time. Such severe life shifts. I couldn't forgive. So much money was stolen from me. Months later, I was still traumatized over the situation.

I had an etheric experience and I was no longer in my house. I was on a cross, hung beside Jesus. I asked, "Why am I here?" He replied, "There once was a man hung there because he stole." I was a bit shocked and replied, "But I didn't steal." Jesus said, "The thief asked for forgiveness, and I forgave him of his sins. How can I forgive you of your sins, if you cannot forgive others?"

Something inside me changed. I was back in my house. I have four nail marks on my body that never go away. I realized that a thief is always a thief, and only knows how to steal. But I know how to make, and I would make back what was taken from me. I turned this financial burden over to God, and let him give out the wrath. I felt lighter and happier afterwards.

I went to my Nana, who I had spoke to about this situation, and said, "I love you! Nothing has changed in our closeness. I am willing to give God this financial situation. When our time here comes to pass, I give you permission to go through my past and see what really happened." Going forward, we never spoke of this situation again. I was as close as ever to my Nana, who told me how proud she is of me, and how much she loves me.

My Nana recently passed. I enjoy her spirit, who visits me often and protects me. I am joyous; she now knows the truth of the past. The full burden has been lifted off of me.

My hope is to inspire and empower others to Let Go and Let God. We may get retested to ensure we are ready to let go. Just repeat the process. It is not always easy but will help you feel more resolved.

Update:

God took care of things once I turned everything over to Him. The person did steal again, and this time everything is catching up to them. Have faith; justice always gets served, in God's time.

Melisa Archer is the National Trainer for Tesla Wellness Energy. She is dedicated to the wellness of mind, body, and soul certified in: Rejuvenation Facials, Pulsated Electro Magnetic Frequencies, BIO Frequencies, Laser, Reiki level 3, Raindrop Therapy, Vita Flex, Dolphin Neurotism, Healing with Essential Oils, Chemistry of Essential Oils, Sound and Light therapy. Melisa integrates her ability to see and feel energies to better understand her client's needs, and is also eager to train generations on the upcoming movement of electric yoga.

Melisa@TeslaWellnessEnergy.com

www.Electricyoga.ca

Brenda Rachel

47

Angels' Cardinal Rule of Empowerment: Stand in Your Own Power!

The angelic quote that I received from the angels, which directly relates to my story is:

"When We Stand In Our Own Power, It Is Powerful!"

Reflecting on my life over the last couple of years, between 2014 and 2016, I was able to correlate this period with one of the divinatory meanings of the Cardinal Bird which is, that when you see one, it may be trying to tell you to lift your head high, take pride in, and stand up for yourself. One definition of the word cardinal is that it can function as an axle where other things are hinged around it.

In my life, I am the center point for the angels to use me as their "Axle as a 'Messenger of Hope'" to impart their inspirational and spiritual messages into the world. The angels had been bringing me the image of a Cardinal Bird for weeks, nudging me to write a story using it as an analogy. The relationship between the Cardinal Bird (telling me to lift my head high, take pride in myself, and stand up for myself) and the word cardinal, (denoting an axle where other things are hinged around it), are in complete synchronicity with the events that unfolded in this chapter of my life which allowed me to stand in my own power and be used as an "Axle" for the angels.

I released my inspirational and spiritual music EP, *"In this Moment,"* in late 2014. The EP was written and produced between 2004 and 2006 during a prior period of disability, and all the music and lyrics were channeled to me by the angels. The EP release occurred while I was going through another very debilitating and disabling period with excruciating back and hip pain that lasted for many months. During this time, I went through a very intense rehabilitation program as a part of my healing and recovery process from one of the lowest points ever in my life.

As I laid on my bed, in my back brace, using an ice pack full-time to keep the pain and inflammation down, I pleaded with God and the angels, sometimes hourly, sometimes daily, to "Take Me Home" if they had no more use for me on the planet, as I did not want to live anymore. I asked them three questions: "What did they want me to learn from this experience? How could I serve them? What message did they want me to bring to others?" I was blessed to have the angels respond by channeling inspirational and spiritual quotes to me, which I posted on social media to bring inspiration to others.

Next, I asked the angels, "What do you want me to do with these quotes?" They told me in very succinct terms to compile their beautiful angelic messages into a book and publish it. I knew nothing about this course of action, but began the publishing process in spring 2015. By September that year, the inspirational and spiritual quotes evolved into my published book *"In This Moment Angels' Sweet Reflections."*

Throughout the publishing process, I went from intense lows to extreme highs. I went from feeling very inept, powerless, unsupported, and unknowledgeable, especially when it came to computer technology, to feelings of elation, euphoria, excitement, and enthusiasm. This was due to the fact that I had found my Divine Purpose and was on a "Mission of Hope" for the angels to get their messages out to the universe as fast as I could.

I taught myself everything I had to do to "birth" these angelic messages. As their delivery date drew nearer, I found myself all over the map with my emotions. I spoke to no one about the intricacies of what I was trying to accomplish, and thus, kept all my emotions bottled up inside of me. I learned all about writing, editing, social media, website design, marketing, publishing, promotion, and communication with all kinds of people along this journey.

As I began writing my story, I now fully comprehended why the angels had been bringing me a Cardinal Bird to use as an analogy for it. I am the axle rod of the wheel, the angels' messages are the spokes attached to the axle rod, and the wheel is the world rotating in a circular motion. It is through this wheel that these angelic messages reach each person they are meant to reach, at just the right moment for their inspirational "direction." This is all in perfect and complete spiritual synchronicity, which I refer to as the "Angels' Wheel of Synchronicity."

In order for me to feel empowered and keep moving forward with my divine purpose on the mission that the angels had tasked me with, I needed to grab hold of the reins to the Angels' Wheel of Synchronicity. I had to trust and have faith that everything was in divine order and I was being guided by God and the angels in a divine manner. When things did not unfold in the timeframe I believed they would, I had to completely trust that the Angels' Wheel of Synchronicity was rotating in the right direction and these angelic messages would reach others, as and when they were meant to.

This was my journey and no one else's. It was up to me to adopt the Angels'

Cardinal Rule of Empowerment: Stand In Your Own Power. It was not up to anyone else to lead my mission for the angels. I became a spiritually empowered human being, thanks to the angels. I allowed myself to totally trust and have faith in the Angels' Wheel of Synchronicity, knowing that the doors would open for everyone who was supposed to hear my story about how I became a Messenger of Hope for the angels. It was in the sharing of my story, finding my purpose during the lowest of the lows of my life journey, and how with the Angels' Cardinal Rule of Empowerment I was standing in my own power and able to heal my body.

I am allowing myself to be a Messenger of Hope for the angels and to be a recipient of their messages in order to be the creator of this unique inspirational and spiritual source that is flowing through me. I am allowing myself to receive God and the Angels' Love, which is so empowering and fills my spirit and soul with passion, vitality, and creativity. I know that I came to the planet to be a spiritual, inspirational, and motivational leader, a Ray of Sunshine that could bring others hope while providing encouragement, support, love, and compassion where it is needed most.

I do know that when I am living according to my Angels Wheel of Synchronicity, I am balanced and centered in God's Love and know this is my Truth. It is when my spokes in the wheel have come loose or one has broken, that my balance is shaky and I fall off this wheel. I do **know** that the angelic quote the angels gave me, "When We Stand In Our Own Power, It Is Powerful!" is what I needed to hear from them to use as my focal and inspirational point of this message I am sharing with you.

The most difficult challenge for me, through this process and for most of my life, has been believing in myself; knowing that I am good enough; that I am gifted and talented; that I am proud of myself for what I have achieved; that I love myself; and it is truly okay for me to be powerful. I do deserve Blessings of Abundance, Peace, Love, Joy and Happiness, just like I wish for everyone else!

I am here to let you know, through my own experiences, that the angels are ready, willing, and able to assist us in handling whatever it is in life we are going through by helping us to believe in ourselves, to be proud of our achievements, and to stand in our own power. They are here to support us in lifting our heads high, to stand tall, and take pride in ourselves. By allowing the angels to assist us, we are able to continue to dream our dreams, envision our vision, and allow the miracles to occur. One thing the angels ask of us is that we request their help directly, as they will not intervene unless asked to do so. They will only step in with a "Divine Intervention" when something is not part of our divine plan.

I experienced a Divine Intervention on February 3, 2016 when I was on my way to work, very early in the morning, as I was almost struck down in a crosswalk by a car going too fast while turning the corner. The young fellow who almost hit me actually drove around the block, came back, and stopped in the middle of the street to ask if I was all right. He, too, was shaken up by how close this call was for him and me.

It definitely was not my time to exit the planet and the only reason I am still here today is the angels intervened and carried me safely in their arms across the street. I wrote an article entitled *"Angels, Thank You for Keeping Me Alive"* about this possible near-death experience, thanking the angels for saving my life.

For any of you going through a difficult time or challenge right now, I invite you to connect to the spokes in the Angels' Wheel of Synchronicity following the Angels' Cardinal Rule of Empowerment by Standing in Your Own Power. You can do this by loving yourself completely; believing in yourself; following your dreams; and by acknowledging that you deserve all the goodness there is to allow your creativity, passion, and vitality to flow through you. Only you have the power to do this, as no one else can do it for you. Call upon your angels and ask them for assistance with any issue you may be dealing with. You are never alone. The angels are only a "Breath Away" and always here ready, willing, and able to help you.

I believe that the Angels' Cardinal Rule of Empowerment: Stand In Your Own Power becomes part of our individual and global spiritual empowerment. This happens individually when we connect ourselves to the most powerful spoke hinged to the axle rod of the Angels' Wheel of Synchronicity which is Love and then we circulate this Love into our own corner of the world. Globally, this happens when we allow ourselves to become the axle rod of our own 'Spiritual Wheel of Synchronicity.'

As we hinge our spokes of Powerful Peace to the most omnipotent wheel in the world, Spiritual Love, our Spiritual Wheel of Synchronicity begins circulating infinite Universal Peace and Unconditional Love into our universe, manifesting in global unification.

From My Heart to Yours, In Peace, Light and Love.

Angel Blessings,

Brenda Rachel

Compiled by Brian Calhoun

Brenda Rachel is a published author of an Inspirational / Spiritual book that was released in September 2015. She composed and released an Inspirational / Spiritual EP in December 2014. As a *Messenger of Hope* for the Angels, she brings messages of Encouragement, Hope, Peace, Love, and Joy to all. The music and book were channeled through Brenda by the Angels during two periods of disability where each time she asked God and the Angels, "What do you want me to know from this experience? How can I serve you? What message do you want me to bring to others?"

http://www.brendarachel4angels.com

http://goo.gl/AyUnh4

Kelly Gregory

48

Bobby's Heart

I saw three different versions of him walking down the hallway in front of the store where I work. They were all him, just with different haircuts and clothing. The third time, he was with a little red-headed girl and I was so sure it was him I almost shouted to him. I realized he was up north visiting family and that there was no way it could be him. Then I got the dreaded phone call. I know now, he was saying goodbye.

On July 24, 2015, my son, unexpectedly and mysteriously, passed away while playing in the water with his seven-year-old daughter, Marley. After a week of waiting and worrying, the autopsy was inconclusive and they requested my permission to retain my son's heart for testing. I was assured at that time that I would have choices as to what was to be done with the organ once all the testing was complete. Nothing would be done until I had given them direction. Due to the fact that he had a sister and a daughter, and that whatever took his life could be hereditary, I agreed. I buried my son's body and returned home to wait for the results.

A month had gone by and I had heard nothing. I really didn't even know where his heart was, where it was being kept, or if they had the right contact information. I was terrified that the pathology department did not know my wishes, as no one had asked by this time. I did not know who to get in touch with to get this information. I tried to contact the original coroner up north by leaving numerous messages, but I did not get any response.

I woke up at 4:30 a.m. one morning, which was becoming the norm by this point, and started googling until I found the Organ Retention Center in Toronto. I emailed them and they got things moving. By that afternoon, I was told that the arrangements were made and Bobby's heart was on its way home to me. I was so relieved and happy.

My intention, from the first day I found out that my son's heart had to be kept for pathology testing, was to have it cremated and put in a necklace, so that I could take him all over the world with me. I wanted him to see

Las Vegas, I wanted him to see the ocean, and I wanted him to be with me at all the music concerts and events I attended. I wanted to keep a part of him with me always. I wanted to give him the chance to see everything he did not get a chance to see when his life was so suddenly taken from him at thirty two years of age.

I was in the process of ordering urn necklaces, one for my daughter Pam and one for myself when I got an email from the head coroner up north. He told me that Toronto had advised him there was no point in sending me the heart to cremate because ashes come from bones and not organs. The cremated heart would leave me nothing.

I was crushed! I felt like the little piece of him I was going to keep alive just died. I felt like he died again. My hands were tied and my heart was broken. There was no choice. The following morning I emailed the coroner back and agreed not to transport the heart – just have it cremated in Toronto.

That afternoon I got a call from the local funeral home I had been in contact with prior to being told it was a pointless effort. They explained that they had been on the phone with the head coroner, they had made arrangements to go pick up the heart, and they just needed my signature. I was totally confused. Why? Why would you go get his heart if I was to get no part of it?

The funeral home was not willing to accept that I was getting nothing. They wanted to attempt, at their own expense, to bring the heart back and cremate it in their own crematorium. They thought that it was possible that Toronto's version of nothing and their version of nothing could be two different things. They understood that all I needed was a just tiny bit ...just a tiny bit to keep near my heart. They actually took the time to bring the form to me at work to obtain my signature. They made no promises but they were hopeful.

They drove to Toronto and got the heart. They did the cremation and surprise, it turned out that Bobby's heart was big enough to put tiny amounts of ashes into not only one necklace, but four! His sister, his daughter, his cousin, and I all have a piece of his heart.

How do I ever thank the people at this funeral home? What could I ever do to make up for what they have given me? There is a peace I can not put into words that comes from having Bobby's heart ashes with me always. It is almost like perpetually holding his hand or having his arm around me. Without the help of these complete strangers at this funeral home, I would never have experienced this peace.

Please take the time to spread the love and gratitude for the assistance that the funeral home gave me by sharing the message contained within my words. I would also like to let others know that despite the odds, always have hope. One just needs to believe in the miracle of a higher power to guide things so all works out sometimes even better than you could ask for.

I know I am and will forever be grateful, from the bottom of my heart, to all involved!

Bobby now travels and sees the world with me, one trip at a time!

Kelly Gregory is a mother of two who was born and raised in Kirkland Lake, Ontario. She is passionate about by traveling, fine dining, and wine making with her husband, but first and foremost her grandchildren. She now resides in Sarnia, Ontario working in fashion as a sales associate.

kelly.a.a.gregory@hotmail.com

Robyn Dewar

One Dimension Away

Ever since I can remember, I have always believed in angels and source energy. I haven't always trusted this knowingness of a loving angelic presence.

I was raised according to my mom's dedicated belief system. It seemed curious to me that her faith, values, and philosophy did not encourage the use of terms like clairvoyant or clairsentient. According to Mom's religion, tapping into this type of "culture" was not acceptable nor appreciated. When my mom took her last breath on February 22nd, 2009, I knew from that moment onward things would be different. During my mom's passing, I received three metaphysical gifts which filled me with so much love. This experience has confirmed my perspective about life. I hold a deep place of gratitude upon witnessing Mom's transition to spirit.

My mom had a beautiful smile. She was kind, compassionate, caring, and thoughtful. During her lifetime though, she suffered privately with many emotional ups and downs. Her lowest of lows took her away from our family unit when I was just a little girl. I could feel Mom's emotions deeply. In an attempt to brighten her day, I made her cards filled with messages of encouragement.

Growing into adulthood, I experienced similar ups and downs that mirrored my mom. I fell into a similar pattern of darkness, hopelessness, and self-hatred. I felt stuck, abandoned, and did not know why I was here in this lifetime. I moved through each day unable to see my connection with my purpose. At one point I was hospitalized. It took many, many years to sort through all that muck and grow into a place of self-love.

In November 2008, my mom was diagnosed with ALS (Amyotrophic lateral sclerosis, commonly known as Lou Gehrig's disease). Three months later, her team of respected physicians and nursing staff made arrangements for Mom to leave the hospital to be surrounded by her loved ones at home.

Since Mom required around-the-clock care, family members took turns rooming in her bedroom during the night. On the eve of February 22nd, I was on night care duty, and it was quiet evening. After settling into the little comfy cot at the foot of Mom's bed, I dozed off.

I remember slowly waking up to the fragrant smell of a holiday turkey dinner. It smelt just like our traditional family feasts. Turkey roasting in the oven filled my nose. I took a couple more good sniffs, and wondered why a vegetarian was waking up smelling a turkey dinner. Strange, I thought, and sat up and glanced over at Mom. She looked peaceful in her bed. I smiled and felt such gratitude for those family dinners growing up. Mom's breathing apparatus was still moving up and down and I was cozy, so I stayed put.

I fell asleep again only to be awakened by the soft sounds of ocean waves. I had been dreaming of a little girl playing on the sandy shore. Her thick, bouncy, light brown curls spiraled into shoulder-length ringlets. She appeared to be collecting tiny sea shells. I perked my head up and looked at Mom. I wondered if that was a smile on her face. My Mom had never seen the ocean. The sounds of the waves were soothing and their rhythmic flow lulled me back to sleep.

The next moment I recall, I was receiving a gentle nudge to wake up. I blinked my sleepy, tired eyes. I was seeing foggy, polka dots. I placed my fingers on my eyelids. I remember thinking I sure could use some toothpicks to keep my eyes open. As I shook my head, I continued to see the thousands of whitish-bluish dots literally appearing in the room. From the edge of my cot, I could still see Mom. The room felt very peaceful, so I didn't have the urge to get out of bed. A sense of calmness came over me as I watched the orbs. They were mesmerizing.

As I continued to hold my eyes open, I said to myself, "I am not seeing things." I felt Mom was going home and this presence was here to help with the transition. I was witnessing Mom's homecoming. I watched the orbs float around the room until I fell back asleep.

Morning arrived and I awoke when I heard my dad's sister lightly shuffle her feet across the bedroom carpet. When I opened my eyes, my aunt was at Mom's side, leaning over and lovingly touching her frail arm. I immediately felt a sense of guilt as I didn't get out of bed during my entire night watch over Mom. She was gently tucking a soft blanket in around Mom and said that she felt cold. She mentioned to me that this was a sign her body was shutting down.

Shortly after, our family gathered for an early morning breakfast in the dining room. It was Sunday morning, so we decided to all go to church to say a few prayers. My aunt stayed behind. An hour later, we all returned and gathered in Mom's bedroom. We sang our family favourites; we laughed, shed many tears, and shared memories. Collectively we said, "We will all be okay Mom, you can go." She took her last breath.

It was a huge gift to have witnessed my Mom's transition. This experience opened my eyes to an even greater connection with source. Seeing the orbs with my own eyes has truly grounded me in peace and tremendous comfort.

Since Mom's passing, I have received many more gifts from this dimension. Feathers and dimes cross my path daily and are two obvious signs that Mom is with me. I am learning to trust my highest self and take such delight in receiving signs from spirit.

We are truly only one dimension away.

Robyn Dewar easily shares her passion for a fulfilled life as an International Singer / Songwriter and Entrepreneur. She is an educator of integrative wellness and savvy network marketing professional. Robyn happily resides in Haileybury, Ontario with her husband Shawn and their two daughters.

http://www.robyndewar.com

Angie Carter

Rainbow Blessings

50

Nothing compares to the pain a parent feels when they lose a child. There's a physical pain that accompanies this type of loss that is beyond debilitating. It's hard to see hope through the lens of grief, but it's not impossible. My daughter has opened me up to a new world by showing me that love never dies.

Bella was a special little girl with a strong presence. She was a child with high needs and had a difficult transition to life on this planet. She had severe colic when she was a newborn and as she grew, she continued to require a lot of attention. Bella had a very demanding and persistent personality; when she wanted something, she refused to give up or let go! She seemed wise beyond her years; I looked forward to one day hearing about the deep thoughts I could see circulating every time I looked into her beautiful eyes.

Bella passed away suddenly in her sleep when she was only nineteen months old. Shortly after her transition, she began sending me signs from heaven. It wasn't until a session with a medium that these signs became clear. I intuitively knew what I was experiencing but it's easy to question yourself. The Medium confirmed that Bella was letting me know she was still with me even though I couldn't see her. Her strong personality became a blessing as she was determined to teach me about her new world.

The day after Bella's transition, I had a near death experience. I stopped breathing; my sister and niece performed CPR on me while my brother-in-law drove us to meet the ambulance on the highway. Meanwhile, I was unconscious and able to communicate with Bella. The next day, I felt her energy surrounding me. I knew she was with me and for the following two weeks, I felt her arms around me, hugging me. Three days after I returned home from the hospital, the brightest rainbow I have ever seen appeared outside my house. I have a photo of my son which I hugged in front of this rainbow and in that moment, I felt as though the three of us were together once again.

The first sign from Bella occurred even before I even knew she had transitioned. My best friend called me while the first responders were at my house working on Bella and we were waiting for the ambulance to arrive. My friend and I hadn't spoken in months; we never spoke on the phone as we would always text. I broke down while we spoke and she met me at the hospital. A week later, at Bella's funeral, she saw Bella running around the church. My friend has since realized that she is a medium and can also see spirits. She has been helping us communicate ever since.

The day of Bella's funeral, I was looking for some lavender essential oil to diffuse during the service. I couldn't find a single bottle anywhere even though I always have many on hand. I asked my parents for theirs, but it was also missing. Instead, I chose a blend called "White Angelica" which was perfect for her service. A few days later, three bottles of lavender essential oil appeared on the shelf in my closet. I know I did not place them there!

When I spoke with the Medium, he mentioned rainbows as well as a special drawing of Bella's that I had put aside. I knew immediately that he was referring to a drawing of a rainbow. I took the drawing to the daycare (where she drew it) and asked to know who helped her draw the rainbow as it was too perfect to have been drawn by a toddler. No one had helped Bella with the drawing. A few weeks later, I returned to the daycare and they had a gift for me. They found a layered "rainbow crayon" that no one had seen before. It was assumed that Bella used this crayon herself to make the rainbow. I brought the crayon home and it matched the drawing perfectly!

Rainbows appeared more often during the first few months after Bella transitioned than I have ever seen. I either saw a rainbow or had a friend send me a photo of one almost every day. It didn't take long before anyone who knew me began associating rainbows with Bella. I also began seeing rainbows where they shouldn't be, such as on walls in houses, around lights, and in television screens. Rainbows surrounded me, often with no logical explanation!

Bella's presence filled my home, which shifted the energy, making the environment feel warm and loving. These higher frequencies were felt by anyone who visited me. The plants in my home responded to this shift in energy; they thrived even though I would forget to water them and plants that hadn't grown in years suddenly began to grow. The very first roses my fiancé bought me lived for weeks; they bloomed and grew new shoots.

That winter was the first time I had a real Christmas tree. We cut our tree in the middle of December and by Christmas, it began budding! We kept that tree until the middle of February because it didn't feel right getting rid of a tree that was so full of life. It was still very much alive when we decided to take it down. We kept pieces of the trunk and made Christmas ornaments so we would always have a piece of this special tree in our home.

In the months following Bella's transition, she would communicate with me. I would hear her in my left ear, and her voice was clear, as though she were right beside me. Bella would talk to me about life, death, and offered me guidance to help me heal. She loved to tell me all about rainbows; I learned that they have always been very significant to her and she carried rainbow energy with her into this physical realm. She often spoke about energy, high frequencies, and the power of love. According to Bella, love is a powerful force that has the ability to heal everything! She would tell me about the state of the world and how I would help her complete her life purpose by telling the world about her. This would help spread love which would help increase the frequency of the planet and help us "heal."

My sisters, niece, and I took a trip to Las Vegas the winter after she transitioned. Before we left, I went to the bank to get money but my bank card was missing. This was strange as I always put it right back in my wallet every time I use it. I reached in my purse for Bella's ashes (I carry them with me and would hold them when I felt stressed), but her ashes were also missing! I emptied the entire contents of my purse and wallet, but they were nowhere to be found. As I was leaving the bank, a friend sent me a photo of a rainbow. I couldn't believe my eyes: a full rainbow in the middle of winter (and it wasn't raining or even snowing)! It was incredible! The next morning when I woke up, I reached into my purse and Bella's ashes were sitting right on top.

The reason for our trip to Las Vegas was to attend a concert but the purpose of the trip ended up being so much more than that. I was on a mission to tell everyone I met and anyone who would listen all about Bella! I made "Random Act of Kindness" cards with an image of Bella as an angel on the front. I handed these cards out and performed as many random acts of kindness as possible. Bella made her presence known the entire time and she kept sending us rainbows (which would appear on the floor or walls of buildings, such as our hotel room and museums). It seemed as though she would send us anything we asked for. We were eating supper one night and talked about wanting Spanish coffee. Minutes later, our waiter brought two Spanish coffees to our table explaining he made extras by accident and offered them to us for free! Bella was definitely helping to guide our trip. Everyone I spoke to was someone who needed to hear my story, such as the couple who were grieving the loss of their adult son and the woman whose friends had just lost their baby girl (who was the same age as Bella and passed away under very similar circumstances). Nothing that happened on that trip happened by chance!

Family members and close friends would often tell me about visits they would receive from Bella. Two friends of mine had dreams about Bella the same night and sent me text messages telling me about their dreams at the same time! She would send other people rainbows as well. A friend sent me a photo of a rainbow she saw in the stairwell of a hospital. She explained how this provided her with much needed hope and she was certain it came from Bella. She would often turn lights and electronics on or off, which happened regularly in my home, but also to my friends and family members. My sister was on her way to work one morning when her iPhone connected itself wirelessly to her car and began playing Bella's favourite song as loud possible. She didn't even have the song on her iPhone!

Bella's presence is still strong in my home, but it's not as prominent as it was during the first year following her transition. She continues to send me signs, but they tend to appear when I need them most. During this past Christmas season, her baby sister's electronic toys would regularly light up and play music when no one was near them. They would wake us up in the middle of the night, but this hasn't happened again in weeks. I have also seen a few rainbows this past month, which is very rare in winter and has always been when I most needed a reminder that she is with me. Just yesterday, while I was at the emergency room with my youngest daughter, a friend sent me a photo of a rainbow around the sun (known as a sun dog). As always, the timing was divine and I felt reassured that Bella was watching over her baby sister.

I am extremely grateful for the connection I continue to have with Bella. During the early days of my grief, her presence gave me the strength I needed to continue to live when I wanted to give up. These signs have helped me heal from this unspeakable tragedy. She is never far from me and continues to guide me. Even though I have physically lost my daughter, I have gained a new awareness and know that I am truly blessed.

Our departed loved ones are not actually gone; they are always with us and let their presence be known in many different ways. Pay attention to the signs that they send. It could be a rainbow, a bird, a song, or anything of meaning for you. Know that when you think of them, it is because they are whispering to you that they are near. May these signs open you up to this beautiful world where love never dies.

Compiled by Brian Calhoun

Angie Carter is a grieving mother and inspirational writer who began her penmanship as a way to cope with the sudden loss of her nineteen-month-old daughter, Bella. Her blog *"A Mother's Journey Through Grief"* is dedicated to Bella's memory. Angie's writing offers perspectives and encouragement to parents worldwide. The strength she was able to find during her traumatic life experiences have been an inspiration to many. She has deeply touched others with her understanding of life after death. Angie resides in Larder Lake, Ontario, Canada with her partner Tom, her son Hudson, and daughter Aria.

www.angiecarter.ca

www.facebook.com/angie.carter81

Fiona Louise

We Are All ONE

51

Oneness is the condition of being unified despite being made up of two or more parts. A jigsaw puzzle consists of many differently shaped pieces made up of the same material, yet each part has a specific place and purpose, and when interconnected creates one image. The revealed image makes sense of all the parts when viewed as a whole. Each piece exists and functions as it is, but when fitted together creates something far more beautiful and elaborate than a single portion alone could. The jigsaw is a tapestry of unique parts functioning as one.

Oneness, as supported by quantum physics, is the unified field of energy from which everything began and exists. It is the organized chaos and the universal laws that govern existence. Literally every particle of the entire universe is conscious and exponentially evolving. Oneness is also known as the field of consciousness or God. By connecting to the field and operating at a frequency of oneness, we can unify mind, body, and spirit, and achieve enlightenment.

Our physical world focuses on duality (day or night, happiness or sadness, good or bad, us or them, rich or poor, and so on). This mind-set of opposites fosters separateness, inequality, superiority, and inferiority…and yet it is all an illusion.

Babies are born into the world from this place of oneness and purity, in a state of love. However, as we age, we are taught how to think and behave, and our identities and self-beliefs are moulded through our experiences. Attitudes, beliefs, values, and prejudices are learned and taught at home, school, in neighborhoods, workplaces, through media, and societal rules. People tend to see the differences between one another (such as religion, skin color, gender, socioeconomic status, educational level, and occupation) as reasons to create separateness, and motives to disassociate and dislike each other. Disagreements, conflicts, and wars arise from this mind-set of separateness and disconnection, and are fueled by egotistical desires to hold all the cards, or get one up on someone else.

Yet in spiritual truth, these differences and disagreements are irrelevant, for we are all one and come from the same unified field. From nothing, came everything. We all originated from the primordial soup as cells divided, sharing complete copies of DNA to multiply and form life. We began from the same energy and matter, and are therefore infinitely interconnected to everyone and everything.

When we take the time to step away from our egos, intellect, reasoning, and conditioning – letting go of the trappings of daily life, and duality – we can focus on the present. It is at this very moment that we can experience oneness. You know that unguarded, indescribable moment that takes our breath away? Like witnessing a beautiful sunset, the blossoming of a flower, or the outflow of unconditional love we feel for our new-born child? This is the experience of oneness.

When we meditate, we quieten our minds, and the gap between thoughts and breath is oneness. As we practice meditation, that same gap becomes longer and we experience this unity for a greater duration. The more we experience it, the more it permeates our lives. In a mind-set of oneness our decisions, actions, and thoughts come from a place of love (not fear) – we lead from the heart.

This oneness state of mind enables us to find peace and balance. The illusory veil of separateness drops and reveals love. From oneness, we see miracles occur, synchronistic patterns emerge, and our highest intentions manifest.

We experience this state of being by first acknowledging and becoming consciously aware of how our thoughts, emotions, and values affect the way we react to situations and people we encounter daily. As we practice coming from a place of oneness, we actively choose how we act or react, how we feel and think, in order to better the lives of all. Isn't it so much easier to treat people with respect, compassion, and kindness? Doesn't our day go faster and become enjoyable when we are exchanging a smile, or interacting, with others? Isn't our work life more pleasurable when everyone is working together and shares in the responsibilities? When we are consciously aware of how our actions affect our lives (for better or worse), we are empowered to change our reality. We can become part of something greater than ourselves or our own ideas; we can transcend our physical selves.

Oneness comes from giving without expectation of return, through spreading kindness and positive intention into the world by paying it forward, or opening the door for another. Creating a community garden where everyone come together to plant, tend, and share the harvest, or by holding a street party with neighbors to share food, conversation, and laughter forges friendships, connectedness, and a co-operation where everyone looks out for one another and develops a sense of belonging.

To be unified and interconnected puts us on a trajectory for heart-filled living and positive evolution. Oneness, as global connectedness, can end suffering, despair, neglect, deprivation, starvation, and poverty. Oneness shares resources to end unemployment, substandard housing and homelessness, to provide an equal opportunity for education and achievement. Oneness focuses on conservation and preservation to end species extinction, poaching, pollution, and desecration of our delicate ecosystems. Connectedness ends disagreements, wars, human trafficking, and displacement of people.

Oneness creates unity without judgement. It fashions co-operation and kindness, fosters philanthropy and connection, generates alliance and peace, and creates inclusivity and commonality. In the state of oneness, we are connected to all living things, to the biodiversity of the entire planet and all its inhabitants, and lends us opportunity to care, to be gentle, kind, and compassionate. Oneness enables us to see that in order for everything to work in harmony, for our ecosystems to recover from pollution, for our hungry to be fed, for our people to be valued, we must work together, and we must pool our resources, dissolve our separateness, and for everyone's benefit, come together, as ONE.

Fiona Louise is a writer, student, natural therapist and blogger of both fiction and non-fiction. She has co-authored three International Best-Selling books. With a background in marketing and management in the science and property industries, Fiona left the corporate world to heal from auto-immune disorders, learn natural therapies, and write. Re-evaluating her life in order to heal put Fiona back on the spiritual path which she now shares with others. She facilitates creative workshops locally as she sees a need for people to unwind from hectic lifestyles, de-stress, and have fun! Fiona is currently studying Educational Psychology.

http://www.fiona-louise.com

Compiled by Brian Calhoun

CONCLUSION

I wish to thank each and every one of you for taking the time to support us in our endeavor to help Light up Heaven on Earth, starting with the consciousness of mankind. Thank you for your support by purchasing our book. I truly hope that you enjoyed reading each of the chapters and received the many gifts held within them.

It is my hope that you took some time to reflect upon the questions that I shared at the beginning of the book as you read through the authors' stories. If you didn't do so, please take some time as they are designed to help you further expand your divine light. If you did so, awesome! How did they make you feel? What new perspectives did the chapters on Health, Abundance, Love, or Spiritual Connections bring you?

Life begins with us and in order to change our outer experiences, we must start with shifting our inner world. Think of it like a garden. If you have a Rose bush in your garden, you can't simple just pick the flowers off the bush, paste Lilac blossoms on it, and expect that it will now be an Lilac tree for all of life. If you want a Lilac tree instead of the Rose bush, you need to have the roots first extracted from the ground and plant a new seed, one that is of the Lilac tree.

Life is very much the same. If something is appearing in your world that you wish to change, you must first go within and get the source of it all, weed the garden, and clear those roots. Only then can you plant the new seeds with love and gratitude. With some time, patience, and nurturing each day they will begin to grow roots, break through the surface of the soil and into the outer world for all to enjoy the beauty of the new plant. This will take some time as you know before you see the results, so keep focused on nurturing those seeds daily, knowing that good things are happening.

The roots are often held within your heart and are tied to the emotions; our past experiences are frequently connected to them. The roots could be filled with grief, pain, anger, fear, worry, or some other lower emotional experiences. However, sometimes the emotional roots are tied to good memories connected in feelings of love, appreciation, and joy.

One thing many people don't realize is that our past experiences are affecting the results in our lives today, even from a subconscious level, despite that we may be focused on positive thoughts. The strongest emotions will be the sponsors of your reality as you know it. This is important to know because when you begin to realize this, you can take your power back and start the process of clearing and releasing the old worn out, so that you can begin anew. Through the authors' stories in this book that is exactly what is unfolding; we are helping you to become conscious in new ways, thus clearing out the old roots to plant and nurture the new seeds.

We are all connected through the energy of the divine source within. We all hold the power to change our world as it is progressing. Everything in life is about choices, so dig in and start nurturing your garden so that you too can experience the Lighting up of Heaven on Earth in Health, Abundance, and Love through the Oneness of the Spirit Within.

Take some time to ask yourself:

- What plants are you currently growing?
- Is this the plant you truly intended to sow and nurture?
- Is a weeding of your garden required?
- Are you even sure what you are growing or what you want to plant in your garden of life?

Please know that it is okay if you don't have all the answers yet.

Start where you are and just take one step at a time. Taking some time to breathe deeply is a good start as you connect to the heart and soul. Then ask your questions and allow the answers to come forth in the perfect way and time. Your angels and guides will make sure that the answers are brought to your awareness, so just relax and go with the flow. If it doesn't happen immediately, know that it will come forth to you in another way and time.

Just by reading this book, you have already begun the process of becoming more conscious. Perhaps you felt inspired, like a weight was being lifted somehow, or more hopeful, or empowered. Did you feel like healing and enlightenment was taking place? Or some other shift or blessing transpired?

If you answered yes to any of these questions, then the seeds that were planted long ago in answer to your prayers, and that lead you to this book, are being nurtured. Trust in the outcome and know that everything is going to work out for your highest good, somehow, even if you aren't sure how yet. Just surrender and go with the energy flow of loving light.

As you have discovered through the reading of the authors' stories, life truly does begin with you because the energy of everything you could ever

Compiled by Brian Calhoun

imagine is within. Know you are truly ONE with Health, Abundance, Love, and Spirit. The same power the created the universe lies within you and therefore there is nothing that is separate from you.

It may appear that everything comes from something outside of yourself, however, in truth, the energy starts within and shows up in your world being returned as required. When we begin to live with our new perspectives and are conscious of the power that we hold inside, we can then start to channel that energy in ways that truly bless our lives as well as the world.

Life is about to take a turn for the better as you love yourself to clear out the old energy and plant the seeds of HALO to Light up Heaven on Earth, starting with you. Live life to the fullest as you go about the day, looking to see the light within all expanding.

I love, bless, and appreciate each of you. Thank you for being the energy of Health, Abundance, Love and Oneness in action daily.

Brian D. Calhoun

www.ingramcontent.com/pod-product-compliance
Lightning Source LLC
Chambersburg PA
CBHW070555300426
44113CB00010B/1256